Born on her grandfather's farm in Co. Armagh, Betty Dawson was the eldest of six children and attended the local schools before joining the civil service and working in London. After marriage, she lived in England and the Far East before returning to UK. After divorce, Betty worked in local newspapers before taking up the role of a public information officer within the UK and then in the Former Yugoslavia. Now retired and living back in Northern Ireland.

I dedicate this book, with lots of love, to my family, Clive, Jane, Conrad and Dessie, whose quiet support I value.

Betty Dawson

REFLECTIONS OF MY LIFE

AUSTIN MACAULEY PUBLISHERS™

LONDON * CAMBRIDGE * NEW YORK * SHARJAH

A CIP catalogue record for this title is available from the British Library.

ISBN 9781398453111 (Paperback)
ISBN 9781398453128 (ePub e-book)

www.austinmacauley.com

First Published 2022
Austin Macauley Publishers Ltd®
1 Canada Square
Canary Wharf
London
E14 5AA

My sincere acknowledgements go to all those family, friends and colleagues who have advised, supported and instructed me throughout my life. Thank you.

Part I

Preface

This is my account of my life. The events that were good and those that were not so good, even, dare I say it, bad. The more pleasant things in my life, I dwell on. Remembering each one with pleasing nostalgia, sometimes smiling to myself as I go over them in my mind. Not all of these events are up for mention, but I treasure them anyway within the recesses of my mind.

I am not claiming that my life was unique in any way, but it was interesting on the whole. I was always curious about people, how they lived and the places they lived in. To me it was all fascinating—and an education. My maternal grandparents had gone to America, both my parents had served in the war and, I suppose, I inherited the gene.

Life is always a challenge, the memories in this account of my life are personal and not intended to annoy or distress anyone. This is my view and does not take into account what others might think or say or do. I make no apologies for this.

This is as I remember it, there is no embellishment. My life was a bit of a roller coaster with some great moments but some very difficult times. The difficult times seem to last longer than the good ones. This was maybe just a feeling rather than reality. I do have a lot of pleasant memories, which I treasure. These memories and reminiscences are mainly of people, young and old, who have brightened my days, and I thank them. The sad times and the bad times, I try to keep to myself but I am not sure that I have succeeded. It was my life but as my grandmother used to say, 'You only pass this way once so make the best of it.'

Chapter 1
In the Beginning—My Parents

As a small boy, my father had been evacuated from the town of Lurgan (about fourteen miles away) during the First World War and had gone to live with a childless family, Sam and Jane Harrison, who lived on a farm in an area known as Teaguy (beside Teaguy Orange Hall) near Annaghmore on the Moy Road leaving Portadown.

My father joined the Royal Navy when he became eligible to enlist (during World War II). On one occasion, when he was home on leave during the war, he was introduced to my mother who was visiting some friends (the Wright family) who lived in Teaguy, about 100 yards down the road from the Harrison home, and they clicked, as we say.

Dad was allocated to submarine and worked in the engine room. He never spoke much about his years of service but Mum could tell us that he had a tough and interesting war. That is if you can call being on submarines and being sunk a few times—interesting. On one submarine patrolling the Mediterranean in the 1940s during enemy action, his submarine was sunk and he ended up in the sea surrounded by burning oil and debris. Somehow or other, he was washed ashore somewhere along the coast of Malta. Dad was found lying on the beach and picked up by some local people who nursed him back to health. He spent a year living in Valletta, Malta, not knowing his own name or where he was from.

Eventually, a former shipmate walking down the street in Valletta recognised him and was able to let him know who he was. At one point, from something that was said by Mum, he had been declared Missing in Action. When he was recognised in Valetta, my father did not remember anything of himself or his past so was very grateful to his former shipmate and was then able to return home and re-join his unit.

I asked Dad on one occasion about his swimming ability and, typically of him, he said you just do it, pretend you are a dog and paddle. Telling me about being shipwrecked, I asked how he could swim and he said, you just do it.

Despite the stoicism, swimming through a sea of burning oil and then being washed up on the shore does not hold good memories and it certainly affected his health. The sinking of his ship off the coast of Malta (1940s) was not the only time he was shipwrecked; there were others that he survived, but all these leave traces. His lungs suffered the most, weakened by the ordeals, and he had bronchial problems every winter for the rest of his life. Dad also suffered nightmares and would shout and wrestle around in his sleep. The nightmares were part and parcel of his life, I suppose now he would have been diagnosed with PTSD, but then, it was just accepted and you worked with what you had. Many of his friends from the services did not survive at all, so you always had that in your mind.

Needless to say, Dad always remembered the people of Malta with affection and remained eternally grateful to those who rescued him from the sea and gave him a place to sleep and food to eat. He also knew some of the British Servicemen who had worked, as prisoners of war, on the now infamous the railway in Northern Thailand, and who were made famous by the film *Bridge over the River Kwai.*

As a serviceman during the war, on demob, Dad, the same as other ex-servicemen, got the usual 'demob suit'—in his case, a rather nice grey check with a fine blue line running through the check. I can recall it very vividly as he wore it for quite a few years.

Dad 1944   Mum 1944

My mother, born and bred on her dad's farm in Cloncore, near Portadown, had joined the ATS during the war and reached the rank of Corporal in a short time. Typical of Mum, she was very precise and always with an immaculately presented uniform. She worked hard and was very well organised.

Before the war (World War II), Mum (the oldest in the family) had been a stalwart farmhand, working for my grandfather on the land. When she joined up, Granda then worked the land on his own. There were always lots of jobs to do. The farm was of the subsistence type, supporting the needs of the family. So a wide range of crops were grown which supplied family needs and in combination with sheer hard work, was the name of the game.

One of the major crops was corn. A useful seed requiring quite a lot of work when ripened. The crop had to be mown when the stalks became golden and ripe. After cutting, partly with a scythe to 'open' the field by the entrance, then by machine. After cutting the corn had to be made into 'stooks', that is, to gather an armful of the cut corn stalks with the seed heads on, making it up into a bundle, tying the bundle together using a couple of the stalks of corn. You would make five of these bundles and then stand them up against each other to form a rough triangular shaped 'stook'. After 'stooking' the field of grain, the stooks would then be lifted, place on a trailer and brought back to the yard by tractor.

A staple crop was the potato or 'spud'. The small seed potatoes had to be planted in rows in spring and then 'gathered' in October when they were dug up from the soil. When I was young, the preparation of the ground for planting and the digging up of the potatoes was done using a tractor. It was hard work, even with the help of the tractor. I can still feel and see the sticky damp soil that stuck to the boots and hands. After the plants flowered and the potatoes multiplied, the tractor dug them up and they were then gathered by hand, collecting them in round metal wire baskets which you moved along as you progressed up the field. This was a back breaking job. From there, they were piled into large 'bings' (heaps).

Shortly after this, they were collected and brought into the barn and covered with straw to be kept over the winter and used as needed. They were kept in the dark so that they wouldn't 'sprout' (produce small whitish stalks from the 'eyes'). Keeping them in the dark helped keep them as fresh as possible and smaller ones were picked out for planting in spring.

Potatoes formed the staple food in our diet coupled with whatever vegetables were grown. We had a variety of vegetables, carrots, parsnips, cabbage and a few rows of beetroot. We also had a few crowns of rhubarb which was lovely stewed and serves with custard.

There was a lot of fruit trees growing around the farm. Dark Damson plum trees were numerous in our local area but we also had the larger red Victoria plum and a couple of Bramley apple trees. The area in Co. Armagh was well suited to the growing of apple trees and it is renowned for the beautiful 'apple blossom' when the trees bloom in May. It is a beautiful sight when the apple blossom is in full bloom and attracts many sightseers. There were a few varieties of apples suitable for eating (my favourite was Kemps) or for cooking (Bramley were best).

Chickens were also part of the life on the farm. They provided eggs and, when they were past laying age, they were killed and cooked. Granny made up the feed for the chickens in a large metal bucket. (Hands were used to mix the mash) Added vitamins were not considered but the mash was a good mix of natural food waste, potato skins, pea husks and general natural waste from preparing food.) The chickens then had to be fed. The bucket of mash was then carried out to the hen pen. The struggle (by me when I had my turn) carrying the bucket out to the hen pen was laughable and hard work but the hens appreciated the food and flocked to the gate when they saw us coming with our bucket.

Granda always had a cow, supplying the family with milk, buttermilk and butter. The cow was usually put out in the field beside the house and brought in every evening to be milked. Milking was Granny's job and the milk had its own special white enamel bucket. I used to love sitting on my hunkers in the byre watching Granny. She sat on her milking stool and I loved to hear the 'whish, whish' sound as the milk dropped into the bucket. During winter when it became very cold and maybe snowed, the cow was held put in the byre and fed hay, but they much preferred the fresh grass and it was much more beneficial.

At one time Granny and Granda also kept a pig or two in the pigsty at the low end of the house. The pig had to be fed mash and then, when the time was right, the 'pig man', a lovely man and fellow farmer called Issac Gray, was called. He would come and kill the pig—a quick bang on the head and a sharp knife did the trick. (No one thought about the feelings of the pig—after all, they were reared for us to eat when the time came.) The 'pig man' or butcher also gutted the pig and split it up into fillets and joints of meat. The meat was then cut into—even smaller pieces. This was done so that Issac could get his cut (payment) as that sometimes was part payment for his work. The 'pig man' was well known to us with his dark overalls and big smile. After he has done his job, he always had a 'drop of tea' with us at the big table in the kitchen. A genial man, he would relax at the table and my Grandad and he would swap stories of this and that, ruminating on local events, the ways of life of those around us and the deaths. This was just our custom, nice and relaxing, just all done with good humour.

Production of food for the family was what life was about and basically that was what happened. Any money earned just bought a few necessary items which included essential clothing, shoes and anything else that was considered necessary.

As children, we never went without but my Granny would often tell stories of her youth when there weren't any cars, just a pony and trap (if you were lucky) and she would remind us of the olden days and the progress of civilisation that she had witnessed. In her youth, Granny had seen poor children who had to run around in their bare feet. Her father had been fairly well-to-do and she was grateful for that. On one occasion, she told us that because of her comfortable family status, she was able to buy a bolt of cloth. Then she had to explain what a bolt of cloth was.

Granny always felt for those who had to do without and impressed on us how lucky we were. In my mother's time when she was young, some progress had been made but there were times when some had to use cardboard insoles to cover the holes in the worn soles of their shoes. These worked well, except for when it rained. Quite often, shoes had to be passed down the line and, more often than not, didn't fit the wearer. They were usually too small and resulted in foot problems in later life. On the odd occasion a few fortunate families would receive a parcel from family in America which would contain a few essentials.

Feet were never measured accurately for size, you counted yourself to be fortunate if the shoe size was nearly right and the toes did not pinch too much. Exact measurements were really too much to expect. One had to be practical. By the time I came along, though we had our feet measured. Sometimes our feet measurements were taken by placing our feet in between the two prongs of the fire tongs and then cutting a small stick to the correct length. This happened on a couple of occasions and then we discovered the Clarks Shoe X-ray machine which took the size of your feet accurately. I remember feeling cross because I was not big enough to look down the window to check my feet for myself. Mum was a bit cautious of this machine as she had heard about the dangers of X-ray machines. So the exercise was not often repeated; the tongs were a safer option.

In those older days, farming was at its self-sufficient basic. There was no running water and no electricity. A different time and different ways. Hard physical work was the order of the day. This work lasted from early morning to late at night. Farmers nowadays would say the same. It's a tough existence but it has its compensations—plenty of fresh air and exercise!

My mother would tell me in later years that it had been a difficult decision for her to join the ATS during the war as she was needed on the farm but she figured that the money she earned would come in useful. In the end, joining up became a necessary decision as the previous year's crop had not been good. (I think that there was a lot of rain which rotted the potato in the field.) Potato was still the staple diet and was cooked every day for the main meal. When the potato crop was scarce, memories of the days of the potato famine and the mass migration came flooding back and individuals took action.

So spurred on to make a decision, my mother decided to sign up.

This decision could not have been easy and Mum had to get the boat from Belfast across to Liverpool. The boat trip across the Irish Sea was an overnight crossing. The journey could be very rough around the area of the Skerries as you enter open water. Mum, as was usual, had never travelled far from home before and definitely never having been on board a ship before and she must have felt a bit overwhelmed by it all. Some people are natural sailors, but Mum was not.

In later years, she confessed to having been very seasick on most of the journeys across to England and back. A problem that she endured with her usual stoicism, making as light as possible of the trials of the journey. Typical of her and her practical 'must do' nature. It was always a case of 'when needs must'. Mum considered herself quite lucky as, eventually, she was stationed at Berwick-on-Tweed. This was a relatively short journey as the sea voyage was only a couple of hours between Larne in the North of Ireland and Stranraer in Scotland. Certainly it was easier than compared to going further to the South of England and it was here that she served as a Corporal and worked in the Officers Mess.

I learned from her laughing descriptions of what happened to the food of those officers who thought they could order the staff around at their whim and treat them as mere servants, that good manners were easily carried. I will not say what was cooked up but let's say I always remembered my manners when, eventually, I became an officer!

Chapter 2
Childhood

According to my mother, I was thoroughly spoilt, especially by my grandfather. I don't remember that bit, but I probably was.

When I was a baby, he did not like to hear me cry so, at bedtime, he would carry me around in his arms, singing a soft lullaby so that I would fall asleep, soothed and content. I did, and this action, plus many others, must have been deeply ingrained in my subconscious as I always adored him.

Granda was soft spoken but firm, gentle and kind. My grandfather was my hero, my confidante. I listened to him intently and he talked to me with a serious intent, answering questions with simple straight answers and explained, in simple terms, some of the expressions/chat that I often overheard.

I remember asking him about rainbows and why they appeared and if it was true, as the fairy story related, that there was a pot of gold at the end of the rainbow. I remember his smile as he explained that the fairy tale was just that—a fairy story. However he added—(something that I never forgot)—if you follow the arc of the rainbow (i.e., your dream), you will find your pot of gold right there at the end of the rainbow. Even at about seven years old, I understood that he was telling me to follow my dreams and I would be satisfied with the outcome. Very wise words, and in his gentle way, a great lesson for life. Memory of that conversation still brings tears to my eyes.

There were many such gems. How Australia was the antipodes of the British Isle, how insects and birds were valuable to the earth, performing their roles and that they were part of the circle of life. He explained that we all fitted into that pattern, in our own particular role as human beings. He believed implicitly in God and His creation.

Chapter 3
The Early Years

I was born on 1st May 1946 at my grandfather's farm in Pin Box Lane, Cloncore, outside Portadown in Northern Ireland. My mother Tilly (Sarah Matilda) was the oldest daughter of my grandfather (Henderson Dougan) and Margaret Jane (formerly) Taggart from the area of the Antrim plateau known as Mosside. Granny and Granda met in America. Granny was a nurse in the hospital in Massachusetts and Granda had gone to America to work and earn money, to send some home to ease the financial burden on the farm and family. He had a job on the railroad. When he met Granny, they got married and planned to continue living in America. Unfortunately, events at home changed and he was asked to return home to run the farm, so they left their life in America.

Farming in Ireland (as anywhere else) wasn't easy and they had five children, of which my mother was the eldest. They worked hard together, working side by side preparing the ground for planting and then throughout the process of growing and harvesting the crops, as well as seeing to the regular chores around the house, looking after the animals, etc. They worked hard and the family survived, but without any luxuries.

Mum and Dad met during the war years, while they were both on leave, and hit it off immediately, getting married after demob at the end of the war, they came to live with my grandparents at the Dougan family home in Cloncore.

It was here that I was born. Mum and Dad lived in what was known as the 'Good Room' of the house, nominally the sitting room.

My parents must have lived with my grandparents for about two to three years—having their bed and personal possessions in the 'good room'. This room was the largest room in the house, at the end of the hall just off the main living room and we had to step up a step to enter. In my mind's eye, I can still see the room with all its detail and I can smell the paint on the walls. Paint in those days was based on a lime wash which was white and had its own distinctive smell and was used extensively.

In the 'good room', there was a lovely large mirror above the mantelpiece which was surrounded by an ornately decorated dark wooden frame that held a few small shelves which contained a couple of 'good' ornaments, china figures of men and women and a few other things. The prized (very fashionable then) china dogs were sat on the mantelpiece. The fireplace was dark and I think made of black metal, worked into a nicely patterned surrounding. The room was not overly furnished but very comfortable. There was the 'Chesterfield Suite'—two large chairs and a settee, a chest of drawers and a large double bed with a metal frame. The mattress was typical of its time, maybe a bit lumpy, and placed on a framework of metal joined together with springs and coils which had a bit of a bounce when jumped on. The chest of drawers was black-painted, again typical of the time, and I think it had three long drawers and two half-width top drawers.

Down in the house, the living room was a good-sized kitchen and living area with a large scrubbed table at one end near the window, looking out on to the back fields. The same plain wooden chairs were around the table and we had a comfortable settle to the side of the open fire. The back surroundings of this fire were white tiles with a fine green tile border and it had a high mantel that held a large clock and some rather nice china dogs and brass candle sticks. The fire also had the normal crook (crane) that swung out over the open fire and from which was suspended hooks to hold the large frying pan and kettle. These items were covered with a healthy layer of crusted smoke and soot. A normal Ulster farm fireside at that time.

Also in the living room, as well as the table and chairs, there was a cabinet, a 'Kitchen Maid' (popular in the 50s) that held all our cups and plates as well as a few larder items like salt, sugar and sauces. HP sauce was a favourite. There was a central pull-down door in this cabinet and it could be used to prepare a few items. In the corner was a large upright churn with its staff and lid (used every Monday to churn milk into buttermilk and make butter) plus a large half hundredweight of plain flour set on a wooden chair.

This was our home, comfortable and basic.

Some years later, my mother told me that the bottom drawer of the chest of drawers in our room was my first 'cot' when I was born. A large blanket cushioned me from the hard edges and it was cosy. The big plus was that I was within easy reach if I wakened at night. I cannot remember that but I do recall the wooden cot that I occupied later. The cot which was bought for me was rectangular, light brown in colour, the sides were made of round bars (like dowel rods) and chrome clips that held the front side up in place and the chrome bars at each end of the moving side.

I also remember the big pram that I was pushed around in and in which I enjoyed my afternoon naps. The pram was large, comforting and cosy and I can remember the feelings of security as I lay listening to the noises around me. The pram was also used by my sister Olive (born 13 months after me) and I think that we had a lot of service from that pram, otherwise I would not be able to remember so much about it.

For my midday sleep, I would be placed in my pram which was usually parked outside the front door, weather permitting. The pram was an imposing 'carriage', high and grand with a shiny chrome handle and gleaming wheels. I can recall the sense of total comfort and security as I lay within the depths of that pram, hearing the birds calling and the soft breeze as it flowed over the sides of the carriage and the fuss to get it inside if it started to rain. When my sister Olive came along, she had the same treat.

These memories are deep in my psyche and I often think of how important it is for a child to experience that kind of love and belonging.

My mother could also tell me later that I had been very spoilt by my grandfather. Granda could not bear to hear me cry and would carry me around the house until I fell asleep. If I wakened and cried during the night, my grandfather would appear and 'walk me' until I settled and went off to sleep again. I was told that sometimes, that took a long time!

After the war, jobs and housing were in short supply but Dad got a job, as did many others after the war, working on the roads. He was part of the crew who built the main Portadownte to Maghery Road (now the A4 and B196). This road was made of cement constructed in 100-yard sections. Each section represented a day's work by the road crew. The sections were then joined together by a thin line of tar to allow for expansion and contraction in the heat and cold. This tar strip also made the surface easier to ride over whilst cycling, reducing the bump. This method of road construction was basic but with a strong foundation. It was long lasting and you could see the ridges in each section where the concrete had been tramped down with the edge of a large plank of wood. As I said, it was basic.

This road lasted for some time and, as a child, I often cycled that road, bumping over the joins. I asked my dad why the road was as it was and that is how I found out that he had worked on it after his return from the war. Later, Dad got a job working on the sand dredging of Lough Neagh close to home. Before that, he worked in Portadown for a company called Wades which became quite famous for their 'whimsies' (a set of small animal shapes in porcelain). Dad had to cycle the seven miles to and from work, Monday through to Saturday. Mum continued to help my Granda and Granny on the farm.

Unable, at first, to get a house of their own, my parents and then with me, lived with my grandparents for about a year, whilst Mum and Dad waited for a 'council' house to be allocated to them. The housing list was long, even though my parents had both served in the war, my father in the Royal Navy and my mother in the ATS. Ex-service people were supposed to have a certain priority because of their service but they still had to wait. My parents wanted to stay in the local area to be close to Granny and Granda. Both grandparents were getting on in years, although you didn't seem to realise it, and both still worked hard every day.

Possibly because we lived there, I was very close to both my grandparents and adored them, particularly my Grandad. I listened attentively to his every word, wandered around after him as he worked in the fields, helping with the weeding and being a general helping hand (maybe a bit of a nuisance at times but he always had time for me). Understanding how hard he worked, I was always trying to help him as I grew older. My grandad taught me a lot about nature, crop rotation, animal life and all aspects of nature around us. There was a 'big drain' running through his land which eventually flowed, into Lough Neagh. The area around us was bog land, peaty and liable to flood so the 'big drain' was fed by smaller drains from the individual fields. This was common in our area and worked well.

As my Grandad worked close by and could keep an eye on me, I was encouraged to watch 'the insects and small animal life' that lived in the boggy waters in these drains. I began to see how the cycles/stages of growth evolved from one point to another, how the small creatures changed as they grew bigger. I particularly loved the caddis fly larvae for some reason. In the 'big drain' there were even eels and pike to be seen at different times, even the odd bigger fish which created lots of excitement in our family if we were lucky enough to catch a glimpse as they made their way to Lough Neagh.

During the summer, the water level would dry out to just a trickle and the clay bottom of the drain was lovely and squelchy, the mud oozing up through your toes when you took a paddle in your bare feet. My mother would get very cross if I dirtied my socks or shoes and they were always carefully set up on the bank, under the small road bridge, out of sight of anyone who chanced to go up or down the road. Again, this was something I was not supposed to do, but if I remained hidden from the house, and was careful to rub my feet well in the grass before putting on my shoes and socks, so I could get away with it. I am sure that my mother suspected what I was up to but she said nothing—as long as she didn't catch me, it was ok!

I was the oldest of a family of six, three girls (myself, Olive and the youngest one, Eileen) and three boys (Henderson, John and David). A happy lot we were, brought up on a diet of hard work, fresh air and plain food. Usually, on a Saturday, Mum would go into town on the bus and take me and my sister with her. It was a great thrill to travel on the old green and white bus, with the green seats and chrome frames. The chatter of the passengers as they exchanged news and views rose above the drone of the engine, and the air that blew in through the door could be quite chilly, but we didn't care. It was a big adventure.

Pictured at the back of our grandparents' home, the Corry children
Betty (me) (left), Henderson and Olive at the back with David, Eileen and John in
front. Circa 1958

I remember the buff and faded-green coloured ration books issued after the war for goods/food that were difficult to get, items such as sugar. It was something that had to be imported so therefore it was 'rationed'. The coupons in the book were always carefully used and the amount of effort that my Mum made to ensure that we could have a couple of ounces (a quarter) of sweets from time to time was much appreciated. The sweets were such a treat and were chosen very carefully after much deliberation, viewing each glass display jar from as many angles as was possible!

During the week, Mum was always dressed for work, sometimes with an all covering cotton wrap that covered all her other clothes or a small apron over her dress or skirt and jumper. She was great at knitting and we benefited from her work with jumpers, skirts, hats, scarves and gloves, even thick socks. They were all beautifully patterned in wool and were warm, especially in winter. Mum knit for all the members of the family and then started knitting for a wool shop in town. She made it seem effortless but, having done it myself, there are a lot of late nights and steady concentrated effort in order to meet deadlines and 'to get it done'.

When we went to town on Saturdays, Mum always dressed nicely and we always wore our 'good' clothes. I loved my mum's half-length fur coat which she wore to go to town together with her much prized kilt. She looked so well and, in my opinion, no one else in our town seemed to have such a grand and lovely outfit.

Mum, Olive and me shopping in Portadown, 1953

Among the memories in our family are the awful memories of the dangers of an epidemic of Diphtheria which rampaged through the area in the 1930s (a killer in those days). My mother's younger brother David had contacted the disease and had been taken over to Lurgan to the hospital (the closest), some six or seven miles further on from Portadown.

According to my Granny, David was twelve years old when he caught this infectious disease in the month of January 1937. His cousin who lived nearby was also ill with diphtheria and was in the same hospital. Granda went over to the hospital every day to see his son but on 7th January, he set off as usual to walk the 10-12 miles to the hospital. David's condition had been improving and Granda was hoping that he could bring his son home that day (he planned to carry him). When Granda got to the hospital, he was met with the news that his son was dead. The shock must have been incredible and mind-numbing. Granda then had to turn around and walk all the way home to break the news to Granny and the rest of the family who waiting expectantly.

The waiting family heard Granda coming down the lane crying and knew the news was bad. Obviously, they were all devastated and Granny told me that Granda never spoke of it again but that it nearly killed him. David was buried in the family plot in Tartaraghan Churchyard. Because this illness was considered so infectious, they could not even bring the coffin home to the house (as was our custom). We would hold a wake, friends and neighbours gathered in the house around the coffin, remembering all the good times, the laughs and the bad times of the deceased. Saying goodbye. In this instance, the funeral procession started off on (then) the main road about 100 yards from the house.

Every Sunday when Grandad went to Church, he would go early and spend some time at the graveside before going into the service. A quiet restrained man who never raised his voice, Granda held it all in, working the land as usual. He worked in the fields, doing what had to be done, where he thought his own thoughts as he used a wooden mallet to break down the lumps of hard soil or dug hard with the spade to clear away weeds or turn over the earth in order to plant the new crops. A strong belief in God and his righteousness, the agony of losing his son must have been beyond description. As an adult, who has experienced my own sorrow and heartache, I can only, now, begin to empathise with and fully understand the depth of his grief and loss. Hard physical effort is sometimes the only relief from inner torment. I know.

I was brought up to respect the authority of the police, law enforcement in general, to be tolerant of others and their views and way of life, but only always to do what was right. I knew that the local GP and District Nurse were to be valued and that there had been a time (not so very long ago) when such services had to be paid for and were therefore only used when really necessary. Local 'cures' were very much in fashion and there was also someone within a few miles who had a 'charm' to cure things like sprains, warts, etc. All old notions and ideas that were effective in their time and even used today on occasion.

Each person had their own 'special' charm. These people were much respected as they looked so ordinary but had these magical powers. After all, it wasn't everyone who had 'the charm'.

Despite the name 'charm' they didn't have to be nice and charming, they could be quite sharp. I suppose if they had had a lot of people turning up on their door, it could be quite tiring. No matter what their attitude, they had the privilege of being set apart for their gift of healing and were treated with respect.

I vividly remember the day the postman delivered my father's war medals to our home in Clonmacate. The medals came in a rough brown cardboard box which my Mum opened and sat down on the bottom step of the stairs of our recently acquired council house. She just cried. She was obviously remembering the hardships of war and fearing that another war could erupt that would decimate families once again. It was a sombre thought and we children only just caught a glimpse of the heartache caused by war.

Mum didn't dwell on it too long but the memory lasted and made a deep impression on me as I began to understand the politics of factions/nations as they vied for who would be top dog.

At my grandparents' in Cloncore, I can also remember the pump, just outside the front door. It was here that we got our fresh water. It was a smallish neat pump, pretty basic, made of heavy cast metal and it was carefully painted every year to keep it 'good'. I loved the sound of that pump as the handle was pumped up and down to draw up the water. The water, which came from a spring way down in the earth, was always fresh, clear and sparkling with a beautiful taste.

The water was pumped into a white enamel bucket kept for the water and was always to be found in the kitchen. The enamel bucket was always so clean and considered a better choice of container in which to store water rather than the metal zinc buckets that we used elsewhere around the farm where it was used to carry feed and meal to the hens and other animals.

Granda's house was at the end of a narrow lane that ran between the main Cloncore Road (a road that would probably be now classed as a 'C' road) and what we called the 'Long Road', so called because it ran very straight and stretched away into the distance, a thin tarmac ribbon beckoning us to explore. Though Mum made sure we never did. The lane to Granda's house was tarmacked in the early 1950s, but only partway, as far as the third house. The 'road' men refusing to go any further. This meant that the last bit was like a rough track with a grassy middle that was raised and caught the bottom of any car that ventured down our way. There weren't many cars in those days, so the grass, weeds and dandelions flourished down the middle of the road.

The lane stayed like that for about ten years before the next lot of 'road men' came and redid the complete lane. It always remained a bit of a mystery to me as to why it wasn't fixed. At the farm in Cloncore, my grandparents also kept a flock of hens, mainly Rhode Island Reds, considered to be a good breed of hen. Our hens were very much 'free range' in that they had a large 'pen' fenced round with chick wire and although they had a house complete with perches in which they slept at night; they laid their eggs wherever they liked. As children, it was our job to find the nests and retrieve the eggs every day. From time to time, there was the odd fox who would turn up and sometimes get into the hen pen but rarely got hold of a hen. Hens were very precious and carefully housed at night when Mr Fox would be about. Mr Fox was very clever and he could manage to get into the hens from time to time. It only needed a small hole in the wall or a bit of a dip in the ground for him to be able to wiggle his way in and create havoc, panicking the hens, so that the eggs were few for a day or two.

A certain number of eggs were kept every year, from which chicks were hatched, under the watchful eye of a broody hen. They were also under the equally careful eye of Granny. These chicks replaced the older hens who, when the time was right and they no longer produced eggs, their neck was 'wrung' and they were prepared for cooking, usually in a broth/soup where the meat was lifted out and drained when it was cooked. This was a great treat, delicious and used on important occasions. My grandmother was the executioner-in-chief but we were carefully prevented from seeing the 'deed' performed, although we were very aware of the feather plucking and gutting process that followed.

Granda always had a cow either in the byre or out in the field. She provided us with milk from which butter was produced. Butter was produced by Granda 'churning' the milk every Monday. This 'churning' or pounding up and down of the long handled wooden 'staff' in the tall barrel 'churn' gave us our weekly supplies of butter as well as the buttermilk which we drank daily. The process took quite a while and was hard work with Granda standing at the big barrel type wooden churn, plunging the staff with the circular open work attachment at the bottom end of the staff, up and down, splashing the milk around in the barrel. Eventually this action made the butter float to the top of the milk. The milk itself had turned into buttermilk by this stage. Buttermilk tastes a little like drinking yoghurt and is quite delicious. Grandad would scoop the butter off the top of the buttermilk, placing it in an enamelled or metal bowl which was then passed over to Granny who would then, using two wooden butter pats (rectangles of wood with broad handles) expertly fashion the butter into rectangular blocks. Granny was very good at 'patting' and shaping the butter into the blocks which she would store in a cool brown and black delph 'crock' full of buttermilk. These butter pats would be taken out of the buttermilk and used as needed. I was always mesmerised by her expert smooth actions as Granny worked the butter.

Granny also baked bread every day using a big baking bowl, throwing in a handful of flour, a pinch of baking soda and a pinch of salt with some milk. The flour was kept in a large white flour bag kept in the corner of the kitchen where it was dry and warm. The brand on the bag was marked in red. It was called 'early riser' flour. The bread always tasted delicious, especially when it was warm, straight off the griddle. The griddle (a large black flat tray with a handle which hung from a hook on the 'crane') was placed over the open fire where the heat cooked the bread. The crane was an 'L' shaped metal bar that was fastened at the side of the fireplace and carried hooks that held the kettle and griddle over the fire, which was sometimes burning turf and sometimes coal.

Turf was cut from the moss and brought home to dry properly before burning. It had its own distinctive earthy smell which permeated the house and was synonymous with home and comfort.

Sometimes Granny mashed leftover potatoes to make potato bread. A speciality of Ireland that tastes good cold or hot. The potato, being the staple diet for pretty much every family in the land, was usually in plentiful supply. I can also remember that when Granda had the pig slaughtered, there was much delight when we had some pig liver cooked for tea or even better, some pork fillet. Either of them, served with tea, bread and butter, were mouth-wateringly delicious. Interspersed with meals of fresh herrings or eels from Lough Neagh, we were well fed. The herrings and eels were brought around by one of the young men from the Cash End, down by the shores of Lough Neagh. The young man had probably caught the fish earlier that day. The fish were carried in a wet wooden box that was fastened on the back of his bicycle, behind the saddle. A young entrepreneur supplying a treat for the family, every week on a Friday, although to us, it was just a case of doing what you had to do to get a bit of money. We always had enough but there were no luxuries as such.

An example of this type of farmhouse living was when at secondary school (in the 1960s), my younger brother Henderson (born seven years after me), made Granny a wooden baking board with a rim which kept the flour and dough containing it within bounds. This was much thought of and as Henderson adored Granny, he was delighted to be able to make this piece for her at woodwork lessons in school.

Granny was really thrilled with this baking board, it was so easy to clean and wash. It also helped keep the flour off the floor!

Granny was a great baker, making all the usual stuff, like soda bread, wheaten and currant sodas. At the end of the summer when the apples and potatoes had been gathered, as a really special treat Granny made potato apple bread. This was where the potatoes were boiled and mashed, then rolled out like pastry and stewed apples were enclosed between two layers of the potato pastry and cooked on the griddle. Delicious!

Most bread was made on the griddle which hung on the crane over the open fire. There was nothing as nice as coming in from school and being given hot potato apple bread, hot off the griddle.

I must admit, though, I adored her 'champ'. This was where she boiled a big pot of potatoes and then mashed them up adding a bunch of chopped scallions (spring onions) that had been heated in a little milk and mixed into the mashed potatoes (we called them 'spuds'!). At some times of the year, Mum would collect some nice young nettles and use them instead of the scallions. Equally tasty. This mixture was heaped onto your plate and formed a mound. We would then make a hole in the top and add a big knob of butter. This melted and ran though the mashed spuds. Delicious! The shape of the mound on the plate was reminiscent of a volcano but at that time I didn't know much about volcanoes. I just liked what I was going to eat, and I still enjoy a good plate of 'champ'.

Granda had always kept a donkey on the farm (the picture of my mother with a new donkey foal which appeared in the local Portadown newspaper). The donkey that I first got to know and befriend eventually got too old, but he was so gentle and had a lovely personality.

As I wandered around after my Grandad, I soon became fascinated and friendly with the donkey currently in residence. As usual, Neddy was his name. On one occasion, Grandad had to get a new donkey but this one was 'skittish' as he had not been treated well and was very grumpy. Grandad warned me about being careful with this one and, as a matter of practice I kept a resentful distance.

Mindful of Grandad's instructions, I spent ages sitting on the grass and watching this new Neddy as he wandered about the field. The donkey was on a long chain anchored by an iron peg in the middle of the field and this ensured that he could get around all of the field but could not wander away altogether. Eventually, Neddy allowed me to come close to him and touch his soft nose. I loved the feel of his furry coat and I was warned to be wary of his teeth when I was feeding him a piece of carrot or grass. As he got used to my presence, he became quite gentle as he gradually accepted me and realised that he would get the titbit and that I wasn't teasing.

I loved watching him, studying his movements and being able to discern his moods. Learning that he had a personality of his own and that there were things that did not please him and that there was a time to keep well clear, giving him a wide berth ('his room'). Donkeys are very intelligent animals with a great sense of humour and I sometimes felt that he was grinning at me as he realised that I was being wary of him or had just been told off by my mother and was going to visit him to find comfort by stroking his nose and snuggling up against his neck. He loved the touch and comfort as much as I did but would cut it short if he thought that I had a piece of carrot or apple in my pocket.

Mum with donkey and foal. Cloncore, 1939

Despite my careful approaches this donkey was easily startled, he would often throw his head up very quickly and scamper off. I would wait for him to settle and he always did, returning to where I stood but hanging back a little as if to say,

I am still a little wary but I think you are ok.

I was told not to get on his back and ride him because of his nervousness, but I was trying him to get used to a weight on his back. It was usually me leaning over on him and walking with him as he moved around. However, one day, my sister asked if she could ride him. Olive was not a regular visitor to the fields, so to the donkey, she was a stranger. I was not very nice and I said 'sure' and I went over and held him at his neck (he had a harness with 'blinkers' on which made him a little less nervous). My sister climbed on his back, I saw his eyes roll as he felt the weight on his back and I let him go.

A big mistake, the donkey bucked and ran and my sister was thrown over his head, rising high in the air, and landing in the nearby drainage ditch. She rose immediately, looking very nymph-like with wet plants draped around her head.

She was angry and yelled. Working on the principle that if you can move and make loud noises, I figured she was alright so I took immediate action—I ran. Of course, I had to face the music later when I eventually plucked up enough courage to go home, but it was one occasion, when, as a child, I wished that I had had a camera to capture her image as she rose out of the drain. The picture still lives with me as vividly as the day it happened. But it was cruel of me and I was well punished. I still (over 60 years later) do not broach the subject with my sister whom I love dearly.

On the farm there, we also had some cats. They kept the mice and rats at bay and sometimes the cat population became quite large, but nobody minded. Some of the kittens were a little wild, as the cats hunted for their own food but as I helped feed them every day (a few scraps of this and that to supplement their own efforts), they got used to me. I had a special favourite. I called her puss. She loved to be tickled and stroked, purring in a most satisfactory manner that was very soothing. She used to come some way up the lane to meet me as I wandered home from school.

On the days I was slow to make it down the lane, distracted by the primroses or violets or even collecting a few 'conkers'/chestnuts, she would sit on the grass verge (usually about the same place each day) and leisurely perform her 'toilette', washing herself as she waited, licking her paws with such deliberation that I knew she had noticed that I was late and wanted to let me know that she knew and was not going to put herself out to walk any further! We always made friends again and she would walk alongside me purring loudly, giving me the odd rub as she pushed against my legs.

Old Massey Ferguson Tractor driven by and belonging to a neighbour, C Woodhouse (since deceased)

Chapter 4
Clonmacate Home

Sometime after my sister, Olive, was born, my parents were allocated a council house, a couple of miles down the road from my grandparents. The new house was part of a small row of four lots of semidetached that had been specially built to accommodate ex-service personnel. They had three bedrooms upstairs, a living room at the front and a small room at the back which could be a dining room or a bedroom, depending on need or choice.

The kitchen was small, basic with a larder in the corner running from floor to ceiling suitable and used for provisions. The few pots and pans were placed in the bottom of the larder and beside it was the sink with a small wooden draining board on one side and a small floor cupboard on the other. Away from the window, on the back wall, there were shelves that would hold the delph and various other bits and pieces, including the 'Tilly Lamp', powered by paraffin with a wick and a glass globe to enclose the flame.

The lamp had to be pumped to keep pressure in the paraffin reservoir to make sure the flame kept burning and lit the fibres of the mantle, the main source of light. This lamp provided us with the light at night accompanied by a soft snore as it burned. On long winter evenings, the lamp had to be pumped a time or two to keep the light going.

Initially, we did not have electricity but had it installed at a later date in the 50s after the Electricity Board brought power lines and put up the large poles on the main road running outside our house. Although the electricity lines were up along the road outside our house, we still had to pay someone to wire it into our home. A friend of Dad's who knew about these things came and ran a few points to a couple of rooms and joined us to the main power.

The installation was basic but to us, it was special. We now had light at the flick of a switch. This was luxury!

Underneath the shelves running along the wall opposite the kitchen sink was a space where we had a small wooden table on which was placed, at first, an enamel and, later, a plastic bucket which held water that was drawn from the outside pump supplied specifically for the row of houses. This pump was large, painted green and sheltered by a tall privet hedge to protect it from the frost.

We had an outside toilet a few feet down the yard and a storage shed, all stone built. The toilet had a smooth-grained wooden seat that was comfortable to sit on and a large bucket underneath. No fancy doodah. This bucket obviously had to be emptied regularly in a specially dug hole down the bottom of the field which was our garden. Running water was unheard of in the country.

Facilities were basic but adequate, it was in the country and we had freedom and space to run around. The neighbours were nice and the bus stop was only about a hundred yards up the road.

Getting to primary school was a little bit more difficult as the nearest one was a couple of miles away and the only way to get there was by walking, but everyone walked or cycled—if they were lucky enough to have a bicycle—so all was well in our corner of the world. Mum would remind us that we had all our needs and luckily, we were only a few miles down the road from my grandparents and a mile or so from Lough Neagh.

In the summertime, Lough Neagh was a great attraction and people used to cycle from town to go for a paddle in the water. There was a field that had to be crossed to get to the Lough but when we got down to the water, the bottom of the Lough was sandy and was soothing to walk on. During the month of May, the air along the road down to the Lough became crowded with May flies, tiny little things that flew up your nose and would get into your mouth if you were talking as you cycled. They were very unpleasant as they were so tiny and travelled in great clouds, but the inconvenience didn't last long and they were soon gone.

There was a regular bus service (the number 75 bus still runs) which we all used, although there were many who cycled the seven odd miles into their work every day. The fat wooden telegraph poles lining the road brought the telephone lines to the red telephone boxes, provided by the General Post Office. Each pole had a cap on top to protect it from the rain and there were white delph mushrooms (made mainly in the Wades factory) attached to the three or four small cross bars at the top of the pole. The telephone wires were wound around the white delph mushroom shapes and the lines would 'sing' as the wires moved gently in the slightest breeze and the signal passed along the length.

Red GPO telephone boxes were located at appropriate locations, mainly at places where there was a collection of houses. This box was where we had to go if we needed to get help, and it was used mainly for calling out the Doctor. Our nearest box was about half a mile away and I remember vividly having to race to the box to call out the doctor for my sister who, it turned out, had a bad attack of appendicitis that turned out to be peritonitis. She was really ill and had to go to hospital for a time. It was very frightening but she got better after an operation and a stay in hospital. We were all very thankful.

Despite the odd minor emergency, there was still work to be done at Grandad's and we still went up the road to Granny and Granda's house every day. There was work to be done in the fields and my mum helped Granny as well, doing the weekly washing every Monday when she would produce two or three long lines of immaculately washed sheets, pillowcases and general clothing.

This chore, in the 1950s, was completed using the most basic of boilers (the Burco boiler powered by electricity, was metal, round and could take a good load of sheets). This was quite a modern item and Mum reckoned she was very lucky to have one. Once boiled, the clothes were rinsed in a zinc bath using a 'blue bag' in the final rise to enhance the whiteness.

We children were allowed to 'help' by tramping the clothes in the zinc bath to squeeze out the soapy water. It was great fun but we had to make sure that our feet were clean, otherwise we would mark the clothes.

Mum was quite fussy about that! She was fussy about a lot of things, including our table manners.

Monday was also the day Granda 'churned' the milk, producing the butter and buttermilk that we used every day.

In later years, I discovered that the glass of buttermilk we had each day with our dinner is called yoghurt in other countries and is recommended as a health drink by the food gurus.

To us at this time, the mixture of smells on a Monday was iconic and as children, we knew the comfort of the routine and helped as best we could, sometimes even just sitting quietly on the sofa or going out to play if the weather was fine. Granny always had fresh bread baked, often from early in the morning, and we wanted for nothing.

Money must have been tight (I realise now that it was) but we were rich. We had love, comfortable smells, conversation and direction. Go out and play, it's not raining or, if it was wet, put on your 'welly' boots and find something to do outside. The wellingtons were mainly black and, if they were used a lot, would leave a dirty looking line along the back of your leg at the calf. Strangely enough, many a calf line was much admired, because it meant that you wore the wellies a lot!

Despite and because of it all, we were content. We always knew where we were and what to do. Boredom was a concept that hadn't even been invented. There was always something to do: playing 'house' with pieces of broken plates or cups or, more importantly, there were chores to be completed, feeding the hens, bringing in the animals from the fields or sweeping the floor.

There was always a lot of excitement when 'corn stooks' were brought from the fields into the yard to be ready for the threshing machine that removed the ears (seeds) from the stalks. This was a highlight as it involved a large 'threshing' machine being towed by the grey Massey Ferguson tractor trundling into the yard. Men came and got busy feeding the loosened 'stooks' into the top of the machine and then making sure to catch the grain in bags tied to the other (front) end of the machine.

I think that this seed could be used to reseed the fields, be ground in a mill to provide flour or sold to a neighbour for his use.

The remaining straw was collected and used mainly for bedding for the animals. In itself the process of threshing was fraught with problems, there was no safety guards around the intake and the men had to be on their guard to prevent accidents. Sometimes the machine broke down and a new part had to be brought in from the supplier and this could hold the process back for a few hours or days depending on the supply of parts.

My sister (left) and I holding the corn stooks.

The haymaking was easier as it (the grass/hay) was cut in the fields, dried, turned over and then shook out with the aid of a pitchfork. It was them built into 'haystacks' before being brought back into the farmyard and built into one giant stack. The haystacks in the field were smallish, no more than six foot high and easily built. The making of these haystacks in the field was always great fun for us children and we made sure that we were down in the field when this was planned. There were always a few additional adults there as this job had to be done when the hay was dry.

The dried grass (hay) was piled up and someone would have to 'tramp' it a bit to shape it and firm it down into a stack. Then the stack would have to be tied down with grass rope thrown over the top. Two ropes were used. These grass ropes were made by spinning lengths of grass on the 'tine' of a pitchfork or on a peg of a long wooden rake. Granda was expert at this with one of us children holding the other end and walking backwards as the rope lengthened. Sometimes I was allowed to 'tramp' the hay, balancing on top of the stack.

These small haystacks were then brought back to the farmyard on the back of a flat-bed trailer trailed pulled by the Massey Ferguson tractor. Once in the yard, the hay would be built into a giant haystack, sometimes two stacks, depending on that year's yield. The shape remained the same as the one in the field, cone shaped, as the rain would run off it more easily. On some farms the haystack would then be covered by a piece of tarpaulin to protect it from the elements. These stacks of hay would be used throughout the winter as bedding and feed for the animals when they had to be kept indoors.

Work was always waiting to be done and we all had to help. Granda maintained our main food supplies for the family but he also grew lots of fruit which he sold in the market. This was very labour intensive as it meant picking the fruit by hand and packing it for the big market in Belfast. So every summer, we spent a lot of time pulling strawberries, black currents, gooseberries, raspberries, apples and plums as they came into season and ripened. Pulling strawberries was the most tedious as we had to crouch down alongside the plants to pick the fruit.

Fruit picking work was, in turn, back breaking and welcome as, when pulling plums or picking apples, we climbed up the ladder and had a great view of the surrounding countryside. The main crops grown at our place were at ground level though and we didn't have many apple or plum trees in comparison to other places.

Strawberry picking team with Grandad on the right

As children, we recognised special times of the year, Christmas when Santa Claus came and we had our stocking hung at the end of the bed and we got an apple and an orange, usually a pencil and a few other small pieces. Usually, Mum found a special colouring pencil that had a mix of colours in the lead so you just twisted it around for different colours. We always had one toy, a doll or a book or, for my brother, some toy soldiers or a small car. Birthdays were special as you got a present only for you.

We also celebrated 'Twelfth of July' with the Orangemen parading, wearing their orange sashes, to 'the field', and on the 'Thirteenth' it was the turn of the Black Men, wearing their mainly black sashes, with decorations, to parade at Scarva. It was always a great couple of days with sandwiches and tea served in the fields. These two days basically commemorated the Battle of the Boyne 1690 where the poorly armed defenders of the protestant faith defeated the Catholic King James

Easter and the Harvest were always celebrated with Church Services and, because they were special occasions, we always had a new outfit for these festivals.

Mum always made sure that we attended the few local social occasions. There were the Guest Teas that were held in halls and school buildings. These were good fun. Local entertainers would come along and there would be music and songs. Usually someone would have a story or rhyme to recite. All acts were presented with great gusto, much enjoyed by the audience. Tea and buns were always supplied to the audience afterwards as we sat in our chairs and were served by the ladies.

We, in the audience, would walk home in a happy frame of mind, having had your 'bun'. On the way home, we would start off as a group of people going a certain direction and family groups would break off when it came to their turn off in the road. It seemed to me that on most of those evenings, the stars would be twinkling in the sky and I remember Mum asking us to identify the few different constellations that we could recognise. The night sky was always jet black, except for the nights there was a moon and the stars were out. In those days there was no big areas of lights to be seen on the horizon. The only light would come from a house and then the light shining from the window was dim, this was the country.

Walking along the road, as our eyes would become accustomed to the dark, we saw the shapes of the hedgerows and bushes and the odd animal scurrying across our path. We saw enough to know where we were and we were very comfortable in this darkness. We could always find our way home.

Sometimes there would be a bit of frost or, on the odd occasion, a smattering of snow. It rarely seemed to rain much in those times.

Those were magical walks home.

Another special event was when we attended the opening and dedication of a Royal Black Preceptory (RBP No.30) District Hall for Chapter No 5 in 1954. It was located at 66 Dungannon Road and we passed it every Saturday on our way to and from town in the bus. The building of a new hall was quite unusual and the opening was much anticipated. The RBP Institutions are based on the Christian teachings in the Bible based on the Reformation and this was quite a moment.

On the day of the opening (a Saturday) we were all dressed in our very best dress, shoes and sparkling new white ankle socks. It was a blistering hot day and we had to walk the four miles along the main road to the hall. There were few cars in those days and we had the road mainly to ourselves and others attending the 'do'. As part of the preparations, I guess, the road was newly tarmacked and the excess tar bubbled in the heat. My sister and I had great fun popping the bubbles with the toe of our shoe. Mum was not happy with us doing this but she was chatting to other mums making their way to the hall, so we popped quite a few bubbles. The event was well attended and the feeling was festive. A service was held and this was followed by tea and buns on the grass outside. A great day out and a happy walk home.

Chapter 5
Starting School

When I became the age to start school, I was reluctant to go and put forward lots of reasons why I did not have to attend a school. I pointed out that I could count and do sums, I was learning to read. What more did I want. Anyway, my Grandad could teach me all I needed to know. Granda was keen on me learning how to count and taught me how to total a page of (then currency) pounds, shillings and pence—and to do it quickly. I could do this and Granda would test me. It was fun and a challenge and both of us (?) really enjoyed it.

I managed to, somehow or other, not go to school for a while after I became five. However, when my sister came of school age (she was 13 months younger than me), I couldn't evade the issue any longer, and Mum put her foot down. I had to go to school.

Looking back, I feel sorry for my mother and the struggle she had to get me, physically, to go to school. I yelled and dug my heels in (literally, kicking up dust in the road) and she had to pull me by the hand along the road. I know that she was embarrassed by my behaviour but it was simple—I really didn't want to go to school! I didn't see any point. My Granda had taught me to count, my Mum had taught me to read, knit and sew. What more did I need.

After much deliberation, Cloncore was the choice of Primary School for us simply because it was a short distance from my grandparents' house. In Clonmacate, we lived a couple of miles from any school, there being three within equal range, but as most of our time was spent at my grandparents, Cloncore Primary School was the natural choice.

As my sister was younger than me, she was placed in the first class and was able to play with coloured paper and scissors. She had a great time. On the other hand, I had to knuckle down to real schoolwork. There was reading, sums, spelling and writing. I enjoyed them but demanded from my mother an explanation as to why I couldn't play like my sister. I was disgusted, she also got to play with the abacus. Mum explained that I was too old for these things and had to move on. I listened and obeyed, but I remembered the sense of missing out. I hadn't seen an abacus before.

After school, I could be found wandering around the farm, following my grandfather around the fields wherever he was working, learning about growing strawberries, corn, potatoes, picking plums, etc. I loved collecting eggs from wherever our 'free range' hens had laid them.

Wild bird nests were a fascination for me with their choice of location, the colour of their eggs and then the appearance of the little fledglings. I was only allowed to get so close and no further so as not to disturb their nesting habitat and the cycle of life.

I learned a lot about plant and animal life from my grandad (being his shadow) and I was fascinated by all aspects of the world around us. I spent many hours lying on the grass at the side of the 'big drain' that ran through the property, watching the animal life and beginning to understand how they related to one another.

The water boatmen skimming the surface of the water were an education in itself. How could this happen? They did not sink and I noticed there was a small gap between them and the surface of the water. Marvellous. At different times, there were eels, pike and small sticklebacks (sprickles) in our drain. Another world to check out.

The plants in the hedgerows were another fascination and I learned all the names, my grandfather making sure that I learned the Latin name as well as the common name.

My grandfather read his Bible every day and listened to the Sunday Service on the radio (if he couldn't get to church). He listened to many religious programmes on the radio and made sure that I understood the enormity of the universe that was made by God and of God's love and power. It was a great education the value of which, remained with me all my life.

Though I must admit, I was not a good Christian at many times in my life and, to my eternal shame, too many times.

During the winter months, the bad weather and the heavy snowfall often meant that we were confined to the house and my mother, practical and not wanting us to waste our time, taught us (before we were old enough to go to school) to read books, to count money by playing 'shop' and 'travelling on the 'bus (a few kitchen chairs upended were perfect) to town'. We used cardboard money that we had been given by Santa Claus. It was great fun and passed the time beautifully. Mum also taught us to knit, sew and embroider, even to crochet (which I just couldn't get to grips with).

As I progressed through school, all these basic lessons at home helped make school easier.

Part of the local scene was the fairly regular 'movement' of pigs across from the South of Ireland to the North and vice versa. There were quite a few pigs involved as they crossed and re-crossed the border many times, making their handlers a lot of money each time. One of the trips made with these smuggled pigs seemed to take place in the early morning. This was a noisy trip as the lorry racing down the road as it was usually accompanied by the siren noise of a 'police chase'.

The lorry load of pigs would hurtle past our house at great speed with the pigs squealing as they bounced around inside the truck.

A few seconds later, the 'oonagh oonagh' of the siren on the police car could be heard as they also came hurtling along in close pursuit. Both vehicles were heading with all haste to the Bann Foot ferry, where when crossing the River Bann, you were on the Lurgan side and a different police patrol area. The simple boundaries were the norm and as there was no mobile phones at this stage and any potential crossover of boundary by those evading the law, had to be anticipated in advance, and plans made to catch the culprits.

The ferry which crossed the river Bann was a simple affair. It was a wooden platform floating on the water and just large enough to carry one vehicle at a time. The contraption was then pulled across the river by the ferryman, Mr Wilson, using a rope tethered on both banks and he hauled the whole thing across to the other side, hand over hand on the rope. It was quite a feat of strength. During the morning run, he would then calmly come back and offer the same service to the waiting police car.

The game stopped when the police on our side had the presence of mind to alert the police on the Lurgan side to lie in wait for the smugglers' lorry.

Cigarettes were also a source of good revenue to those interested in making a quieter living transporting their loads of contraband goods.

Bannfoot Ferry, 1950s (Mr Wilson was the ferryman)

Chapter 6
Primary School

I started Cloncore Primary School in September 1952. I did not want to go to school but I was told that I had 'to learn'. Our home was a few miles from the school so my sister and I bicycled part of the way, and left our bicycles at our grandparents' house and walked the rest. We were not troubled by bad weather, we just wrapped up and went on.

Cloncore School, in common with most country schools, was made up of two 'rooms'—the small or 'Wee' room was used for the youngest ones who were taught by a Mrs Jean Stewart. Mrs Stewart was married to a Justice of the Peace and was my first teacher. She was an excellent teacher who taught the younger ones, from five to ten years old. She had to teach a wide range of ability in various stages of learning and development, a job which she did with ease and grace.

The latest intake in the 'Wee Room' started their educational career by played with coloured paper and scissors, simple words on pieces of paper and, to my mind, a magnificent abacus consisting of a light wooden frame with rows of coloured wooden beads that took us through counting up through units, tens and thousands. I was not allowed to do this—I was too old by a whole year (I was a late starter to Primary School) and I had to apply myself to the serious stuff of learning the 3 'Rs'—reading, 'riting and 'rithmetic. The reading books featured the activities of 'Janet and John' and took us through the various levels of learning the new words.

Mrs Stewart had a great method of teaching us our tables. She would draw a large circle on the black board and divide it into 12 sections, labelling each section with its number (1-12), but not in consecutive order. To the side of this circle she would then write the number of the table that we had to learn and practise—3 or 5 etc. We then had to take it in turns to stand up and rattle off our appropriate tables. She would decide which number that we could start with and going clockwise or anti-clockwise. Making it fun for all and I know that I enjoyed this game.

After a couple of years, I was sent into the 'Big Room' where Mr B K Thoms was teaching. He was the headmaster and a strict disciplinarian, who, once again, taught a wide range of ages from about ten years old to fourteen, which was the school leaving age at that time.

The Big Room was roughly divided into two halves, the side nearest the connecting door to the 'Wee Room' where the youngest ones in the 'Big Room' were placed which was towards the back of the school building. At the side nearest to the front of the school, with its large windows letting in the light, were the older pupils who were arranged with their backs to the windows facing into the room. The oldest pupils had their seats nearest to the door, thus signifying their eminent departure from school life. This door led out into the small hallway which also had the cloakroom area. This was simply a row of pegs on the wall for holding coats and scarves. This corridor also led to the main door into the 'Wee Room'. This entrance always looked a little dark and lost to me, being as it was, at the end of the row of coats.

The toilets were outside, up the back of the school yard. They were a draughty and smelly area with the three or four old-style dry toilets. These toilets were eventually replaced, in my time at the school, by a row of modern flushing toilets.

In the Big Room, the desks were arranged in rough pattern ranging from the youngest who were seated close to the connecting door to the 'Wee Room'. The desks on this side of the room were lined up facing the Blackboard and the Headmaster's desk which was over on the right near the big windows. We were arranged so that the tallest ones sat in the big desks at the back of the room, near the large open fireplace, where a fire would burn in the really cold days in winter. This fire heated the room until the arrival of a potbellied stove that was centrally placed to give out a more even heat.

Initially, when I was transferred to the Big Room, I was placed near the connecting door to the 'Wee Room' and being quite tall for my age, my desk was at the back of the class, sitting between two boys, Victor Neill and Roy Turkington, of a similar age who were also tall.

Needless to say, we became good friends and enjoyed 'racing' each other around the school at break time. We could also help each other with our spelling tests and work on sums. Much against the rules, and it was a hit or miss affair because we had to be careful not to get caught.

The blackboard was the focus of our interest and Mr Thoms would position the blackboard at the appropriate angle for the group he was teaching and we would sit up and pay attention. He would take us through what we had to learn and then set us a 'piece of work' to do which we then handed over to the person at the next desk, who would, under supervision by Mr Thoms, mark the work. Spellings were a key part of learning, we had five new spelling to learn every night and we were tested on this the next day. Again the answers being marked by the person in the desk beside, behind or in front of us. It was all depending on what Mr Thoms decided would be the order that day. He walked up and down the rows, making sure that there was no cheating, checking each person's work.

We also seemed to have daily tests with 'sums', with marking being done in the same manner. We then had to give out our results—some of us were braver than others—depending on how we had done. But everyone knew the results— there was no hiding place, but we accepted our placings as a matter of course realising that there were 'horses for courses' and there was no shame attached to poor results. This was the way life was—a mixture of good, bad or in- between'ers.

Reading was another daily lesson. We had our reading books and we all had to read aloud from the prepared piece, some of us were more fluent than others but we all made the effort, stumbling over the new words and learning how to build up on the basic words

I was very keen on talking to my two friends at the back of the class— somehow thinking that Mr Thoms, who would be busy elsewhere, wouldn't notice. I was wrong. The man had eyes in the back of his head and we were nearly always caught. The one time I wasn't talking, I got 'the blame' by Mr Thoms and, despite my protestations of innocence, I was called up to the front of the class and had my knuckles rapped—with the sharp edge of the ruler whistling past the tips of my fingers (he missed!) to come up sharply from below and connect with my knuckles. It hurt.

There were good times too when Mr Thoms encouraged us in the Friday test—he would give sixpence to the one who got most of the spellings or 'sums' correct. If there was too many of us getting a good percentage of the answers correct, then he raised the stakes—we would have to be 100% correct. It was a great incentive, and I got my fair share.

We also had an annual visit by School Inspector, a Mr Dick Little. This visit was part and parcel of the school year and Mr Little was a much-respected figure, although a little remote from us pupils. The visit would pass nearly unnoticed by us pupils; his focus of attention was the teacher, we just observed.

As the visit by the Inspector came without fail, so did the visit by the dentist and the nurse. These were important visits as we all had to be 'seen'. The nurse checked our heads for lice, injected us against polio, whilst the dentist inspected our teeth, often having to do an extraction, usually without anaesthetic (or so it seemed). It was a painful process that enlivened the daily routine.

Summer was always welcomed as it meant that we would go out and play a few games of rounders, run a few races, maybe practice the high jump. This was in addition to the games we normally played in the school yard—skipping being a favourite where rhymes were chanted as you ran in and out of the twirling rope, sometimes alone, sometimes in friendly groups of two or three. All we needed for hours of fun was a rope and friends.

Sports Day was always the highlight of the summer—Tartaraghan No.1 PS, Tartaraghan No. 2 PS and Milltown and us (Cloncore PS) would meet together in a nearby farmer's field for the day and we would compete in our different groups, running, jumping (long jump and high jump) and relay races.

Usually, the cows had been taken out of the field a few days before and the 'cow clap' would have dried, but there were still a few remnants that could catch out the unwary. It was not good to step in the cow clap, it smelled bad and it messed up your shoes and socks. But accidents happen.

There were other little side events going on with hoops and things. These additional side shows ensured it was just a fun day with winners and losers enjoying themselves. I don't remember any parents coming to our Sports Day, but it wasn't something we expected to happen. The teachers were in charge.

An important event coming up to Christmas was the Nativity play. As many pupils as possible took part and it was a great honour to be picked to play a part. Costumes were basic with a piece of silver tinsel serving as a halo and pieces of white sheets were easily transformed into garments suitable for the Wise Men and the Shepherds. The scene was pure magic to us and got us into the Christmas spirit. It was the signal for the forthcoming visit of Santa Claus, a few days off school and maybe even getting snow! Blissful anticipation.

I do have one particularly bad memory of a trip to the dentist. I was about seven years and having bad toothache. The man in the white coat was nice and friendly but decided I had to have the tooth removed. They used gas and that large smelly black rubber mask was terrifying but the toothache was gone. My jaw just ached.

I had to go back for a filling but as it didn't need gas, so I was OK with that. When I saw the large awkward needle, I shrank back in the chair. When the dentist gave me the first injection, it hurt. The second jab was just too much; I bit the man's fingers—hard. Needless to say, I was in disgrace. Mum was mortified and we were asked to leave and not come back.

I can still feel those fingers and smell the faint smell of tobacco from where he smoked.

It was a long time before I went back to see a dentist.

Small rural schools are now a thing of the past and, following the current governing trend, there are many more schools that are due to close because they are not economically viable. In the following of this ethos, we are successfully losing the spirit of kindness and fellowship that bound us together as a community, leaving us, the people, feeling as if we are more of a statistic than a contributor to the human race. Integration was never a problem under the old system, newcomers were greeted, accepted and joined in our games. Maybe we could learn something new from them. We always lived in the hope that some new event/game/tradition would be brought into our lives.

After all, our grandparents' generation had gone to America to join the 'brave new world' and some returned with news of other people with strange sounding names and funny accents. (At that time, the Northeast of England was a funny accent to us, Ulster born folk!)

Cloncore Primary School Photo 1955
(Small Room and First Grades) Infant Teacher Mrs Jean Stewart (married to a JP)
and Headmaster (Big Room) Mr B K Thoms (A Welsh man)

Back row L-R: First grade teacher Mrs Jean Stewart, George Brennan, Roy Turkington, Victor Neill, Davis Turkington, Vivien Brownlee, Harry Matchett, Fred Jackson, Brian Odgers, Ernest Cassells, Robert Forbes, Wilson McAdam, David Neill, and Headmaster Mr Brian Thoms

Second Row from back L-R: Derek Odgers, Desmond Castles, Elizabeth Matchett, Elizabeth Cassells, Dora Turkington, Marion Forbes, Betty Gray, Anna Rainey, Netta Lutton, Rachel Cassells, Betty Corry, Maurice Lyttle, Noah McAdam

Third Row L-R: Samuel Johnston, Doreen Odgers, Doreen Gray, Dora Strain, June Castles, Olive Corry, Elizabeth McAdam, Evelyn Odgers, Peggy Stewart, Evelyn Humphries, Hester McAdam, Hazel Cochrane, Elizabeth Ann Neill, Mildred Brennan, Esther Cassells, Victor McAdam

Front Row L-R: Earl Cassells, Kenneth Thornton, Thomas Sullivan, Matthew Gray, Bertie Neill, Cecil Turkington, Tommy Troughton, Billy Troughton

During school holidays, there was usually work to be done on the farm, particularly in the summertime, we had fruit to pick that were to be sold in the market in Belfast. When the chores were completed, we were free to go and explore. This meant, for me, wandering around the fields and 'drains' watching out for the small plants and animals that interested me. Grandad was always somewhere around to ask, what was this or that? He was very knowledgeable about nature and he even allowed me to go across the fields to the 'moss'. This was peat bog that had once supplied local families with the turf which was burnt in the grate to heat the house and on which the cooking was done.

I loved the moss. I could wander around it all day. There were plants of all descriptions, indigenous to the moss habitat. Then there was the acid black water in the drains that crisscrossed the moss. They too had their own specific plants. It was, to me, a world of magic and mystery to be explored. My explorations were a little bit dangerous because the drains/ditches had steep straight sides where the turf had been cut out. They were full of black peat bog water. It was impressed upon me that if you fell in, there was nothing to hold on to get out and you could easily drown.

My mother warned me not to get my feet wet, so, in the wet boggy areas, I used to jump from one solid lump of grass to another, balancing precariously at times until I could make the next jump. But I had to be fast, the tufts did sink under the weight.

Between this and watching out for the different flowering plants that were indigenous to the moss environment, I could spend all day wandering around. I never felt hungry and only came home when I heard the 'coee' shout by my mother, signalling that we had to have tea or make our way to our own house a few miles away.

Chapter 7
College Days

When I came to the age of ten years old, I was reckoned to be a suitable candidate to sit the 11+ examination, which would allow me entry to Portadown College. If I remember correctly, there were five of us selected from the school and we just had a couple of extra homework to do to ensure that we would be prepared for the wording of the questions and the fact that we would be working to a timed schedule. We had to travel to a school in town (I think it was the Hart Memorial Primary School) to sit the exam.

My friend's mother drove us in her car (a treat in itself). The setting for the exam, with lines and rows of desks, was awesome (to me) but I was able to complete the papers—set on a series of three separate days.

As soon as the exams were over, I forgot about them and, much to my surprise, I passed and got a place in Portadown College.

As the College was in Portadown, it meant that I had to catch the local bus every day. The bus service was number 75 and ran between Portadown and Maghery (a few miles further on past my home). The other people using the bus were mainly office workers and other students going to different schools.

We quickly got to know each other, being regular travellers. It was a small community and the noisy chatter rose above the rattle of the bus engine as it chortled and groaned it way up and down hills, grinding to a stop at each bus stop to pick up passengers.

In Portadown, the College buildings were centred around an old house (formerly very grand) and set in its own ground on the banks of the River Bann. There had been additional buildings added to accommodate the various classrooms for the different additional subjects that were then part of the school curriculum. The catchment area for the school, spread over the surrounding countryside and meant an increased number of pupils each year. For me, this was a very large school when compared to my school out in the country with its two rooms.

The change of school could be considered a traumatic experience, as the numbers were vastly different from what I was used to.

As well as getting the bus every morning for the 20-30-minute journey, I had to play hockey—a game totally foreign to me, who had been more used to skipping ropes, marbles and playing house with broken pieces of discarded pottery. But it was an exciting prospect and there was much discussion over the uniform that I had to wear and what type of hockey stick I would need plus the hockey boots (made of a heavy woven material) that I needed for the game. I wasn't much bothered by all of this, as it was just school and I had accepted by now that I had to 'learn' and do what I was told.

The first day on the bus into school was exciting—I loved the bus journeys, the rattling old bus with its unique smells and draught swirling round my feet from the open door (even when the door was closed there was a draught). Sometimes on frosty mornings, the bus had to crawl carefully up and down the small hills along the way. The passenger door was at the back of the bus and the draught had free rein around all the passengers within. The driver was nice and snug in his closed off cabin at the front.

Inside the very back of the bus there was a very definite draught and when the door opened when it snowed, the flakes of snow drifted in along the passageways. The effect was quite magical. The bus got me to school so all these things didn't matter, it was all ok with me.

When we arrived in town, I knew that I had only a short walk from where I was dropped off in the centre of town to the school. Even the walk through the town was a novelty and I remember feeling a sense of being grown up and responsible.

Arriving at the school gates that momentous first morning, I looked up the drive at all the other pupils milling around, I felt strange (maybe slightly sick!) but honoured somehow. Maybe even a tiny bit lost. Cars were stopping at the school gates and students were getting out, most were smiling in anticipation of seeing their friends and catching up with the news of the summer just past. There was a sense of confident anticipation in the air.

Everyone seemed to know where they were going, so my friend Elizabeth, who had travelled in on the same bus as myself, was more confident than I was, having had her brothers as past pupils, led the way. I just followed her amid the main throng going up the steps through the nearest door. Somehow or other we found our way. To be fair, there were people directing the new pupils. Looking back, I think that I didn't expect it to be this easy to find out where to go and what to do.

Once through the doors, we entered a dark corridor among a sea of black blazers and black jumpers over blue shirts (the colours of the school uniform) but I felt strangely at ease. I was astonished when the Headmaster, Mr DWJ Woodman, came along and spoke to each of us by name. I was startled, even though I knew that I had sent in a photo of myself into the school as part of the preparation for entry. What a memory the man had! I felt reassured after that and just knew that I would find out the rest as I went along!

Going in to First Assembly was an *eye*opener—there were about 600 pupils gathered in the Assembly Hall, all in rows, according to their year and subdivided into classes. We had all been notified in advance of all of this detail and I finally started to remember what the letter had said. At last, I was getting a grip of things.

There was a lot of noise but the excited chatter died as the Headmaster, Mr DWJ Woodman, in his black teacher's gown (an imposing sight to my way of thinking), strode into the hall and mounted the steps to the platform to conduct the morning service—a hymn, a short prayer and a few announcements.

It was reassuring and everything fell into place after that as we dispersed to our different classrooms for our formal College education to begin.

It was all so new to me. The different subjects, changing room for each class—I just followed my identified classmates. The school was mainly an old building with lots of stairs and many rooms all dedicated to different teachers and different subjects. I loved the smell of the wooden floors that the cleaner had swept with some sort of disinfectant granules the night before, leaving this gorgeous aroma.

Outside of school, the headmaster was an easily distinguishing figure. He rode around on a bicycle, in all weathers. He used bicycle clips to stop his trousers from catching in the chain and he had the most wonderful highly polished light-coloured wooden briefcase, more like a suitcase, which he used to balance on the cross bar of his black bike. A much-respected individual, he was easily identifiable. In my mind's eye, I can still see him cycling up or down the drive at the College.

The number of subjects I was going to study were much expanded, in comparison to the Primary School I had just left. 'Sums' became Algebra,

Arithmetic and Geometry. Geography opened a wide new world and my sense of curiosity made me want to learn as much as I could about the world, its countries, its people and its natural resources.

The production of food crops throughout the world was so logical and in tune with the prevailing climatic conditions of the regions that that its very logic astounded me.

I was much struck by the details of this awesome natural world of volcanoes, earthquakes, ice fields and tropical rain forests, it was wonderful and inspiring. History was fascinating, even a bit bewildering as we went back to the beginning of man's journey on earth.

The Stone Age, the Bronze Age, etc. seemed a bit useless to me until I realised that this was just progression as each age learned new tricks (just like me and moving schools). French and Latin were complete new doors to me, as did the constant changing of rooms and teachers for each class. It was really quite pleasant, as it was interesting to me, and I quickly settled into the new routine.

The books of the Bible (which I knew well from Sunday School) took on a new and wonderful meaning as I began to understand, not just, the significance of the Forty Days and Forty Nights Jesus spent in the wilderness, without food and shelter, but I also now understood the difficulties experienced when coping with the different climatic conditions, which up to this point, I hadn't really thought much about, merely accepting the words but without going into the meaning or the reality. I was fascinated by this new world of learning.

During my first few months, I learned a lot. We had 'cloisters' at our school and the central playground was the 'quad'. All new to me.

I was an avid reader from an early age and the exciting adventures I had read about in the Famous Five and Secret Seven books and others, all paled in comparison to this new world. I had often sneaked away to read Dad's cowboy books and murder mystery novels, but they were just words on paper. This was real.

This realisation got me started to read even more. To the irritation of everyone at home, I read the writing on the sauce bottles on the table, I read the details on the biscuit tins we had got at Christmas time. If there was writing on it, I read it. It must have been really annoying but I was oblivious. Going to College had opened my mind to a new reality. I had a lot to learn.

I played hockey in the winter and a little tennis in the summer. Athletics was probably my favourite and it was popular at school. We had an Olympic

Champion, Mary Peters, as one of our past pupils. She was a great inspiration to all. I loved athletics and was quite good at running but didn't have the dedication to take it anywhere, despite an offer to train me by an expert coach, Mr McClelland. I was more interested in books.

During the better weather, usually for a couple of weeks in May, I would be bold and cycle the seven miles or so into school, but usually, I was the idiot running up the road to the bus stop with an armful of books and sports gear trying to make it to the stop before the bus left. I looked ridiculous and it was very funny to those looking out the back window as they grinned down at me. But I was training for athletics (not!), I just didn't get myself organised in the morning. My mother often asked me what I was doing but I could only mumble.

Shortly after my first couple of years at college, the family moved to live in the town. It was purely for financial reasons as the monthly bus pass was expensive. I don't think that it was a popular move but my other country cousins also moved to the town. We had running water there and electricity. A proper bathroom with a bath, wash hand basin and toilet. To us, used to more basic conditions, this was luxury. If we lit the fire, we had hot water and didn't have to depend on boiling a kettle. Maybe sounds a bit incredible as this was in the late fifties, but it was reality.

In town, I was also able to walk the few miles to school. I still carried my armful of books and sports gear (when needed). Instead of just walking, I usually ran to a lot to places simply because I wanted to get there. Unknown to me until recently, the neighbours had nicknamed me 'the runner'. I was oblivious of all of this, my thoughts were wrapped up in the information contained in the latest book I was reading.

After some years, I left school with my 'A' levels and entrance to Queens University Belfast and Trinity College Dublin. Due to restricted family finances, I decided not to go to Uni but to start work instead. My father had serious health issues and I figured that further qualifications could come later. I felt that this was only fair to the rest of the family, especially my mother and father who were having such a struggle just trying to feed and clothe us all.

Chapter 8
Work

After my final exams, one afternoon, as I was walking home from school, I noticed a job vacancy notice pasted to the glass in the door of the Post Office (GPO) in Portadown. The job was for a Postal and Telegraph Officer which meant working as a member of the counter staff, paying out pensions and allowances, selling postage stamps, money or postal orders and licences for radio and television. It was a Norther Ireland Civil Service job, using local staff.

I filled in the application form and got the job fairly quickly. I was sent for three weeks training in Belfast at the GPO Training School in Fort William Belfast. This was my first time away from home, so quite an experience for this naive teenager. It was only about 30 miles from home, but it might as well have been a trip to the moon, as far as I was concerned.

On the Sunday prior to the start of the course, Mum organised me and accompanied me to Belfast. She had organised a car to take us there and just wanted to make sure that I was ok. Mum checking out my landlady and digs, before leaving me on my own. The place was quiet, especially, after the busy boisterous home that I had just left. I lay on the bed, feeling a little bereft and a little excited about the future.

My digs weren't far from the Training School, so making sure I had the correct directions the next morning, I set off. I was the only one on my course, so I had the full attention of the instructor and we got through fairly easily.

GPO engineers were also being taught at the centre and we only saw each other at break time. As my digs were fairly close, it was a short walk home, before the evening meal. Where I was lodging was quiet but the other residents, a traveller for something and another guy who lived there permanently, were pleasant, though I didn't see much of either of them. The traveller was a fairly regular resident and the permanent residents were, like myself, quiet.

I got the train home every weekend, returning on Sunday night after having had my washing done. This was alright and wonder upon wonders, I was being paid to do this!

After the three-week course, I reported back to work and settled in quite quickly. It was a good job and they were great people to work with. It was fairly routine. You handled cash and dockets all day and you balanced your till at night. We were busy at the counter and worked in shifts to give continuous coverage. People used the Post Office a lot in those days, picking up different types of allowance, buying Postal Orders, stamp, licences for guns, radios and TVs. There was a lot of letters posted, some using Special Delivery, some, containing items of value, which went Registered Post.

The Post Office was, at that time, a very busy place. I enjoyed meeting the people and dealing with their requests, but I was not so happy at the balancing. I was always a penny or so 'out' and had to check everything again. But it was part of the job, so I got on with it and soon learned to be careful with the change.

After a few months, it was decided that I could do better for myself and I was advised by a senior member of the Post Office Writing Office Staff, Mr Kennedy from Portadown, to aim higher as he felt that I was capable of doing a much more difficult job. Wilbur knew my father well and he came to our house and spoke to Dad, telling him that I was capable of a higher grade in the Civil Service which meant that I had to go across the water to work in London. My father didn't object and Wilbur agreed to set the process in motion.

It was with some trepidation that I applied to the Imperial Civil Service for a job as an Executive Officer (I was just over 17 years old at the time). I was granted an interview and had to travel to Manchester.

This was my first visit to the mainland UK and I had to plan how to get there. I didn't have a clue so I went to the local travel agent, Lockes, in West Street Portadown and Connie Locke organised my trip. I boarded the train in Portadown at the then Railway Station in Watson Street and made my way to the Liverpool bound boat in Belfast Docks. This was an overnight journey, sailing across the Irish Sea (a journey my mother and father had both made at different times during their years of military service during the war). I was seriously nervous and after boarding the boat, I went down to my cabin and, surprisingly, had a good night's sleep. The nervous tension of the preparations for travel had tired me out!

Arriving at the docks in Liverpool early the next morning, following the throng of passengers, I found my way to the train station and boarded the train for Manchester where the interview was going to be held. I was a bit scared that I would get lost or make a mess of the directions around Manchester and had arranged to meet an old school friend who was already working in England (in the RAF) and who knew Manchester. I was pretty relieved when we met at Manchester station and was even more relieved when I got to the building where the interview was going to be held and with lots of time to spare.

Scared as I was by all this newest of experiences, I was still enthralled by it all and, much to my surprise and awe, even enjoyed finding the way around the massive (to me) streets of Manchester and seeing some of the magnificent buildings in that town. I had a good relaxed exploration after the interview before making my way to the bus station.

I don't remember much of the detail about the Civil Service Building in Manchester in which the interview was held but I do remember that the interview was held in a large and imposing room, typical of the time, and although a bit intimidating and bewildering to me, I somehow wasn't worried at all. After all, I did have a job and was earning the essential salary—so, no bother!

I found my way to the correct room and waited patiently. My grandparents had instilled in me that if I did my best that was all that could be done. My mother and father had echoed that instruction as I left for the interview, so I felt no stress.

I do remember, quite vividly, that I was interviewed by five people sitting behind a large table. They fired lots of questions at me—all at once! In the arrogance of youth and innocence, I listened calmly and answered the questions in turn. Taking each question in turn and answering it—as calm as a cucumber! I remember feeling that this was a lovely challenge. I clearly remember them firing the questions at me and then, holding my nerve, I managed to answer them in turn. I even remember answering them, starting to my left and going down the line.

Surprisingly, I felt that we had a great chat and I thought that they were very nice people who knew what they were doing! The ideas of youth and arrogance. The fact that they told me that there were University graduates also competing did not bother me at all.

After the interview, my one thought was that I had to return home as I had to get back to work the next day, starting at 11.30. So following the plan as arranged by travel agent Connie Locke, I caught the airport bus, took a flight from Manchester to Belfast and then travelled the rest of the way by bus.

A lot of firsts for me—my first time crossing the Irish Sea and my first flight. I remember just looking forward to getting home.

The next morning, I was still in bed at 8.30 when my mother came into the bedroom with a letter for me. It was from the Civil Service telling me that I had passed the interview and was selected for a post as Executive Officer. I was quite surprised that the word came through that quickly. I was surprised, not just by the speed of the response but, as they had said at the interview, I had competed against others who had passed through university and gained their degrees in various subjects.

The Postal Delivery service in those days was first class and fast.

Nevertheless, at home, it was all low key and I went off to work as usual.

Chapter 9
London

When I moved to London to take up my post, it was a nerve-wrecking experience as I had only been in England once before when I had gone for the interview in Manchester. As was the usual way to travel to England at that time, I travelled to London by boat and train, arriving on a wet Saturday in the capital.

I met a friend who had a cousin living near Battersea Power Station. Pat (the cousin) was married with a daughter (Josephine) and she had agreed to put me up for a few days until I could find somewhere to live.

After initial greetings and a cup of tea, I was keen to see a bit of London and get my bearings. I needed to find out how I was going to get to work on Monday and we went out for a walk to find out where the tube station was in relation to where I was staying (I was going to go by tube as travel was easier that way as buses could get snarled up in traffic). The lady lived in Chelsea just off the embankment and the view of Battersea Power Station was impressive. This view emphasising the enormous size of the place I was now in.

Walking past Cleopatra's Needle reminded me of the book *The Third Man* and I visualised the scene with the mist rising from the river, and I looked for the steps! Walking along beside the Thames was the thing of books and adventure stories. I was very impressed, awed by it all, in the middle of my own adventure...

We continued our discovery tour and somewhere about Putney Bridge, the rain, which had been falling steadily all morning, became heavier and we decided to catch a bus. Again, I was awestruck by the continuous and fast-moving traffic flow as it went over the bridge and down onto the High Street.

The iconic red double-decker buses synonymous with the London scene convinced me that I had arrived in the capital!

A bus slowed and drew up alongside us as we crossed Putney Bridge and, as we had decided to catch a bus, I hopped onto the platform. Being new to the scene, I forgot to hold the pole provided at the corner of the platform and fumbled in my bag for money to pay my fare. Engrossed in what I was doing, I didn't notice that the line of traffic had started to move. The bus started off with a jerk, I slipped on the wet platform and fell off backwards. I heard the frantic 'ching' of the bell and as I lay, flat on my back looking up into the concerned face of the conductor leaning over and holding onto the pole, I felt so stupid, a real idiot. I leapt to my feet and jumped back on the platform of the bus, this time holding on to the pole.

What an introduction to London and its traffic! Trust me! Though I was very lucky that the traffic behind was slow moving, otherwise my first day in London could have ended quite differently, in a bit of a disaster!

On the Monday morning, I presented myself, as directed, to Shell Mex House in the Strand. It was here that I got my introduction to the Civil Service and London.

After the initial meet and greet, I was handed a street map of London and asked to report to another office, near the British Museum. The walk was enjoyable and I noticed many famous street names as I followed my route. There were a few other designated stops and eventually, I arrived at my final destination in Holborn.

This was, to me, an exciting introduction to the Civil Service. I revelled in the challenge of navigating my way around using a street map and I enjoyed the sights of London on the way. It was a great way to introduce a newcomer to the city, I was quite delighted, both with myself and my achievement at finding my way and in not getting lost. A great confidence boost.

Eventually finding my way to St Georges Court in Holborn, I was assigned to the Contracts Division of the Ministry of Aviation (which later merged into the Ministry of Defence). My role was to deal with civilian contractors who supplied the Ministry of Defence with spare parts for the large aircraft, mine was the then iconic Comet 4e transport plane.

The job was a relatively straightforward one and I was given a quick induction session by the outgoing incumbent, focusing on the daily routine and instructed on what was required of me before I was on my own.

Dealing with my opposite numbers in the civilian aircraft contract business, spare parts division, I was working exclusively on the contracts for the Comet 4e which was an imposing beast, that, in later years, I had the privilege of having a flight in one of those iconic planes.

Some 20-30 years later, it was still in service with the RAF, monitoring the weather from up in the sky.

Meanwhile, I worked with the contract division of the Hawker Siddeley Aircraft Corporation and the British Aircraft Corporation. At the desk facing me was the executive officer for the new Concorde who dealt with all aspects relating to the functioning of this aircraft. This was impressive. The officer had loads of experience and I learned a lot from him.

Dealing with spare parts for aircraft, whatever make or type, might not be everyone's idea of a great job but I was delighted and fascinated. This was so new, technical and intriguing, that I felt I was in seventh heaven. I learned about mechanical parts, electrical parts and Doppler radio aerials. All new stuff to me. My contacts in the aircraft industry were important people and they treated me well. It was great.

However, I was seeing Reg who was in the RAF. He would come down to London at weekends and we would wander around, visiting the sights. We decided to get married and it was evident that I had to give up my job, very reluctantly, as he was moved around often with his job. This was fairly common in those days, but, in hindsight, it was not a good decision. But then as I found out later in life, 'hindsight is an exact science'.

I was there for a year or so, enjoying it, and fitted in great shopping expeditions in the West End at weekends. After a couple of weeks, I was fortunate enough to get a small bedsit in Putney, just behind the High Street. At the weekends, I walked around the sights (sometimes with Reg in tow), enjoying the bustle and noise of the Strand, Charing Cross, Regent's Park, etc.

Working and living in London also meant that we (some friends and I) could get last-minute tickets for the various shows in the West End. (These tickets were ones that had been returned due to the ticket holders not unable to attend for that night's show, so it was always very last minute). These were much cheaper tickets, thus allowing us to see some great shows currently running.

In work, I was also sent by my office to attend various civil service courses, as well as to attend finance and parts committee meetings that were, to others, tedious, but to me they were exciting and allowed me to see other offices and meet fellow civil servants.

I loved it all, the courses, and the band concerts on Sundays, usually going to the one in the park beside Charing Cross station. I loved seeing the families enjoying a stroll along the footpath beside the Thames at Putney, the Boat Race in which I supported Oxford because I preferred the dark blue colour.

This was London and I gloried in the atmosphere, the hustle and bustle of the markets, and the never-ending stream of people hurrying along the streets. I used to play a childish little game to myself—watching the people walking along the street and trying to identify those who were new to London (they usually bumped into others as they navigated the crowds) and those who were more at home in the city. Those more at home in London were able to navigate the crowds more easily, following the unwritten, unidentified rule of the pavement. Intriguing.

Chapter 10
Marriage and Singapore

After a relatively short period working as a civil servant, I got married to Reggie Dawson with whom I had gone to college and who was now RAF aircrew (air signaller/radio operator), flying in Hastings Transport planes, which was at that time considered the workhorse of the RAF. He was based at Colerne in Wiltshire and he insisted that I move to Bath and therefore give up my job in the Civil Service. This was a fairly normal occurrence in those days, but I hated to have to leave my lovely job in London. But this was the way it was then.

Because of the nature of his job as aircrew on Transport Command, he went on many assignments to the Caribbean and other exotic places. I stayed back in the flat and looked for a job.

As the Squadron was based at Colerne RAF station, we lived in Bath, one of the nearest large towns. Bath is a beautiful city, with many ancient buildings and touristy spots like the Pump Rooms, the ancient Roman Baths, Bath Abbey and the Royal Crescent and many more.

We found a top floor flat near the Centre of Bath but found that Reg then had to travel through traffic in Bath centre to get to work at Colerne. So after a reasonably short stay there, we then moved closer to the RAF base having found a ground-floor flat in a beautiful old Georgian house at the other side of Bath, near Batheaston.

The flat was lovely, old style, with high ceilings and lovely wooden floorboards. The floors moved as you walked on them and they weren't totally level. But the flat had character. There were large, old carpets, that covered most of the floor and the surrounding visible floorboards were painted black. There was a large open fireplace in the large living room which had tall bow windows and looked out over a large part of the town. Some modifications were made to the back of the flat and a small narrow but modern kitchen had been added with a handy alcove suitable for the large fridge which we purchased second hand. The fridge was 20 years old at that stage but worked efficiently and held a lot of stuff. There was a lovely archway joining the kitchen to the dining room/small living room. I loved it.

The door to the unused basement was in our hallway and the impression of darkness and cold that came up from that basement scared me half to death. On one occasion, when my husband was home, I was brave enough (with him) to go and explore the basement. It was dark with many rooms and had obviously been the servants' quarters.

This was a glimpse into the past and the times of large houses and servants' quarters. There was really nothing to fear.

My husband was away a lot of the time and friends, telling me stories of ghostly happenings, did not help me at all as I spent most evenings alone. But I was just being silly.

After a short search, I got a job in an Insurance Office and the times spent on my own passed quickly. I made friends with some nurses and physios who lived in the flat above and we sometimes went to the cinema together. I discovered the local 'scrumpti' in their company. It was a pleasant discovery but as they didn't have much money to spare and neither did I, we were well matched.

The garden outside the front door of our flat was small and overgrown but after a bit of a clean-up it was quite pleasant to sit in during the nice warm days. It was a pleasant time. During that time, hubby spent a lot of time on trips to the Caribbean but after participating in one trip, I think it was something to do with Rhodesia and Zimbabwe and airlifting of supplies to that area, he suffered a collapsed lung and after receiving medical checks after his trip, sometime later, he was hospitalised (starting off in Swindon before being moved to a specialist hospital in Midhurst, King Edward VII). Reg had to remain in hospital for the most part of a year.

It was a difficult time (I had to give up my job) as the specialist hospital was in Sussex. It was quite a long way away and as I was having to use and rely on a mixture of the local bus service and RAF Transported, visiting took up most of the day. There were problems associated with the then treatment of a collapsed lung and life became very serious and it all became a bit of a struggle for both of us.

Eventually, I moved down to Midhurst in Sussex where the hospital was located. I was in lodgings there for most of a full year. The people with whom I lodged were very nice but the situation was serious for Reg. However, despite the challenges, he survived and we then returned to Bath.

After my husband came out of hospital, he had a lengthy period of recuperation before returning to work. By this time, our financial situation was not in great shape. The whole episode had been an emotionally and financially draining period. We were wrung out and broke.

Fortunately, I was able to get a much-needed job in the gas board in Bath working in the Wages Department. The gas board in Bath was responsible for the workers in the southwestern area and the many employees were paid on a weekly basis. Recording hours and calculating payments was where I and a few others played our part.

Each wages clerk was responsible for a dedicated area and the system was that the wages section, received the completed time sheets from the workers in each specific region. Each desk had this very large tidy block of wage/time sheets in the centre of the desk. The information coming in from the field was then manually transferred onto the larger weekly wages' sheets. After completing the week's entries and calculating overtime and allowances, the information was transferred to a computerised wages slip. Impressive to us but awkward and naive by modern standards. One day each week, we then had to be secured in a closed safe room and physically count out the wages for each employee.

This was my first experience of the new technology—computers (1965-66). Though the computerised part was minimal, it was highly regarded in those days.

After a few very enjoyable months, I had to leave this job as my husband, because of having had a collapsed lung, was transferred to helicopters and posted to Singapore for a tour of duty. The tour was normally for two and a half years and we were to be based at RAF Seletar on the northern part of the island. Excited to be going out to the Far East, I still felt a little disappointed at having to give up my extremely interesting and well-paid job.

Both of us liked the idea of travel—and the warm tropical climate was a big attraction! We were due to leave immediately after Christmas and temporary accommodation and the travelling to Singapore was organised by RAF Movements. We were being flown out on RAF transport. All we had to do was to follow instructions.

Suitable clothing for the tropics was difficult to find in December but I remember investing in two new dresses, a pink and white stripped one in seersucker material and a blue dress in rather nice smooth fabric. I was very skinny (about size 10) at that time and the dresses were a little big—fitting me where they hit! I wasn't very concerned with dress and style so I wasn't bothered. I would get some more sometime later.

Chapter 11
Singapore

The posting to Singapore was for two and half years, but we ended up living there for five years, the equivalent of two tours.

We left the UK for Singapore in January 1966, flying out from Brize Norton. The flight was approximately 23 hours long with one fuel refill stop in Bahrain where, although it was the middle of the night, we experienced our first taste of the heat as we disembarked the plane. The wall of heat hit you like a sledgehammer as you stood on the top of the aircraft steps.

I don't remember staying there very long before we boarded the plane, this time destination was for Changi Airfield, Singapore.

Among the passengers was a family with three or four young children and I felt sorry for them as they tried to settle down for sleep. Their Mum was a lot more experienced in travelling than I was and she had changed into a cotton dress for arrival in Singapore, thus remaining cool in the intense heat.

Whereas, arriving at Changi, I suffered, dressed as I was in my UK winter clothing. Though, honestly, I don't remember caring very much as this was a new adventure!

On arrival in Singapore, we were met and transported to our hotel, the Pasir Ris, off the Tampines Road, near Paya Lebar. The taxi was comfortable but parts of the road were rough, travelling over the red laterite clay road was a thrill. (I had learned about this when studying geography at school, so I felt comfortable with the condition of the road and marvelled that I was actually seeing and feeling what it was really like at first-hand!) The road was rough and during the rainy season, it would degenerate into ruts that held the water and it would be difficult to travel over but I wasn't worried. This was what it was like in the new (to me) environment. The luxuriant jungle growth pressing in on both sides was impressive. Here and there the sight of a small house was intriguing. Sometimes a couple of curious onlookers could be glimpsed through the undergrowth. This was my new world so I settled back in my seat in the taxi and enjoyed the journey.

The hotel had been booked by us from the UK on advice from the RAF Movements people, so we did not know what to expect. The journey along the red laterite road running through the jungle was a surprise but not unpleasantly so, this was what we had, so 'hey ho', relax and soak it up.

Arriving at the Pasir Ris hotel, we were delighted to see that the building was quite traditional Far Eastern style, open, welcoming and apparently deserted. I could glimpse the sea through the garden as the hotel backed onto the water.

Obviously, we were expected and the young man welcomed us with the offer of a cup of tea or coffee. I can still see the chunky white cups and saucers with the chicory smoky taste of the coffee, which to me, seemed so much right for this place and this time. The tea was 'delicate' and very English, i.e., not strong like in N Ireland.

After refreshing ourselves with drinks, we were shown to our room, not in the main part of the hotel upstairs, but down a small winding path to a house right on the seafront. There were about four such houses in the row looking out to sea and they were quite magnificent in their situation. The facilities were basic but lovely and neat. The door to the room opened directly into a large bedroom with adjoining shower and toilet. The accommodation was so appropriate for the location, in this exotic setting with the sound of the waves lapping the sand.

Outside our room, the wide ribbon of sand stretched off in a slight curve and came to within a few feet of our doorstep. On the sand, hairy coconut shells and hermit crab shells were scattered all along the beach. The sand was beautifully white and fine with small short fronds of coconut palms scattered around that had been blown down by the last storm.

The room was plainly furnished, very clean with its adjoining toilet and shower. The louvre doors opening out to the magnificent shoreline and the room window was fitted with shutters for privacy of the occupants and for protection from strong winds.

The water lapped gently, soothingly along the shoreline. Magic. It was even magical a few nights later when, during a storm, the thunder of the waves on the same surf competed with the roar of the strong winds.

It was another world and I felt thrilled and delighted to be here and appreciate these sights and sounds that I had only read about in books.

I fell in love with Singapore right there and then and when Reg was away at work those first few days and weeks, I donned my bikini, picked up a towel and wandered over the sand, paddling in the surf, examining the debris on the beach and watching the small crabs scuttle along the sand. It was pure bliss to me.

Reg, on the other hand, was more prosaic about things, he had to travel to work by taxi and he was keen to find a house for us to live in which would be closer to the Squadron at Seletar.

The hotel was about halfway between Seletar Camp and Changi and the journey time each way was at least half an hour and he had to get acclimatised to the heat and humidity as he worked and travelled. It was easy in a bikini on the beach.

There was one other Forces family staying at the hotel at that time. They had arrived on the same flight as we did. The husband and wife had three boys ranging in age from about twelve to three and they were housed in the main part of the hotel. I did not see much of them as I was spending most of my time exploring the beach and they, being practical, were busily engaged in finding a home so that the boys could get back into school. After about a week, they moved to a house in Serangoon and we kept in loose contact, meeting at the Seletar Camp swimming pool whenever we had found our accommodation and gotten sorted.

We had arrived in Singapore at a very auspicious time. A few months after we arrived and settled into our place in Seletar Hills, we heard about Singapore's first Independence Day celebrations.

Singapore, under the Presidency of Lew Kwan Yiu, was celebrating its Independence from the rest of Malaysia. It was a big move for the relatively small island and it had to be celebrated in style. A huge parade and a display of National talent and expertise was being planned with lots of razzamatazz.

The inaugural National Day Parade to celebrate separation from the rest of Malaysia was held one year after the separation. So on 6th August 1966 we went downtown to see the parade. A big occasion, it started in the morning at 9.00 a.m. There was a great buzz of anticipation and we knew that this was something we just had to see. We got an early taxi downtown on the day so that we could get ourselves stationed at a good viewing point to witness all of the parade. Following the advice of the taxi driver, we were not disappointed. We had a place across from the Padang near the centre of town, which was where they normally played cricket. My mind was agog with the sights and sounds. I was in a new world that was old, yet new, and full of historical sights. I could hardly take it in, I had read the book, *A Passage to India* by EM Forster based on the days of the Raj (1920's) and India's Independence, and I felt as if I had stepped into a similar book. It was a different nation and location, but the same atmosphere. I was enthralled and hooked.

Then there was the parade. It was huge, noisy and went on for ages. There were rows after rows of people parading, carrying flags and dressed in all sorts of glamourous costumes. There was drums and lines of Chinese Lion Dancers weaving their way across the road. The parade was colourful and joyous. The cacophony of sound was pure magic to my ears, the colours and noise all melted into one big assault on the senses. It was magical. This was my first experience of seeing the lion dancers, the local bands and large groups of people carrying poles with chiffon flags that wove around in amazing patters as the bearers demonstrated their strength and expertise.

The heat was tremendous but those on parade had endless energy and big smiles to accompany the loud clang, clang of the bands. The dancers just kept going, apparently not noticing the heat. I hardly noticed the heat myself. Lew Kwan Yiu must have been very proud. We were enthralled onlookers, absorbed in the magic.

Seletar Hills

After a couple of weeks and a little bit of searching, we found somewhere to live. The houses were lovely but as Reggie would be away quite a bit, I wanted somewhere that I could feel safe, so we opted for an apartment above a shop. The place we found was in Seletar Hills Estate, close to the garrison, and the shop below belonged to the local grocer, Neo Sung and he owned the flat. The grocer and his family lived behind the shop and we reasoned that he would be security conscious and we would be secure with the shop below and the family living at the back. It was a good arrangement. We had to wait a few days for them to repaint the place but it was ideal for us.

Entering from the street door beside the shop, the stairs led up to a large square hallway. This was a one-bedroom apartment, leading off from the large wide hallway at the top of the stairs. The sitting room overlooked the main street outside, there was a dining room with a balcony, a small neat kitchen and a bathroom facing out the back. The sitting room had a very comfortable bamboo frame settee and two chairs with lovely red comfortable cushions. Also there was a bamboo coffee table with a glass top. The bedroom had a large bed and wardrobe with bedside cabinets. There was a large blue Formica table in the dining room with six matching chairs. It filled the room nicely. The only issue I had was with the cockroaches that I discovered breeding in the nooks and crannies underneath the table-top. I found this out when I realised that the young roaches were falling onto my knee while I was having dinner! I quickly turned the table over and laid it on the floor pouring insect killer on the underneath of the table. It worked! No more cockroaches! A few did reappear in the large storage cupboard in the hall but they were swiftly dealt with by me and the insect repellent. I just didn't like opening the door to meet any large cockroaches with their beady eyes watching me and waving their front feelers in my direction! But that was a small price to pay for the experience of living in Singapore.

We had got fitted an ornate security grill on the front door and on the balcony at the back to help delay any unwanted visitors, of the human type. The floors were cement and painted cardinal red and needed to be polished once a week with Cardinal Red floor polish.

The place came with its own small brown lizard (gecko) or chit chat as we called it. About 6-8 inches long, it would chitter as it made its way around the walls and slip outside using the air vents just below the roof which were part of the air-conditioned design of the building. He was acceptable, keeping a low profile as it were, and I became quite used to the little fellow with his bright beady eyes watching from his various vantage points on the walls.

As was usual, we were encouraged to employ help, so we got an Amah. She was a lovely person, with a big smile. The Amah was called Fatima, a lovely Malayan Singaporean girl, who did the housework, working three days a week as there was not much to do. There was only the two of us. We were told that an Amah was essential because of the heat and that it was the best thing to do as it also provided a local family with some income. Fatima was married and lived off the Tampines Road, not too far away. She arrived in the mornings, perched sideways on the back of her husband's scooter and he collected her when she finished work in the afternoon. Her English was limited but gestures worked well, from both our viewpoints.

This place was ideal for Reg to get to and from work. It was about 10-15 minutes in a taxi, and the pick-up taxis prowling up and down the main road a few yards away, provided a very frequent and satisfactory service to and from the base.

After a few months in Singapore, we bought a car from a fellow member of the Squadron. He was going home at the end of his tour and sold his black Humber Hawk for a very reasonable price. In its former life, I believe, it had been a London Police Car and it certainly looked the part. A beautiful strong black bodywork with a minimum of chrome decoration, a chrome badge on the bonnet and luxurious brown leather covered seats. I believe it was well over ten years old, having been brought out to Singapore by a previous owner and passed from one new owner to another. A real icon, even for me who knew nothing about cars.

Of course, we had to get it all registered with the Singaporean authorities and get licences organised, but that was a real adventure too. Going downtown to the appropriate departments and getting registered was just another treat, dealing as we did with such lovely friendly people.

During the time at Seletar, I became involved with the Seletar wives club, going to the regular meetings and various outings organised by the group. I started to play netball two mornings each week for the Seletar Station team. I was the goalkeeper for the first team and, in the game following on immediately after, I played Centre for the second team. We played matches against other teams from different areas across the island. I thoroughly enjoying the games and the friendships.

In the afternoons, particularly after netball, I would go to the Seletar Camp swimming pool where the families congregated to enjoy the swimming and to sunbath around the pool. I was usually on my own and if the tables were full, I often sat on my towel on the grassy bank at the edge of the pool. It was so very relaxing and enjoyable, especially with a cup of OXO (the cube dissolved in hot water was very refreshing).

It was quite an experience travelling on the local buses and the pickup taxis which ran continuously along the main roads. It was so free and easy; you just picked a spot and hailed a taxi and got off where it suited you. The taxis drivers were cheerful and friendly and the fares were cheap. The buses did have their recognised stops but a free and easy atmosphere permeated the air. This attitude reflected the overriding attitude on the island. The taxis were also very safe and got you to your destination in good time.

During the two and half years at Seletar, I only had one bad experience and it was on the bus.

It happened when I was coming back from a day downtown and it was at rush hour, when people were making their way home from work in town. I had spent the entire day shopping and sightseeing and got on the bus in centre of town. The bus quickly became very crowded with standing room only. I was quite content to stand, but after a few stops near some blocks of flats, I got a seat, sitting side-on facing into the aisle. Among those standing, hanging on to the pole, there was a lady standing in front of me with her handbag over her shoulder, one arm holding it down close by her side.

As I watched, I saw a guy slide his hand down to her bag, inside the partially open flap and start removing her purse. I leaned forward to tap her on the arm to alert her and suddenly, a shiny stiletto knife was pointing close to my throat. I looked up and the thief gave me a very hard look. The knife was concealed within his big hand and the look was menacing. No one seemed to notice the little drama so I slid back in my seat and remained where I was. We stayed like that until the bus stopped and the lady and the thief got off the bus. I didn't see any police around and decided that I had to leave it alone.

The bus had arrived at the local market area near Serangoon and I didn't fancy creating a scene. A few weeks earlier, at this location, I had seen a crowd quickly gather around a local taxi driver who had done something wrong. They were banging on the car sides and top. The driver looked terrified and his danger was very obvious. I decided that, as the sole international on the bus, I wasn't going to create any upset or take any chances, I didn't want any bother. The rest of the journey was uneventful and I never had any more bother or witnessed anything that was in any way doubtful.

We lived in our flat in Seletar Hills for over two years, feeling safe and secure. We were really enjoying life in the Tropics, close to the base but not on it. The village was a few minutes' taxi ride up the main road and we could get anything we wanted there. We could purchase anything from a new watch (Rolex or Seiko) to a wooden carving (money permitting) and we enjoyed the weekly Amah's market every Thursday evening.

The grocer shop downstairs was great, obviously very convenient and they even delivered. Perfect. The shop opened early in the morning and didn't close until late in the evening and, as the grocer lived at the back of the shop, I never had any safety concerns when I was on my own.

In the evening, when the shop closed and they were making their evening meal outside under the awning at the back of their shop, I enjoyed the delicious aroma of the food as it was being cooked in the wok (circular cone-shaped cooking pan) over a fire bucket of charcoal. I can still hear the swish, swish of the metal spatula against the sides of the wok as the cook continuously stirred the food around. It was all part of the magic of Singapore.

We used to sample the different meals on sale in the restaurants in the village and made quite a few stops at the 'maken' stalls. The food, always freshly cooked, was very tasty and satisfying—egg fried rice, noodles, sweet and sour chicken, fish or pork and all manner of oriental dishes. These were mostly cooked over a charcoal fire and always using fresh ingredients. All the ingredients were on display, and individually they were added to the other fast-moving ingredients cooking and being swished around in the pot—a pinch of this and a sprinkling of that—all added up to make a delicious meal.

Malaysia

Soon after we moved to Seletar and after buying our car, we decided that we would take a trip across the causeway into Malaya. The first stop of Johore Bahru in Malaya was very different from Singapore as it was more rural (Singapore was a definite city) and we noticed the different ambiance as soon as we drove across the causeway. It was quite exciting to us as we made our way over. Across the causeway, we had the choice of a road one to the left and one to the right. On our first visit, we decided to take the road going to the left, running up the West Coast.

In Malaya at that time, life was quite simple in that there was not an elaborate road systems or large hotels scattered around the countryside with glaring glass fronts reaching for the heavens. There were many 'Rumah Persingahans' (Rest Houses) in the towns, always neat, clean, friendly places and gentle beaming Malay staff to greet the visitor. They were a real pleasure to stop at—restful and soothing, a lovely escape from the heat outside.

The road system was basic with one main road running up the East Coast and one on the West Coast with a road halfway up the west coast running across to the Central Highlands. There wasn't much traffic on the roads, there were the large logging Lorries usually carrying three huge tree trunks. The other main road user were the pick-up taxis that serviced the routes, picking up passengers. These taxis were usually Mercedes, of varying ages and conditions, but they all seemed to be in good running order and I never came across one that had broken down. The main bulk of the traffic were the large logging Lorries carrying the felled trees to the saw mills. The cabs were basic, not luxurious in any way, with the long trailer the length of the tree trunks. They seemed very rough, robust and were certainly very reliable.

There were many rivers crisscrossing the arterial routes and, on the odd occasion there were bridges but mainly the rivers were crossed via wooden ferries. Though ferries were not overly large and only held a few cars or a couple Lorries per trip. It was a tight squeeze on the platform but everyone remained cheerful and it all worked. Sometimes there would be a small queue to board the ferry so I was able to get close up views of the Lorries which rattled cheerfully as they sped along the road. Air conditioning was effectively supplied via the lack of doors on the cabs. These Lorries never seemed to break down despite their outward rundown appearance and in that way, they were a reassuring sight with their drivers grinning widely down from their 'air-conditioned cabs'. Everyone was friendly and helpful, no doubt amused to see these visitors enjoying their relaxed and very green landscape.

I can truthfully say that I always felt perfectly safe travelling these relatively deserted roads, sharing it with taxis and logging Lorries. The long distances between signs of habitation never bothered me. The Malayan people were friendly and hospitable. As time went on and I became more of a regular on the roads, I think the locals viewed this lone female, driving an old black Humber Hawk, as one who was a bit of an eccentric and gave me a free pass.

However, back to our first trip into Malaya and we decided to go to Kota Tinga Falls and have a swim in the cool green water. Despite the sparse traffic, we seemed to have a bit of difficulty finding the falls or maybe, the distance was farther than we had been led to believe! After a bit of a drive, we found the falls. We were the only Europeans there. The rest of the visitors appeared to be locals, out for the day. The area around the falls was bathed in a soft green light and it was cool. The many children splashing and laughing under the falls created quite a magical scene and a cool retreat from the heat of the sun. It was a very refreshing day out and one we voted to repeat.

We were both interested in seeing around the region and visited the many places of interest both in Singapore and Malaya. The beautiful Botanical Gardens in Singapore with its magnificent array of plants was worthy of note and was a great place to view the local plants and flowers growing alongside beautiful roses.

I was on my own a lot and often took the car across the causeway into Malaya to see what was of interest. I loved the little shops selling their more agricultural related merchandise and fell in love with a couple of wide brimmed coolie hats (which I purchased) used by workers in the fields. I suppose this reflected my farming background in Ireland as I mentally compared the various tools and equipment. In Ulster, we used our raincoats with hoods to protect us from the elements!

After reading an article in the Straits Times on sea turtles, we decided to visit Kota Bahru and Terengganu in the Northeast of Malaysia, specifically to see where these loggerhead turtles would come up onto the beach to lay their eggs. By this time we were living in Bedok near Changi and took a couple of friends with us.

Our trip to Terengganu was planned to take a few days and when we arrived at our location, we booked into the local hotel for a few nights. We got directions to the appropriate beach and explored our surroundings by day.

When it became dark, we found our way down to the beach and sat down on the sand and prepared ourselves for a wait. The idea was that as the turtles came up on the beach only at night, our intention was to spend the night on the beach to see the turtles come up out of the sea to visit their breeding grounds and lay their eggs. As we waited for the turtles to appear, we took a walk across the sandy beach. Kicking up the fine sand with our feet, it showered little red sparks of light from the glow worms we disturbed. It was mesmerising to see the spray of glow worms in the sand spray. It was truly magical and I felt as though I was in the middle of a fairy story and this was the fairy dust.

Waiting for the turtles to appear, we had quite a long wait and were even thinking that we would have to come back another night, when, with a splash of water, the first of the turtles started to emerge from the sea. They lumbered slowly up the sand, making wide tracks with their front flippers. The turtles didn't seem to notice our presence or were bothered by our presence. I suppose because this was a protected beach and where local people who were employed to guard these animals, we were a normal presence. These guardians protected the nests of eggs that had been laid in the sand. They had established a proper nursery for the eggs with a fence set up around the nests area chosen by the turtles for their eggs. We were incredibly close to the turtles and the only non-Malaysian presence on the beach. The others were the appointed guardians.

A turtle laying its eggs on the beach in Terengganu, Malaya

As the turtles made their way over the sand, we could have reached out and touched them. They ignored us and we knew not to stand in their path. I felt very much like an intruder on a very private moment as I watched these lumbering turtles, scrape a hole in the sand with their back flippers and dropped their eggs. The eggs were smooth white and about the size of table tennis balls. The turtles then covered the nest of eggs with sand. They then steadily lumbered back to the water and swam away.

As the turtles were a protected species, the local nursery men did make sure that the turtles had space and peace to carry out their business.

We were fascinated with the process and went back, about a month later, to see the eggs hatch and the small turtles make their scampering trip down the beach to the sea.

This trip was one of the highlights of our trips across to Malaysia.

We made many more trips across the causeway joining Singapore to Malaysia, sometimes I went on my own, sometimes with others. I was never concerned in any way. I had become a familiar sight along these roads and the taxi drivers were used to meeting the car. I felt that I'd be ok. I often travelled alone and was particularly fond of Malacca with its pink dashed walls. It was easy to get to, only a couple of hours away, and it was quite a beautiful town with a Portuguese influence and pink painted buildings.

The East Coast was equally well explored during our time at Seletar. We visited the many isolated and beautiful beaches just off the main road behind the Kampong houses (small village house). The beaches were close to the road, and we just parked the car off the road and wandered down a track that led to the sand.

The beaches were always deserted and the fine sand stretched away in the distance. It was unbelievable to us to walk along these beaches and to enjoy a swim in the gently moving waters of the ocean. Mersing was a regular stop for us and we enjoyed many meals there. See attached meal receipt from that time.

We didn't go up to the Cameron Highlands and Kuala Lumpur as we enjoyed the heat so much and the Highlands were cooler.

Among the many great events that I attended during my time in Singapore, there was one particularly outstanding festival that I went to. It was a privilege to be able to attend the Hindu Fire Walking Festival, sometime about the end of October at the Sri Mariamman Temple in the downtown Chinatown district. A Tamil temple (agamic temple), it is built in the Dravidian style and serves the majority of the Hindu population in Singapore. This is the oldest Hindu Temple on the island, built in 1827. The significance of the temple and its architectural style with the beautifully ornate carvings on the facade mean that it is a significant tourist attraction.

On the day of the Fire Walking, we found our way through Chinatown to the temple very easily and was immediately struck by the beautifully heady smell of incense. We spoke to a few devotees near the entrance to make sure that we didn't offend anyone but were invited inside. We stayed there all day experiencing the heady reality of the event. Throughout the day, I didn't notice any other internationals attending and we were careful to check, from time to time, that we weren't offending anyone's sensibilities.

The festival starts at midnight at the Sri Srinivas a Perumal Temple where the devotees take a ritual bath. After the cleansing process, following Tamil traditions, they don their 'kevadis'—a heavy semi-circular metal frame which they carried on their shoulders. It consisted of the semi-circular shiny metal framework with metal rods piercing the outer frame at intervals and extending to stab into the bare flesh of their upper body. Small metal pins pierce their nostrils and cheeks. Many had pierced tongues. These rituals are performed by the devotees who are wanting their prayers and wished granted for the coming year and these actions are viewed as a purging or cleansing ritual.

The devotees, starting in early morning, carried their load to the Sri Mariamman Temple which they reach in the afternoon. Throughout the heat of the day, they only had the odd sip of water dribbled over their mouth. This is no easy feat and says much for their level of determination and devotion. I was just standing in the heat and felt quite faint!

During the day, in the centre of the inner courtyard, a fairly deep fire pit, about 12 feet long, was prepared. The heat and fumes rising from the burning coals mixed headily with the strong smell of incense and the noise.

Around the outer edges of this inner courtyard, people were continually making their offerings to their selected deities at the individual shrines dotted around the perimeter.

As dusk settled, the level of anticipation increased and the coals glowed. The heat was tremendous. This was the main event. The coals are raked over in the pit and the chief priest of the Sri Mariamman Temple, garbed in a white garment, after making his special prayers and rituals (pujas) walked over the burning coals, from one end of this long pit to the other. He walked quite slowly and was followed by the other devotees, both young and older, who wished to take part in the ritual. No one hurried.

I think I remember them stepping in a trough of goat's milk at the end of the pit. It was a very impressive display.

Chapter 12
Hong Kong, Kowloon and New Territories

Whilst at Seletar, Reg was sent on Detachment to Hong Kong and I was fortunate to be offered the opportunity to spend a few weeks there as well. Reg arranged that I should stay with a friend's family in the New Territories. It was very kind of them and I tried not to be a nuisance. When the opportunity arose for me to visit Hong Kong, I had booked a seat with Qantas but I was then offered a seat on an RAF Transport aircraft that was making the trip up. I gratefully accepted the seat on the RAF which meant that I conveniently arrived at the military side of Kai Tak airport to be picked up.

It was November time in Hong Kong so it was cooler than in Singapore so the first stop was the local market to buy some warm clothes. The market was known as 'Stinkies' and it was located among blocks of high-rise buildings directly under the flight path of planes coming in to land at Kai Tak airport.

It was awe-inspiring to be standing in the market and looking up to see, in close proximity, the large planes with the incredible detail of the undercarriage lowered for landing. The noise itself was deafening and knowing that the length of the runway was limited, as it was running out to sea, made me appreciate even more the skill needed by the pilots to carry out this manoeuvre. No one could fail to get a sense of the intense feelings and adrenalin flow of the pilots as they guided the planes in to land, all the time feeling as if they could touch the tops of the buildings as they pass over.

I was totally awestruck by the fascination of what was going on over my head, humbled by the expertise needed by the pilots.

Despite my awe, I had to quickly buy a couple of skirts and a couple of angora woolly jumpers to keep me warm. In those days, although quite tall, I was skinny and size was not a problem, although, if I remember correctly, they were large size and the skirts were two different shades of brown with a self-coloured rib running around the skirt and they were stretchy. Great. Simple and practical, they did the job and even lasted me for years, even back in the UK.

Reggie obviously had to work so I went sightseeing, going out for walks and taking buses into the centre. I loved going on the Kowloon Ferry, seeing my fellow passengers going about their business and wondering what they did for a living and where they lived.

Hong Kong was then, and still is, a fascinating place with many small streets, large luxury hotels and then, the large shopping complex of the Ocean Terminal Building, so called because it was beside the docks where the large liners docked. A mecca for tourists, it was full of shops in the terminal building, where luxury goods were sold, shirts and suits were made to measure in a few hours. There were all sorts of material shops with bales of brightly coloured materials, exotic designs, silks, ivory carvings and Chinese medicine shops.

Eyepopping splendour with oriental mystique, it was magnificent.

Reggie treated me to a purple pattered Thai silk dressing gown beautifully stitched with gold thread. It had a cotton wool padded lining quilted to the pattered silk outer layer. It was lined with exactly matching plain purple silk. The gown was finished with self-made buttons made with little stitched ropes of self-patterned material twisted into a rounded shape. It was exquisite. That dressing gown lasted me for many years and I wore it when I went into the Royal Hospital in Belfast when I had my brain tumour operation on 10th March 1974. I still have it in my wardrobe as a keepsake.

Whilst in Kowloon and Hong Kong, I spent my time visiting the tourist areas, crossing on Star Ferry between the island of Hong Kong and the Kowloon and the New Territories. Lantau Island was close by. Star ferry ran constantly and always seemed to be full of people and their belongings, some quite unusual. I wandered around the smaller back streets seeing the market where live chickens and other animals were for sale, the shops selling precious stones and ivory carvings. The small shop owners and street vendors were an interesting lot as they touted their wares. The craftsmen carving away at ivory, wood or stones were always intent on their task but equally quick and intent on trying to make a sale from a passer-by.

Though I will say, that in those little shops lining the small streets, we, the tourists and service personnel, were all potential customers. The variety of goods on display were so tempting—and relatively cheap, that they were hard to resist. Friendly and hard working the shopkeepers were an education to this stranger from across the seas. These traders were wise to the ways and purchasing habits of the military families who were on the lookout for this or that item which would be a lasting reminder of their tour of duty in the exotic Far East. Always alert to the possibility of business, the traders worked hard talked a lot and smiled often.

During one of my trips in downtown Hong Kong, I wandered a bit far off the main areas, I believe I started out on Nathan Road, and, as I noticed less and less people walking along the street, I also became aware that I had run out of shops. Feeling a little obvious I realised that there were two policemen walking down the pavement on the far side of the road paying me some attention. Deciding I was not in a particularly good area for non-locals, I quickly retraced my steps and lost my police escort. I felt a little shocked that it could so easily move from tourist area to nearly empty streets and I retreated quickly with a lesson learned. It was quite safe, but I could so easily get lost.

At the weekends, with the support of Reggie's friend as a willing guide, driving his car, we were able to tour around the New Territories. There were ancient looking villages, and to my delight, paddy fields where the people were hard at work planting the rice crop in the designated and obligatory few inches of water. This was something I had learned about at school and I could hardly believe that I was seeing it in real life! The workers all wore wide brimmed hats to shield them from the elements. These hats were usually tied down on their heads with a navy band of cloth. As a young girl, I too had worked in the fields at my Grandad's farm so I had an enormous amount of empathy with these workers.

The area of Aberdeen (located in the Aberdeen Harbour in South Hong Kong) was famous for its floating village of houseboats and floating seafood restaurants. The Tanka people who used to live on these boats in the Aberdeen Harbour, were generally associated with the fishing industry. The area had to be seen to be seen to be believed. At that time it was a teeming mass of junks (name for local boats) where families lived out their lives and where you could step from one boat to another as they were so tightly packed together.

Situated in among the junks, there was the odd restaurant trying to establish itself and they were quite an attraction, an adventure of eating out where the fish could be caught by leaning over the side of the boat. Depending on where you stood, the smell could be quite powerful and it was disputable if there was a waste collection service. But this was Hong Kong and teeming with life.

Another main attraction was the Peak funicular railway which ran up to Victoria Peak at the back of the main street. Up at this level the air was fresh and the view over Hong Kong was worth seeing. The Peak Tram is the steepest funicular railway in the world. To me as a passenger, the carriage just seemed to go straight up. The journey takes about seven or eight minutes and is a great visual experience as you glide past the skyscrapers on the way up and then again on the way down. The tram journey was awesome, as the assent was so vertical, straight up and straight down. Standing in the carriage, I felt as if I had to lean forward on the way up and lean back on the way down!

The peak itself was a great tourist attraction and I remember some guy trying to chat me up as I wandered around admiring the view. The approach by the guy spoiled my trip to the top—I was just plain scared and quickly dodged away.

On the way to the railway and my trip to the Peak, I had stopped for a coffee at a rather nice hotel on the main street and a guy had thought that I wanted company and followed me. I didn't want company and was far from impressed. With a bit of difficulty, I was able to lose him whilst walking the peak.

Whilst on our tour around the New Territories in the car, we saw some of the famous walled towns. Very private and closed in. I nipped in through an open doorway in one but a very small Chinese lady chased me away as I was trying to take a photo. I think she wanted some money but I didn't stop to find out!

Our host also took us right up to the border with China and we could just see glimpses of the famous wall with its red splashes of paint.

Hong Kong, Kowloon and the New Territories is a magnificent array of high-rise tenement building and glamorous hotels interspersed with small shops, mini factories and farms. It is a busy place where everyone is engaged in some type of enterprise. A real melting pot of culture, hard work and ingenuity.

Returning to Singapore, I found it to be quiet and restrained in comparison to Hong Kong. Independence had changed things as the vision for the new Singapore was unfurled and had started to evolve. The new concept was that the island would be more commercialised and establish itself as an area of financial importance.

The British servicemen and women, with their families, stationed there, were being numerically reduced and this left those who had worked on the bases and for the military with having to find alternative means of making a living.

As part of the process and the drawdown of British involvement in the Far East, the camp at Seletar was scheduled to be closed in 1971. This left many local people without work—gardeners, cleaners, shopkeepers and craftsmen of all types who had serviced the needs of the military.

The Amah's night market at Seletar, held every week on a Thursday, became less busy and eventually closed. It was at the Amah's market that you could buy all types of knickknacks, towels, sheets and any household article you needed—and many that you didn't need. The items were displayed on cloths on the ground and the market was light by snoring paraffin oil lamps. The flies used to gather and dance around the globes of the lights.

The smiles and muted voices on all sides, stall holders and customers were all part of the ambiance and is intrinsic in my memory.

The closure of 110 Squadron in 1968/9 at Seletar, to which hubby had been posted, was a sad occasion, signalling the start of the draw down of the British presence in Singapore.

As it was a very formal occasion, the families were all invited to witness the proceedings. As part of the formality, we all had to get dressed in our best attire to attend the closing ceremony. It was quite an honour to be there. There was a flypast of the helicopters (whirlwinds/whirlybirds) and Reggie had to hang out the door of the aircraft to fly the flag. Nerve-wrecking for him but quite spectacular.

All the families turned out for the ceremony. The occasion called for us all to get dressed up and, as it was so special, it called for the wearing of a hat to match the outfit. I had an orange and green pattered Thai silk dress and a matching Thai silk emerald green sleeveless coat. The material for the dress and coat were easily bought down Arab Street, renowned for its selection of shops selling all types and patterns of materials. My outfit was made to measure by the local dressmaker in Seletar village near where we lived. The dressmakers were excellent and there was never any doubt relating to style or fit—it was guaranteed to be good.

A hat was a little more difficult. I couldn't find one so I had to improvise. I decided to use a natural-coloured straw sunhat and spray it with orange car paint to match the dress, shoes and bag that I had. I'm not sure what the other wives did (some sent back requests from family in the UK) but I felt that my outfit was OK, very passable, and I enjoyed the occasion.

On the closure of 110 Squadron at Seletar, in 1969, Reg was transferred across to 103 Squadron at Changi and we had to find another place to live nearer the base. After a short search, we found a small terraced house at the back of the shops at Bedok Corner, a short distance from the famous/infamous Changi Gaol made famous during the Second World War.

It was also located on the way from Paya Lebar to Changi Village and also an equally short distance from the sandy beach where the Japanese had rounded up the Nursing staff from Changi Hospital, marched them into the sea and shot them as they waded in the shallows.

I visited the beach a few times, it was mostly deserted, beautiful with deep soft sand that was difficult to walk on. It was so peaceful and it seemed such a desecration of its peace and beauty when it had witnessed such an atrocity during the war. I thought of what had happened there and realised that this was one beach where I could not sit and enjoy sunbathing in the wild beauty of this glorious sand.

Whilst living in Bedok, I became the proud possessor of a small tree monkey I don't know what genus and species this monkey belonged to, but I think maybe a Macaques, but I'm no expert and I stand to be corrected. Daisy. She had been rescued by a member of the RAF Regiment, who was on exercise in the jungle. The baby had been orphaned and in a bad state. He rescued her and then asked us if we would look after her as he had to leave Singapore. We agreed.

I called her Daisy and she was a bundle to handle. She could, and did, break free from any restraint.

She lived in the front garden of our house and was the best 'guard dog' anyone could have. The grocer boy, coming up the path with my groceries, would often throw them in the air as Daisy jumped out at him. She wanted to inspect the contents box to see if there was anything she liked in the box. Daisy loved a drink of coca cola or a cold fruit lollipop. Daisy would often escape from where she was tied up. An expert at picking locks, she could manipulate the most complicated lock. Then I would be called by one of the neighbours to retrieve my mischievous monkey. I usually grabbed a tumbler of coca cola for her to drink and often, as I proffered the drink with one hand and grabbed Daisy with the other, she would throw the glass of cola around me. 'Chittering' in frustration at me for stopping her fun. Life with Daisy had its moments!

Living beside us at Bedok Road were a lovely couple, Graham and Cath, who had a young daughter. Graham and Cath were originally from the Isle of Man and Graham was a keen sailor. Cath did not enjoy sailing but went along to the Yacht Club as a social member. Graham had a sailing partner called Bill, who was from Belfast. They were both Ground Crew on the Squadron so were around all the time, unlike Reg who was always away on trips.

My neighbours kindly invited me to join the Yacht Club and learn to sail. Reg and I accepted the invitation and joined the club. Reggie was more of a social member, not having any interest in sailing. He enjoyed the food there and the lunchtime meals were a real treat.

An older workmate of Grahams had a lovely wooden dinghy, and as he had no sailing partner, I was asked if I would be interested in learning with him. Of course, I was! This guy was a Chief Tech and he took quiet enjoyment just sailing around and he didn't mind teaching me the craft. The wooden boat was a slow mover out in the water but it was a great craft in which to learn to sail. He was a keen sailor and we were out on the water most afternoons, especially at the weekends when he was not working.

The South China Sea is a wonderful place to learn to sail, the sea is lovely and warm and even out in the Straits and the sea is calm. When my instructor went home, our next-door neighbour on Bedok Road, who had introduced me to sailing, kindly arranged that I get some time crewing in their lovely 20-foot fibre-glass boat (Osprey). The Osprey was a beautiful boat and flew over the water with exhilarating speed, especially in comparison to the older wooden dinghy which had been a bit slower, more sedate.

Graham and his friend were expert sailors and often raced in the Regattas. I was not proficient enough, being such an amateur but it was a great spectator sport. I enjoyed sailing, finding it very relaxing as well as exhilarating. After some further tuition from my friends and a few tests, I was considered to have gained my crew category (B Cat) qualification.

Sailing at Changi Yacht Club and going swimming in the camp swimming pool were my main past time and very enjoyable too. However as Reg was away quite a bit, I needed something else to do so I decided to become an Avon rep in the area. A Chinese lady had called at the house trying to sell me some items and got me to sign up as an agent. This was a good way to keep me busy and I was soon making contacts and selling Avon products to most of the international service families (only the ladies anyway). This was something different as I had to go and see if anyone was interested in the product. It meant some walking and talking and it passed the time. I received commission on what was sold—but not a lot! I suppose I wasn't dedicated enough, I just enjoyed going out meeting the people, New Zealanders, Australians as well as British.

Living in Bedok made me more aware of the local culture as we lived across the road from a local Buddhist Temple. The Temple was also used for other purposes and we were then able to hear and watch the Chinese Opera when it came to our area. A fairly regular occurrence, it was very colourful with all the elaborate costumes and make up. It was also very loud, with lots of clang-clanging, but was also very enjoyable. We tried to follow the story on stage but only got the gist of the story. A real cultural experience.

Living at Bedok corner, we were more knowledgeable about local life. One of our neighbours was a local Police Inspector who lived in one of the larger houses and had a wonderful ability to grow orchids. They were beautiful and he took great pleasure in discussing tips on orchid growing.

Next door was the director of a local construction company. The family was really nice and was eager to explain their Chinese customs and festivals. At Chinese New Year, we were invited around and participated in their festive meals. Some of the items were very unusual but pleasing to the palate. They were all washed down with tumblers of raw whisky. I couldn't keep up with these guys. The drink went to my head immediately and I had to retire early.

I also witnessed the Chinese Funeral Processions that took place from time to time. They went up to the Temple and seemed to always form quite a large procession, being led by the group of professional mourners wailing, dressed in what appeared to be to sackcloth and distributing Hell Money to pay for the deceased path to the afterlife.

A sample of Hell Money distributed at a Chinese funeral which pays the way of the deceased into the next world

Each nation has its own way of burying their dead. In Ireland, we usually 'wake' them by gathering in their home and talking about their lives, often telling jokes. It's all a matter of form and respect for the dead.

Chapter 13
Thailand

Whilst stationed at Changi, we decided to take a trip to Thailand, mainly to visit Bangkok but also to see the famous Bridge over the River Kwai. The bridge was built from October 1942 to October 1943. The Japanese army wanted the railway to be built to link Thailand and Burma. They made use of 60,000 prisoners of war (POWs), including 13,000 Australians and approximately 200,000 civilians, mostly Burmese and Malayans. The effort was immortalised in the epic 1957 film 'Bridge over the River Kwai' and based on the 1952 novel by Pierre Boulle. Some of the friends who had served in WWII with my father had worked and died there and, before we left the UK, he had asked if we could visit it in memory of those he had known.

Always cautious with our finances, we decided that travelling by train all the way from Singapore to Bangkok would be a great adventure. We would also find out first-hand a lot about the people and the culture. Getting an aeroplane from Singapore to Bangkok would probably have not been much more expensive but it would not have been such an adventure.

Reading up on Thailand, we also decided to go on up to Chiang Mai, Kanchanaburi Province in the North because of its cultural history and the famous ornate Buddha Temples of Wat Phra Singh and Wat Chedi Luang of which we had been told that were worth visiting.

We spent a few weeks thinking and making plans of what we wanted to do and see. This railway journey would be an epic trip. We would see a lot of the countryside as the train wound its way over the mountains and plains. Much better than going by plane in our opinion. The train would be stopping off in a few larger towns on the way and it would only take a day to travel by train from Bangkok to reach Chiang Mai. We planned to stay about a week in Bangkok before starting off for Chiang Mai and we read up on all the places of interest we wanted to see. Overall, we planned to take three weeks for the trip and wanted to make the most of this wonderful opportunity.

Booking our train tickets at the railway station in Singapore was a joy as the clerks were so helpful, advising us on best practice regarding availability of food, carriage class of travel etc. It was preparation and planning made special!

We exchanged Singapore dollars for Thai Baht and we were ready to go!

We started our journey in Singapore early one morning. We were travelling first class as we had been advised that the regular class had quite uncomfortable narrow wooden slat seats which would not be pleasant for the length of time it would take us to reach Bangkok, our first stop. This first part of the journey would take two days and included an overnight on the train, so it was essential that we were comfortable.

When we arrived at the train at Singapore Railway Station, we were shown to our seats in the carriage. When we saw the interior of the carriage, we could hardly take it in. It was so grand. The inside of the carriage was pure Victoriana with comfortable padded seats plus a lounge car that we could use. (I think that this car was specially attached as we had booked first class, the only first-class passengers on the train.) The lounge itself was amazing, it was like a luxurious, if slightly old-fashioned, sitting room on tracks. Comfortable easy chairs plus side tables with lamps. We felt extremely pampered. It was all immaculate. All this was to be available to us all the way to Bangkok. Boy, were we pleased that we had decided to go by rail! Air travel had nothing on this.

Needless to say, the beds (bunks) on this train were quite plump and luxurious. After all the newness of the sights of the day, we had a very comfortable night's sleep. The train rolled on through the night, an easy soothing motion that lulled us into a deep slumber. I still can't get over this very luxurious method of travel. An aeroplane journey, with all its speed and convenience, could not compare to this luxury.

The trip up country was very smooth and the various vendors at the side of the track sold a huge variety of food and drink. Trade was always brisk as the train only slowed down and stopped for short periods. Most of the stopping points were mere Halts on the way. There wasn't a platform in sight at any of these stops. The Halts were really clearings in the lush green growth with bare pieces of earth. As the train slowed down at a halt, the passengers were jumping down on to the side of the track even as the train slowed. They were very sure footed and I didn't see any one of them even stumble as they landed.

The first main station on the route was at Kuala Lumpur. A truly spectacular edifice, reminiscent of a bygone era. It was very grand, lofty and elegant. Elaborate and very Victorian in appearance, it reflected a former age, glory and style. Imposing and impressive. Magnificent architecture, huge columns and arches. It just took your breath away and I felt as if we had stepped back in time.

Crossing the border into Thailand was uneventful, we hardly noticed the transition. I remember producing our passports and being viewed with some surprise by the border guards, but no comment was made—none that I understood anyway!

As we continued on our journey, it was hard not to marvel at the differing way of life as it unfolded along the railway line. We saw a few low roofs of houses, much greenery but few people. They seemed to be moulded into the background. As the train would slow down at a 'halt' (usually seemingly in the middle of nowhere but obviously pre-determined), there was no platform for the people to help them get up or down to or from the carriages, but the food vendors were waiting, walking up and down the length of the train. Their wares were displayed on the flat woven baskets balanced on top of their heads.

These baskets were filled with homemade sponge cakes, curry puffs and skewers of cooked meats and vegetables. Fresh bananas, pineapples and nuts were plentiful, as were bottles of soft drinks.

In between these stopping places, we passed through large areas of greenery, banana plantings, loads of rubber trees, many with their little cups attached to collect the latex rubber resin (only collected in the mornings) and lots of groundnut palms.

When we crossed into Thailand, the scenery remained much the same although there was a subtle discernible difference, difficult to describe, more of a sense than a reality. The whole scene was interesting and exciting to us. It was an honour too as it let us see what local life was like, as it actually was—no frills or pretensions.

Arriving in Bangkok in the late evening around 10.30 p.m. amid a flurry of activity with people scurrying up and down the platform. We hired a put-put (local taxi) for the journey to our hotel. These little open-sided mini cabs sputtered their way very efficiently along the streets and probably took us the longest way to our hotel. We didn't care. It was our first view of Bangkok and we revelled in every spectacular sight, sound or smell.

Next morning, we were eager to get out and about. We were staying in the New Nana Hotel and the receptionist was eager to help us see and experience the sights and sounds of the city. They showered us with information and advice, all of which was received gratefully by us. Guided by their advice and a few street maps plus a card with the details of the hotel, we set off. We were young and full of wide-eyed enthusiasm and determined to see 'everything'.

There weren't many other internationals around, but we became friendly with an elderly couple from Australia who were also having a ball. We came upon them a few times on our wanderings around the tourist areas. Our sightseeing was at a different pace to theirs but we did enjoy a sit down together at one or two places and agreed that we were all enjoying ourselves and marvelling at what we were seeing.

I can't remember seeing any other international tourists around. The streets were wide but other than a few Thais going about their business, we saw few people. We approached a few Thais on the odd occasion to check directions and we found them to be lovely friendly helpful people, pleased to practice their language skills. We found that the Thais are genuinely really gentle and kind people.

The week spent in Bangkok was packed full of sightseeing trips, shopping and exploring. We enjoyed the smell of the food being prepared at the stalls along the side of the street. Used to this activity in Singapore, we compared smells of the different food being cooked and even had a few snacks as we wandered along. We were young and enthusiastic just wanting to see all that there was to see. We eagerly absorbed as much as we could see, taking taxi rides, smelling the beautiful scent of the small garland of flowers that were draped over the taxi's rear-view mirror, fresh every day. A striking scent, I can still smell it as I write. I think it was hibiscus.

We visited the Floating Market, the Grand Palace and were very in awe of the elaborate finery of the design and the gold decorations on the roof. There is much glamour and protocol associated with everything in Thailand. We wandered around viewing the shops where precious stones were sold by weight and clarity. The beautiful iridescent Thai silk was eye catching shimmering in the sunlight. Thai silk is beautiful, light, colourful and beautifully pattered. The standard of the material ranged from hard wearing, strong weave, to fine gossamer silk. Thai made goods were a wonderful attraction, they looked so honest and sincere—if you can say that about goods for sale in the shop windows.

Brass was a favoured ornament, all shapes and sizes glistening in the sun. The ornamental grandeur could be seen everywhere, from the Grand Palace to the Royal Barge to the inside of the hotels. The magnificence took my breath away. The Thai ethos of design and colour permeated every aspect of life, thus making this country so unique. Throughout this you could smell the beautiful perfume of the flowers (I think it is Hibiscus) and be aware of the tinkling of the wind chimes which were hanging at every entrance.

The food stalls lining the streets were busy, particularly at night when everything looked so appealing in the lights hanging at each stall and combined with the chatter of the diners, this all added to the unique appeal. Based on our Singapore experience we quietly noted the ones that were operating with an eye for good hygiene and avoided the rest. The variety and selection of food stalls, shops and tourist sites was vast. We were young and full of energy, so we walked a lot, only using taxis for the longest distances.

The taxis were another treat, always smelling beautiful from the garland of strong-smelling flowers bought fresh every morning. One taxi driver explained that they got these flower garlands each morning after their meditation where they chant Pali stanza from the cannon before an image of Buddha (Vandana). These flowers, draped over the rear-view mirror, wafted their sweet smell around the cab enveloping the passengers. Researching for our proposed visit to the Bridge over the River Kwai proved to be a little problematic so we enquired of the hotel staff how to make this trip. They appeared quite surprised by our request but after many questions and much discussing with the very helpful staff, we were advised to hire a car and driver to reach the Bridge over the River Kwai. The staff made the recommendation and organised the transport for our trip. The taxi driver seemed nervous so I guessed that this was not a usual arrangement, but we soon became better friends as, on advice from the hotel staff, we paid in advance for the day. I could quite understand that reassurance was needed. We just had to trust.

The taxi driver spoke a little English and, wanting to make our visit to Thailand a memorable one, he stopped at a few notable Buddha shrines for us to appreciate the ornate splendour and solitude. This was seemingly, to us, in the middle of the jungle, but were obviously there to serve some ideological purpose. Those stops were well chosen and we had a great tour of the shrines.

Limited English or no, the driver managed to explain the main rational of each Buddha shrine. We thoroughly enjoyed the whole experience and learned a lot. Usually at each stop there were a few Thais, sometimes one of the young ones spoke a little English and this helped us understand the significance of each shrine. On one memorable stop a young boy offered to give me a good time, explaining that he was very good. I declined his offer but gave him a few Bahts telling him his English was very good.

The way to the River Kwai Bridge wound its way through some pretty wild countryside—jungle really. The green fronds from the undergrowth brushed the sides of the taxi, sometimes the greenery grew across the road—we were basically travelling along a jungle track. We didn't mind. Being young and green, we trusted our driver implicitly (the hotel people had recommended him) and we just enjoyed the experience. The driver was a great guide and took his role as trustee very seriously. We had a great day sightseeing, visiting shrines that had not had many European visitors but were obviously revered by the local people. Each of the shrines was spectacular, the edifice rearing up out of the green jungle growth, startling in their cleared jungle areas in the middle of seemingly nowhere. Obviously well-cared for shrines that were not being overrun by any vegetation.

After a few stops, mainly at the quite magnificent shrines situated at different points along our way, we arrived at our destination of the famous Bridge. It was then that we realised why we had had to have a taxi. There was no sign of any tourist development here. It was simply a clearing in the jungle with a couple of kampong houses built near the bridge and beside the river. A few local people were sitting on the steps at the front of the houses. No one was in a hurry.

No hassle was the order of the day. We received a few curious glances but no one rushed over to sell us anything. It was so peaceful and laid back, nothing disturbed the peace of the day. Obviously there had been the odd visitor before us but nothing startling. Visitors may have come and gone, but nothing had changed the peace and tranquillity of this place.

The railway had been built through the jungle here by the prisoners of war but that was long ago. This place and the bridge were respected, the memory of the builders was remembered but not revered and the potential as a tourist site had not been identified.

The site itself was plain. The original railway locomotive, which was small and painted green, was on a cement plinth inside a dull painted fenced enclosure, half hidden by weeds. The old bridge was there too and we stood for quite a long time looking at the scene before us, paying a silent reverend homage as we reflected on the lives lost in the construction of the bridge and railway line. We also walked some way across the bridge and looked down on the river. The railway line seemed to be still in use and was in good condition. The quiet inhabitants of the couple of houses nearby watched quietly and waited patiently to see what we would do next. Opposite the two houses was another one to our left and we could see through the open sides that a small attempt at tourist attraction had been made and a shelf held pieces of bamboo fashioned into a rough drinking vessel with the name River Kwai burned into the base. I bought one for my father. Simple and significant.

I also bought a small piece of wood fashioned in a small plaque and painted with the scene of the bridge. It was beautiful. I still have it.

I think I remember having a drink of coffee at one of the houses but there were few facilities and I didn't care. I didn't need or want anything more. I just felt good at having achieved this journey because Dad had asked me to do it. That was all.

I, as I often did on many occasions, felt very privileged to be able to get to this place and see it as it was, treated with respect but not idolised. I was just pleased that I had been able to fulfil my dad's request and I looked forward to relaying the details to him, knowing that he would be pleased, visualising him as he ducked his head and smiled at the memory of those he had known who had worked on the railway.

On the way back, we stopped at a couple more Buddha shrines, sturdy and remote. I think our driver just wanted us to feel that we were having a good trip and this was his way by making sure we had a good itinerary. He was right. We felt very satisfied with the day out and humbled and honoured at what we had seen.

We spent a few more days wandering around Bangkok, sampling the food and the sights and sounds. I can still smell the small garland of flowers (hibiscus) draped over the rear-view mirror every morning and still hear the ching-ching of the chimes that were suspended from doorways and windows everywhere, as they were ruffled in the slight movement of scented air. The main streets were wide with little traffic and we walked everywhere, full of youthful energy and enthusiasm for this enigmatic culture with its wonderful sounds, golden decor and architecture.

Scenes from the film The *King of Siam* danced before our eyes and we were spellbound. The splendour of the Royal Palace and the Golden Barges was breath taking as it resembled a scene from a Fairy Tale of long ago but it was there in front of our eyes. I, for one, just held my breath and wanted to remain there forever, enthralled by the beauty of it all.

Soon, it was time to move on to Chiang Mai. We were reluctant to leave Bangkok and consoled ourselves that we would be back this way, even if it was only for a few days.

The train for Chiang Mai left early in the morning and we would spend all day travelling. We were due to arrive in Chiang Mai about 10.30 that night and we didn't know what to expect when we got there. We were told in Bangkok that it was very different up there, very rural with no night life. We weren't night owls so that did not bother us.

The hotel staff gave us some pointers on what to expect when travelling by local train and arranged our taxi to the station. As we made our way to our carriage at Bangkok station, we realised that this train was very different from the one that brought us up from Singapore. This train was very ordinary to look at, very basic in design but it did have a kitchen car, so food would be available on the journey.

The guard was very helpful and showed us to our seats in the correct carriage. Each carriage was clean and tidy and would seat about 50 people. Climbing into the carriage we had another surprise—the seats in the carriage were made of narrow wooden slats and, when seated, our knees touched those of the passengers on the seat opposite. The seats were obviously made for the shorter slightly built Thai traveller. The toilet was at the end of the carriage and would give off a strong smell of ammonia as the heat rose during the day.

We choose a seat near the entrance to the carriage, only realising a little later that we were close to the toilet. It was thus that we had full benefit of the facilities as the day progressed. Settling into our seats and looking around, we saw that there was only one other non-Thai in our carriage—and I believe on the entire train. This guy was American and deliberately ignored us. He was accompanied by his Thai girlfriend or wife who remained equally distant. The other occupants of the carriage were more friendly, smiling and nodding at us, speaking in Thai, and maybe fortunately for us, we didn't understand a word.

The railway line to Chiang Mai was definitely rural and, once out of the station, we realised that the line was a single track. We speculated that there weren't many trains using this line and that passing places would be only at certain points in the journey. In fact, I don't remember meeting any train on the day journey. We were due to arrive at Chiang Mai at 10.30 at night when it would be pleasantly cool. On advice from the hotel, we hadn't brought any food as the train had a dining car. Somehow or other, I just didn't go looking for the dining car.

Foreigners travelling on this train were unusual and the Thais tried not to be too curious but obviously chatted about us. As we didn't understand a word of their language, we just smiled and nodded.

As our fellow passengers got into the carriage, I noticed an old lady who took her seat nearby. She was accompanied by her extended family and they were a noisy cheerful lot who occupied about three rows of seats. The old lady chewed betel nut, occasionally spitting the juice into an old Ovaltine tin, carefully replacing the lid after each spittle.

Because of the betel nut her smile was very red-rimmed. She tried her best to chat with us, using sign language and we all laughed a lot, but we didn't have a clue what was being said.

There was the usual 'halts' along the line and the food vendors plied their trade. The food smelt good but we were being cautious and hesitated, not wanting to chance it. We couldn't see the dining car so didn't bother getting anything. The old lady had kept an eye on us and decided that we needed something to eat and passed over a couple of sponge cakes that her family had bought at one of stops. Not wishing to offend, we bit into the proffered cakes and found that they were delicious and we smiled our thanks.

Delighted with her efforts, the old lady tried conversing using finger pointing and hand signals, I tried to understand and reciprocate with my own attempts at sign language. I did realise that she liked my gold (?) watch and was keen to trade but I shook my head and exaggeratedly held on to my watch. She laughed delighted at my response. We each exaggerated our reactions to different things and we laughed frequently. By the end of our journey, the old lady and her family were our firm friends. We didn't understand a word they said and they didn't understand us but the friendship was there in our laughter and smiles.

This friendship helped later when we visited an Umbrella Village outside of Chiang Mai. Walking around the village with a couple of other international (who had arrived by plane) plus a local guide, we met the old lady. She was out for a walk with some friends. This was her village and she was delighted to see us. She ran over to me, jumped up and flung her arms around my neck, talking excitedly all the time. It was obvious she was telling all around us that we had met on the train and that we had had a good laugh along the way. I was equally delighted and purchased three beautifully hand painted silk umbrellas—at what I found out later, to be at a very good price! I wish I had bought more as a mark of encouragement for the local industry.

The umbrella displayed were in every colour and hue of silk and laid out like coloured shells along the edge of the drainage ditch at the side of the road. The painted design being allowed to dry off in the sun. It was a beautiful sight in the sun.

There were a few other notable incidents of that train journey that springs to mind. During most of the journey we seemed to pass across a flat plain described as the 'breadbasket of Thailand'. Once across the flat fertile plain, we started to climb. The train line climbed steeply to what was pretty much a jungle area. As the train struggled up the gradient, we saw some working elephants with their handlers who stopped for a moment or two to watch the train pass. Further along, I caught my breath as we came on a magnificent tiger, standing motionless beside the track. The still and watchful tiger was obviously curious, and he stood beside the track, watching us with an unblinking stare. The sheer majesty of that animal as he stood unmoving at the edge of the track was breath taking, awe inspiring. I held my breath in sheer delight at what I was seeing. A truly regal animal, idly curious to see what the train was bringing through his domain.

I'm sure the other passengers were as impressed as well but I didn't really notice. This magnificent creature held all my attention.

Continuing on our way, we reached the top of the gradient and started down the other side. This side was equally steep. Going down this side of the very steep gradient, the brakes got too hot and started to smoke. The train, with a squeal of brakes, was forced to stop. Immediately, all the passengers, including us who followed them, climbed down from the carriages and crowded around the wheels to have a look at these heated wheels.

We all crowded around and I was suddenly startled to see that the engineer/driver on the train was trying to make his way to the brakes. The man had to struggle, fight and push his way through this crowd to inspect the wheel and check for damage for himself. Incredible, in the heat of the moment, we, the passengers, were all experts.

Deciding that a cooling period was all that was necessary, the engineer/driver decided that the train should remain stationery for a short time before resuming the journey. Talking to himself, the driver/engineer made his way back to his cab.

We, the passengers, all made our way back to our carriage and climbed on board. Resuming our seats, I listened to the pleasant chatter in the carriage, no one seemed bothered by the delay.

Obviously, this was a regular occurrence. After a short delay, the train started up again and we were on our way. There wasn't any further incident that I remember.

Eventually, in the evening, arriving at our destination, we found that, as promised, Chiang Mai was very different from Bangkok. A former capital of the region, its main influence seemed to be religious. It was very rural and the streets were quiet with a few small shops. The journey from the station to the hotel did not take much time.

At the hotel, which was less elaborate than the one in Bangkok, we were impressed with the cleanliness and the welcome. After a very comfortable night's sleep and a good breakfast we were ready for the day ahead.

Consulting with the hotel reception people, we organised a few trips out with a local guide to see around the area.

One of the main trips was to visit a nomadic tribe, the White Meo, who had only just encamped nearby. There were only about six of us all together in the party (the others had flown in) and we travelled in a small minibus with the local guide and his driver. The guide was helpful, explaining a little of the history of the tribe and warning us that they were of a warlike disposition.

The driver was able to find the entrance to the encampment quite easily—I suspect that the guide had been there earlier that morning to make sure that we wouldn't miss out on this opportunity. As the guide explained—these people moved frequently and we were just lucky that they were easily accessible.

The encampment was as I had imagined—a collection of huts where life and buildings were simple and basic. It all seemed low lying and not visible to the casual passer-by on the road a few yards away.

The village was built in a small depression at the bottom of a hill. It was well organised with the small buildings, made mainly of bamboo and grasses following a defined pattern, obviously well practised by the tribe members, and it was neat and tidy. There was an ample supply of running water. The water was supplied from a mountain stream further up the side of the hill. The water was caught in a series of split bamboo drainage 'pipes' that fed into each other down the slope, they were carefully graduated down the slope supported where appropriate by small Y-shaped branches. So simple and so effective.

Obviously, the tribe had to be self-sufficient for food and they hunted animals and gathered plants together as a group. The people were very supportive of each other, very caring of their fellows, helping each other and taking care of the weaker members of the group.

The tribal people made their own clothes, simple wrap around pieces of cloth made of a rough linen/cotton like material, rough, off-white in colour. These pieces of cloth were colourfully decorated with basic dyes and print shapes using cut out patterns, carved in what seemed to be bamboo. These patterns were sometimes rolled on over the length of material and the garment fashioned accordingly. The colours were natural dyes, simple, brown, blue and a reddish colour (if I remember correctly) all items made as they were needed, colours made from whatever plants they had to hand.

The tribe did barter with other tribes apparently and among the items bartered was opium. The raw opium was collected up in the hills where the plants grew wild and then the stuff was processed for use. I was offered a piece of the solid opium. It looked like a liquorice sweet and about the same size.

To the astonishment of the guide, I declined the offer and he explained that this would be worth a lot of money but I was scared of it being discovered at the border crossing as we travelled back to Singapore. There were no mobile phones at that time and I could just imagine being arrested at the border, not able to communicate and maybe vanishing without trace. Even if I could get word out as to what had happened to me, the scandal would be too much for the people at home. No, thank you.

It appeared that the benefits/drawbacks of opium were well recognised and understood by the tribe. It was solemnly explained to me that opium was dangerous and that there were many addicts in the tribe but they didn't live long once they became an addict. These people were kept in a separate hut where they could smoke as much as they wanted. I was taken over to the hut and the fumes from the opium smoke were really strong. The smokers were very much under the influence, some worse than others.

The guide also told us that some people became addicted very easily, whilst others could smoke the opium pipe just now and then, without ill effects, merely for relaxation. The rest of the tribe looked after and provided for the addicts in their separate hut. The tribe members accepted the problems associated with the production of the drug as well as with the benefits of barter. Their compassion, understanding and caring for their fellow unfortunates was admirable—truly NHS Thai style.

During the visit, I was challenged to a shooting match by one guy who was obviously very proud of his accuracy with the homemade 'crossbow' and selection of arrows. The wood was dark grainy and any joining bits were covered in a black sticky substance I would call 'pitch'. It was very effectively holding the various pieces of the bow together. The young man took aim and scored a hit on a wooden target he had been practising on and then he offered me the bow. I was reluctant but I was told that it was rude to refuse the challenge.

Our guide cautioned me that if I beat the tribesman by hitting the target better, I would get the bow, but said quietly—best to be diplomatic and not shoot well because he will get upset and lose face with his friends. I laughed and told him I had not used a homemade bow and arrow set since I was about seven years old so that I doubted if I would hit it at all. Unfortunately, I hit the target spot on. Much to my embarrassment, the challenger then presented me with the bow and I had to take it. The guide was really quite concerned and advised us to get on the minibus and beat a hasty retreat as he didn't know what way they would react as this was a warlike tribe and likely cut up rough.

A few days later, we heard that they had gone on the warpath over something or other and I wondered if I had anything to do with it as I had made that mistake! I figured it was best not to ask.

During one of our trips out, we were also invited to go to a Thai village where they had working elephants. The Thais were great hosts, providing us with food and a display of Thai dancing—the girls were very graceful, dressed in their shimmering silk dresses gracefully floating as they danced. Part of the dance costume was the long extended false fingernails which they flashed around pointing and bending the fingers as part of the dance. It was quite mesmerising.

We were also treated to a display by the working elephants and were much impressed by their slow steady strength, tremendous bulk and gentle nature. Their affectionate nature was evident and their handlers treated them well. I was the youngest one in the small group of about six so I suppose it was inevitable that it was me who was lifted up by the trunk of one elephant and placed on his back and taken for a little walk. Much to everyone's amusement, I was scared sick. After the walk, and on instruction from his handler, the elephant caught me in his trunk and carefully lowered me to the ground. I was struck by the gentleness of his actions as much as I was impressed by his great strength. Wow!

There were many venomous snakes around the area and we saw them being milked for their venom. They also were very careful to explain that they also had an antidote for those unfortunates who had been bitten. The snake experts seemed to really enjoy working with these creatures and treated them with great respect. We were invited to handle the snakes. To me, handling the snakes was not a treat but I tried to smile and make the best show possible.

The Thais were very keen to show us how they lived and entertained themselves, to give us tourists a real flavour of the Thai way of life. I can truthfully say that they were successful in that respect. They were great hosts.

I remember one morning, a couple of days before we left Chiang Mai, at breakfast time, I really fancied some toast. Foolishly, I asked the waiter if I could have some. I had to explain what toast was and the poor guy was totally astonished. When I further explained about toasting/roasting a slice of bread, the waiter just could not believe his ears. Burn bread, he repeated. No, that was food ruined! I insisted and offered to show him how it was done.

With his permission, I followed him to the kitchen and, in my turn, I was so impressed with the facilities before me. There was a very basic large open fire surrounded by a plain whitewashed stone to contain the heat. It was on this basic hearth that the kitchen staff had produced all our very delicious meals. Breathtakingly basic, it was brilliant in its simplicity. I did enjoy my toast that morning, carefully watched by the attendant waiter.

I also did do a little shopping but there wasn't much to be had. Brass rubbing was the major past time and I did get a rather wonderful brass rubbing of a Thai Dancer. A basic rubbing of an image on paper, I was very taken by their efforts and purchased one. The imprint was attached to a rough orange fabric framed in a teak frame. To me, this was rather special memento of a wonderful visit to a wonderful place.

Having exhausted ourselves and seen as much of local life as we could, we then had to make our way back by train to Bangkok. We started off early in the morning and on the way back down to Bangkok, I decided to be very brave and try some food prepared in the dining car which we had located. I studied the short selection on the menu and decided that a salad was a good idea. I could have that with a bottle of coke (my favourite drink in the Far East). The dish was quickly prepared and it look good. A plate of white rice with little red and green chopped vegetables mixed through it. I took a forkful. I had just put some in my mouth followed by a drink of coca cola when I realised what the vegetables were— chillies! Hot chillies. I can easily say that my mouth actually sizzled. The coke on top of the chillies, I would not recommend. What an experience. That was the end of breakfast.

A few more days in Bangkok and reluctantly, as the adventure came to an end, we made our way back home to Singapore and RAF Changi.

A short time after our return to Changi, Reg was transferred to Tengah and shortly after that, it was time to return to the UK with a change of weather and lifestyle.

Returning to the UK, my husband was based at RAF Odiham and we found some accommodation in Alton Hampshire. I got a job, working for Harp Lager, in the lab and was able to enjoy testing and tasting the lager. We were there for about a year or so, when, due to ill health, Reg left the RAF. We then decided to return to Northern Ireland and we had three lovely children.

In 1974, after a significant operation in the Royal Victoria Hospital in Belfast to remove a rather large meningioma type brain tumour and with the marriage in difficulties, we divorced eventually, after some crippling discussions and court appearances which pretty much destroyed both of us.

Part II

Chapter 14
Preface to the Military Side of My Life

Protracted divorce proceedings left me with a very jaundiced view of life and people around me which lasted for many years. However, I carried on as best as I could. Financially, I was not very secure in that I needed to stretch my salary as far as it would go—plus a little more! I managed but with difficulty. I was no different from a lot of others trying to make ends meet but I think that I felt it a bit more, exhausted as I was continually attending to the court proceedings involved with the divorce. I think that I had emotional trauma and a feeling of failure stemming from my perceived sense of waste of a huge chunk out of our lives. It was all part of the 'down' feeling that most people feel after such a momentous episode and it has to be ignored and overcome—but it is difficult so to do.

By this time, I was working in a local newspaper in the advertising department. I was enjoying the job but money was tight and I was frantically trying to think of what I could do to earn some more money. As part of the job, I attended a social/work event at the local Territorial Army (TA) base. It turned out that the TA were trying to recruit media representatives—reporters—to try and promote the worth and balance of the part-time activities of members of the TA. The main emphasis was on the benefits of getting and keeping fit, whilst earning some extra cash for doing so. I was immediately attracted to the idea.

Unfortunately, the officials were focused on reporters and I was advertising! Bummer! Maybe fortunately, my companion from the newspaper—a bona fide reporter of some note—was not really interested. He was still living at home and therefore did not have the same demands on his salary. I was interested (desperate nearly) so they reluctantly 'considered' my expressions of interest. Within a short time, the wheels were set in motion and my expression of interest was duly forwarded through appropriate channels.

At this point however, as well as this need for some extra earnings, our family had been subjected to the terrorist-related shooting and murder of my brother, John Corry. John was a pacifist, not wanting any trouble, but he was the owner of a small garage and he saw a way to make some extra cash to help him establish his garage.

Other local businessmen had noted the opportunities that had arisen through the need of the security forces to contract local enterprises. They were being used for various types of work required in the establishment of their bases including— building work, electrical, plumbing etc. These entrepreneurs had contracted to work for the Army and John decided to try this too—in a small way. He saw an opportunity where he could be involved in this establishment of the Army bases around the area. Being in the motor business John decided that, if by hiring large Lorries suitable for the purpose, he could move some of the large quantities of soil and stone being used in the building work necessary to establish the bases. John reckoned that others were doing similar contract work in this and other fields, and although there were risks, surely, he was just one of many and wouldn't be noticed.

Religion and bias were not important to him, he treated everyone the same— live and let live was how he viewed the world.

Unfortunately, someone we knew who didn't see it that way, decided to inform the IRA and a contract was taken out on John, ostensibly due to the work he was doing for the Army. The underlying reason that the informant had was simpler—John had had to 'let a garage worker go due to his unwise attraction to strong drink'. As in many other cases of killings by the IRA at that time, simple spite and revenge was often the reason for such actions.

Thus, after a long year under threat of death, my brother John was shot whilst standing in his place of work, in his garage, in front of a customer and his employees and workmates. Gunned down by three men dressed in workmen's dungarees, buoyed up by hate, who had nothing better to do in an afternoon just before Christmas 1988.

Understandably, this event was hugely significant to our family and it was this that was the spur that helped me determine and direct the media message in relation to what was really happening among the average Ulster man and woman. My simple message was dedicated to the ideals of law and order as opposed to the very high flying IRA 'cries of freedom' propaganda emanating from such sources as meetings in the White House, Washington DC, freedom fundraisers on the streets of New York to local 'ghetto' politicos protesting their rights to freedom of the underdog, willing to kill to underline their demands for 'equality'. From the far-flung politicos, there was no feelings of sympathy or remorse for the death, just speeches on revenge and determined collections of cash for the 'cause'.

My brother, John Corry, was shot by the IRA in his place of work at the garage that he owned in Portadown. This killing, on 13th December 1988, was carried out by three members of the IRA who, subsequently, were caught and tortured by others (possibly of their own organisation) and their naked bodies were found in black plastic bags somewhere near the border in South Armagh.

John was the fourth of the six of us. A genial character who loved life. He worked hard and was well known for his kindness to those who needed help. My other two brother supported him and knew that there was a threat out on his life, but my mother and my two sisters knew none of his concerns. Our brothers, Henderson (older) and David (younger), were the only ones in the family with whom he shared this threat. In their turn, they supported him with their presence as much as was possible.

I was working in the Banbridge weekly newspaper when the news came in. In the newspaper office we knew there had been a fatal shooting, but the name was kept from me by my colleagues. They felt it best that I heard from a member of my own family.

My sister did call me within a few minutes, but couldn't get the words out. Someone did try to tell me over the phone but I didn't seem to understand. All that I can remember was my sister telling me to 'come home'.

The editor, Joe Fitzpatrick, who obviously knew and had confirmed the details, organised for me to be driven home. I went directly to my mother's house (with the driver) and when I entered the home, I will never forget the sound or the scene. My mum was crying like I'd never heard before. Her agonising grief was so utterly unbearable to hear and to watch. She was beside herself with grief, crying bitterly. John was such a loving son, a peace-loving person, a dedicated businessman, absorbed in his motors. John was an avid support of the 'stock cars', he drove his stock car every week, providing it was in a fit state to be driven, (sometimes a bit of a wreck after the previous outing!) My two brothers, Henderson and David, along with a few extra friends and associates, were his back-up technical/mechanical team. Stock car racing was a popular sport then and it drew great crowds of supporters. John had also designed his own car. It was sitting in his garage when he died. Meant to be noticed, it was bright yellow.

John was a softie in the home, Mum's favourite son. Always the soft answer. To mum, his death and murder was really unbearable.

Just before I had arrived home, Henderson, my oldest brother, had left the house (I was the last one of the family to get there). Mum sort of collected herself and sent me to look for him and my other brother, David. I just knew where they would be—down at the garage where John had been shot. They were there—along with some of John's friends. Huddled together in a group, all looking very shocked, not quite knowing what to do. I still cannot remember how I got down to the garage.

I didn't see my brother Henderson at first but I did notice the police who were guarding the entrance to the yard. It was a dark night and they had the entrance to the yard, roped off with tape. There was a pile of media types there, just hanging around waiting. Sombre and subdued.

When I arrived at the police cordon, I explained who I was and was allowed through. By this point, I was in a bit of a daze and I walked down to the entrance of the garage where the police were gathered. I wasn't quite sure what I wanted but a very kind detective came over and introduced himself and asked me if I wanted to say 'goodbye' to my brother, explaining that it would help my acceptance of events. I said 'yes' and he led me over to where my brother lay in a pool of his own blood.

My knees buckled underneath me and two policemen held me up. I stood there for a few minutes, looking at my brother's body, his features were relaxed in death. I just cried and stood, the policemen on either side of me holding me upright. This was my little brother whom I loved. With the two policemen holding me up, I said my silent and quiet goodbyes.

The media were at the entrance of the cordon, held back by the police—The policemen, escorting me out, told me that someone needed to speak to the press to stop the pressure and I agreed. The policemen steadied me and stepped back. In that glare of the lights, I told them that this was a private family tragedy and asked for privacy to grieve and for the media to give us 100 yards from the house as the funeral cortege left the house to go to the church, explaining that point was one of the most difficult (they usually zoomed in on the faces of the family as the coffin left the house). They agreed.

As a family, we accepted Archbishop Eames and local Priest and Nuns into our home to show that we had always lived side by side with other faiths. Being Northern Ireland with its strong Protestant Roman Catholic divide, this was important at that time, as we all knew which organisation (the IRA) was responsible for John's death. Everything, especially a shooting or death of a person, as popular as my brother was, was highly politicised and neither, the authorities nor our family, wanted anything to take away from the memories of John's life. So we accepted their sincere condolences. Archbishop Eames was our Archbishop and highly respected. My brother Henderson and I felt that it was important and as the oldest boy, Henderson led the tone—I supported him followed by the others. My mother was silent and my dad was dead already.

My brother Henderson had also spoken to the press on the night John was murdered—defiantly telling Gerry Adams (the leader of Sinn Fein and the IRA) during the media interview that he would not get away with this forever. A strongly defiant, typically Ulster Protestant approach to a sinister and evil leader and his prescribed organisation.

The IRA immediately issued a death threat on the family. John had lived with a known death threat for at least a year, so we as a family just shrugged. Although my brothers took precautions and moved around various houses quite a lot.

The day John was buried, our town came to a standstill. John was very popular, everywhere. Crowds lined the pavements through the town and I was told that many shops had shut. There were many policemen on duty along the route and I remember one opening my car door at the church.

Though to our family he was 'just John'—and much loved. We grieved.

I had already agreed to apply through the TA for a Public Information role with the British Army and the killing of my peace-loving brother was the decider.

This family tragedy just added to my resolve as I pursued the public information pathway.

After Divorce

After divorce, life had changed drastically for me and I had to give up my part-time job at Craigavon Area Hospital plus my very enjoyable child-minding job. There were very little social security benefits handed out in those days. I applied but was told that I didn't qualify for any. My family were not in a position to help me so the choice was simple. It meant that I now had to work full time.

The most important thing I had to do was to make sure that I could support myself and the children. I knew that there would be difficulties, it was inevitable in the circumstances, so I just had to knuckle down. Most importantly to my mind was that, even in the short-term, I needed money to survive—for food and electricity basically. A full-time job was therefore essential. (Previously, I had worked evenings and a few nights in the nearby hospital as well as 'minded' children at home, during term time.) Good money but I had no one to child mind during evenings and nights.

Moy Park, the local chicken processing plant located a short distance away, was hiring office staff so I applied and got a job in the accounts department. At first, I was sent to the invoicing section but this was in the initial period when computer programming was basic. I was not a qualified typist so had frequent finger trouble. It was always quite difficult to recover from these basic and simple errors as, for some reason, the numbering system would go back to the beginning of the work session and, if the mistake occurred towards the end of the day, you had to redo all the invoices which you had typed that day! It was a fairly common error but as I seemed to commit the sin more frequently than others, I was quickly moved to sales.

Fortunately, I was more successful as a telesales operator, so was able to keep the job.

After a few difficult instances where I felt that things could have been handles better by the supervisor, one of the other salesgirls (there were only three of us in the team) decided to apply for a sales job advertised in the local farming related newspaper. The hours were slightly less than what we were working and the wages were better. It was a no-brainer but I was too late with an application, the job had been awarded to someone else.

As luck would have it, a week later another advert appeared in the local paper for a similar job, this time in a different local newspaper some six miles away. I sent in an application and was granted an interview. There was only one problem, how was I going to get to the interview in the next town? I didn't have a car and as I had taken quite a few days off already, I couldn't take any more time off work. Those six miles loomed darkly. I really was going to have to give up on this potential opportunity.

The interview was scheduled for the Friday. I hesitated and didn't say anything and then fortune smiled on me. Friday was the day that the sales reps came into the office to submit their reports. Almost without thinking, I asked one of them if I could borrow their company car for an hour. As I was working for the company, I was covered by the company insurance. This man, Mr White, was a real gentleman and after assuring himself that this loan was for just about an hour, he handed me the keys

I went to the interview, got the job and started working in the newspaper two weeks later. Cheek!

Before I left Moy Park the gentleman quietly asked me if I had borrowed the car to go to the interview. Mutely, I nodded.

Work in the newspaper business was a different way of going. Instead of cycling the short distance to work, I had to catch a bus. The bus service was quite good but I had to work late one evening and had to ensure that I finished work in good time so that I could catch the appropriate bus home. There weren't many buses in the evening so this was a bit of a stress.

In my mind, to compensate for this stress, I had a day off. This was like heaven to me.

Starting work in advertising sales, I was placed in the classified section. As a new girl, I had to become known on my patch so this meant going out around the many small businesses in the town. This was really good practice for me and after a spell in Classifieds, I was transferred over to features—this meant going to a business and persuading them to take space, usually a couple of pages, mainly ads, promoting their business. These features were aimed at showing the level of support the featured business had gained within their local business community. These other businesses…usually all came in with small supporting ads.

Gathering the information was interesting and a reporter always followed up and wrote the editorial but I was hooked. It was enjoyable, interesting and very satisfying when you could see the results of your efforts in the local paper at the end of the week. The 'thank you' from the businesses were also very gratifying.

After I started in advertising, I was told that I could have had a job as a reporter, which I would have loved even more, but the die was cast. I was in advertising sales and I loved it.

I was pretty much forced into thinking about buying a car. This was mainly due to the one late night at work and the difficulty that I had trying to get the weekly shopping done. I had to be careful with the money but the additional amount of money that I was earning did allow me that little bit of luxury. My luxury could not afford to cost too much so I scoured the weekly newspaper to see what I could get. After some searches, I picked up on one. It was £125 for a mini. It was a bit old, obviously, and I contacted the telephone number. The owner lived in the district that really 'belonged' to the 'other side' (Ballyoran Estate) of the religious divide! I was cautious but not put off. I had nothing to fear but knew that it could be potentially awkward for both sides.

I contacted my brother John who owned a garage (later shot dead by three IRA men from that area) and he agreed to come with me to check out the car. The car was an older mini and would suit my very minimal budget. We went to the agreed house in Ballyoran and the car owner recognised my brother and, on that basis, even offered me additional items, spare parts. I couldn't refuse. We had to pick up these items at another address, this time in a more 'hard line' area (Garvaghy Estate) and he jumped in the car with us to guide us down.

This was also a good move, as, when we entered the estate, the car owner leaned out of the window and shouted, it's John Corry! At this information, the anxious onlookers who seemed to have come from nowhere melted away and we went to the guy's house undisturbed. I felt proud that my young brother was so respected by the 'other side' as this was the way we had been brought up by our parents—'take people as you find them', without bias.

My car was not the best buy I ever made. It wouldn't start the next morning, because the battery was flat and it had obviously been primed for the sale. But I had my brother, who knew what to do and he helped me—frequently over the following months! When told about the problem, John just smiled and repeated one of our Granny's sayings, 'you get what you pay for'. I had.

However, despite a few issues, the car did its job. I called it my character car. It was an electric blue mini with a white roof. It had also been hand painted and there were a few dents in the bodywork, but it got me from A to B, so it was great. Part of its charm was the rubber buckles attached to each side of the car bonnet with the related straps attached to the car body. Obviously, the bonnet catch didn't work too well! The car had had an accident and had rolled over a few times. The repair was basic. The head cloth had been slit open at various points and the dents in the roof had been punched out by hand. Still, it was mine and I was thrilled with my purchase. There were images of the Virgin Mary stuck on the front dash—obviously a prayer for saintly protection—I left them there.

One morning on my way to work, I passed a guy who was obviously desperately trying to get a lift. He had missed the bus and the look of desperation on his face was so telling to me that I stopped and offered him a lift. He was a total stranger to me. He got in and then realised I was on my own in the car. He told me off for being so trustworthy! As he said, these were bad times. I excused myself saying that I could have been the one who missed the bus and trying to get to work.

I appreciated his word and promised that I wouldn't do it again. I never saw him again. There's not many like him around.

After I settled into the job in Lurgan (the town six miles from where I lived) where I was started at the bottom doing classifieds before moving on to working on features. I worked there for about a year and was approached by another local newspapers, this time in Banbridge. This was about ten miles from where I lived. This time I was offered a company car and that prospect was too appealing. The hours were full time but more money so I moved newspapers and joined their advertising departments.

I really enjoyed working in Banbridge and got to know the town well. I did all classes of advertising in this newspaper and thoroughly enjoyed it all. Later I moved to another local newspaper, this time in Dromore, a few miles further away but still within the same local area and still with a company car.

I enjoyed the job but found that I really needed a little more money as my home required a few much-needed repairs. It's strange how things happen because, just about this time, I had a golden opportunity presented to me. It was in 1988 and the local branch of the Territorial Army invited representatives from the local paper where I worked to come to an 'Open Evening' at the Banbridge TA camp based on the Scarva Road. The staff there told us that they needed more members and wanted an article in the paper to let the local people know about their recruitment drive.

Paul, the young reporter, and I agreed to volunteer although my suitability for a role was doubtful. Having volunteered not quite knowing what I could do, I decided that this was my opportunity (if at all possible) to earn the extra money that I needed to help maintain my home and add a little to the family finances. I would give it a try and see what would happen.

I was a little old for joining the Territorial Army, I was then 42 years old (the energy needed for part-time soldiering is a young person's game) and it was with a bit to my surprise that, after the event in Banbridge, I was contacted by Headquarters Land Command in Salisbury and asked if I would work as a Public Information Officer, providing I passed a Selection Board. I didn't quite know what that meant but agreed anyway—thinking just an interview.

As part of the selection process, I was asked to write a short story on the demographic balance in the UK. I wasn't too sure about the topic but wrote some words anyway.

I also agreed to go across to Salisbury for a weekend of interviews. I was a bit mesmerised by all this and doubted my commitment to this project. However I was persuaded by my need for potential extra earnings to take a trip over to Salisbury. Simply, I was not going to have to pay for my travel and the Army would accommodate me overnight.

On arrival in Salisbury on the Friday evening, I discovered that, I was one of a class of about 28 people, competing for a position. I hadn't thought of asking for details. Accommodation had been organised and I stayed in a hotel close to the Headquarters (at Army expense) and was due to be picked up by car early on the Saturday morning. The car was late and I began to think that my journey had been a waste of time. So I called the army number and asked if they were going to come for me. I think that this cheeky person daring to question their punctuality was a surprise to them but they politely told me they would arrive soon. I did not realise that the others who were competing for the job were already members of the TA and had been accommodated on the base. I was the only civilian.

Arriving at HQ Land Command, I was escorted to the interview area where a selection of short presentations was being made by some knowledgeable guys in military uniform. This series of presentations were then followed by intensive interviews by a board of military bods. It was all very well organised and intensely interesting.

I remember feeling impressed with all this organisation and information, whilst, at the same time, wondering if this was all my cup of tea. We had a few presentations from respected journalists who were already members of the TA in UK. We had a few simple English language tasks to complete, including comprehension and a short essay. The whole thing was all very interesting and I relaxed a bit. This was straightforward but a little bit of a challenge.

I always enjoy a challenge and the proceedings was made more so, sometime in the afternoon. This was after some of the interviewees had departed from the classroom, presumably because they had decided or were told that this was not for them.

I felt quite comfortable with the information being given but the challenge became more defined, particularly when one of the Senior Officers told us that it was no shame if we failed the selection process. My reaction to that announcement was that, I had had to make serious arrangements to get here and I'm not giving in that easily!

Some more did leave but I stayed and, maybe because I was the only candidate from Northern Ireland. I was selected as a suitable candidate. One question posed during the interview process was a bit of a stunner—asked if I had always wanted to join the Army because my parents had both served in the Forces, I replied—'No, I never thought of it!'

I think it was pointed out at this stage that if I was selected to do the job, I would have to know some very basic things, like going on patrol, order of rank, tabbing and some basic tactics. They felt that unless you had experienced these things, it wouldn't be possible to write about them. I think that, at this point, I smiled and nodded, thinking to myself, well, that's that then!

However, on my return home, I was notified that I was regarded as suitable and was appointed to the job. All I can think of was that they really needed some media representation in Ulster when I was selected as suitable.

After a short period of me wondering what was going to happen, I was instructed to attend basic training at the Royal Signals camp in Belfast. The Army are very thorough and I had a few very helpful calls to let me know what would happen next. I was a little overwhelmed by it all but went along, taking day by day.

I received a call from a female officer giving me detailed instructions on where exactly to go for training. 40 Signals Regiment in Belfast was apparently the only suitable place for me to get the necessary training.

I really had no idea what was required of me though. I was fit because I had been running most evenings but I did that alone and there was no gauge for my level of fitness. This unit suited me well as my ex-husband, had been a radio operator/signaller in the RAF and I had picked up a lot of information from him as he had to study radio and communications subjects in order to pass his Category Training exams for Signals and Radio every six months to maintain his 'Cat' standard operating procedures for aircrew. Apparently though, according to the Army, because I had no idea of Army protocol, I had to do the basic training, teaching me how to march, recognise rank, etc. I was a little taken aback but agreed with the plan. It did make sense but I hadn't thought that far ahead.

The goal was that I was to become a Public Information Officer with a Headquarters (HQ) in Salisbury at the British Army HQ Land Command. I was going to have to promote the media profile of the TA units based in Northern Ireland. My Selection Board had been held in Salisbury. But first there was the training to get through at the base in Northern Ireland.

As instructed, I reported to the unit in Belfast for training. This was scheduled for two nights per week with a commitment for the odd weekend away, working with the different units based in Northern Ireland, familiarising myself with their different roles. As a complete novice I had no idea what I was agreeing to do.

On reporting to the unit, I was somewhat bemused by the constant running, parading up and down, about turns, right wheel, left wheel and halt. On one occasion, we were standing around waiting for the evening session to start and, as I had completed a hectic day at work, I leaned up against the wall.

Before I knew what was happening, an irate Sergeant was roaring into my face telling me I could not slough (lean) against the wall! Startled, I leapt to attention and gaped at him. I'm pretty sure he smiled but quickly recovered himself and walked off. Memories are made of things like this!

One of the shocks I received was the Army concept that when you felt that you couldn't do anything else, well, you just turned around and did another task. As part of the training, we had to run around the camp every training evening and often, when we had reached the finish line, the Sergeant or whoever was there would order us to run back to the start.

Quite a lesson and I often remembered it as I went through tough times in life.

On another occasion, I was part of the squad and we were marching up and down, doing our drills. The Corporal who was taking the drill thought that I had made a mistake on the 'about turn' and screamed at me to get 'down for ten'; i.e., do ten press ups. I did the necessary but he was not happy so I had to do the same number of 'star jumps', still not satisfied he demanded I do a further ten 'press ups'. I was a bit fed up with all these moves and as I wasn't at all phased by the effort required, I decided I would clap hands between the down and the up. The Corporal, by this time, was down beside me shouting his instructions into my ear. When I started to clap my hands, it was too much for him, he burst out laughing, but I knew I had to complete the sequence although I was well pleased with my little stunt.

On another occasion, in a classroom scenario, we were being taught how to iron our kit. This is very serious as kit has to be immaculate, clean and ironed precisely with only specified creases. I was sitting back enjoying the demo when suddenly this same Corporal told me to get on my feet and demonstrate how to iron a shirt. Startled, I repeated, 'who me'! Satisfied, he beckoned me up to the ironing board. Swallowing hard, I obeyed.

As I started to demonstrate, I had this vision of an Amah (housekeeper in Singapore) I once knew who would iron the collar of a shirt very carefully and then, turning the collar down, she would very carefully pull her finger and thumb of her right hand along the crease to define it even better. The amusing part for me was that she held the little finger up in the air as she did this. Without giving it much thought, I copied her action, grinning at the assembled squad. They grinned back and the Corporal ordered me to 'sit down'. Basic training had its moments!

WRAC 'Passing Out Parade' at Guilford Barracks

Tapio

An essential element of my induction into the Army was the rigorous physical training schedule two evenings per week. Meanwhile, still working hard at my regular job which held body and soul together plus family and household needs. The work with the Army was meant for weekends and the two nights training every week. The plan was that I would attend the training and unit exercises and write up the articles at home. I would then send or take these articles to the appropriate local newspaper requesting their support and for local publication. This would keep me busy.

I was destined to become an Officer but as an unknown and 'older' candidate, my fitness level was in doubt. The schedule was enjoyable and I became very adept at 'Star Jumps' and 'down for ten'—i.e., press ups. As part of my general attitude to the personal difficulties I was experiencing, I ran four or five miles three or four times each week. I had always enjoyed running, finding it relaxing and energising and was reasonably fit so this new fitness regime was very acceptable.

I had to attend a basic soldiers training course. This was held at the Woman's Royal Army Training Camp in Guilford, Surrey. During the training I managed to hold my own and tried not draw attention to the fact that I was so much older than the others who were in their late teens and early twenties.

However, during one of the runs at the Signals camp in Belfast prior to leaving for Guilford, I had torn a calf muscle as I hadn't warmed myself up properly. I heard it go so I knew straightaway and it hurt!

I had booked the time off work and felt that I couldn't change any arrangements and as I needed to be on reasonably fit form, I decided to attend a physio. The guy tried his best but time was against him. There wasn't really anything he could achieve as this happened just the week before I went on the course. As I couldn't change my leave dates, I had to think of something.

The only solution I could think of was to strap my ankle as tightly as I could inside my army boot. The combination of boot and strapping acted like a splint and gave me the support I needed.

During the course, I did this every morning and took a few painkillers to ease the pain. The course was not that easy and included camping out overnight, enduring a dawn raid, a long tab over rough ground, an assault course and a lot of tough walking with a heavy rucksack. All these activities also included perfect bed making, boots polished to mirror sheen, perfectly ironed kit and clean soap. It was busy.

During the course, I managed all tests/lessons, including map reading and tactics. It also involved the two-mile run, in which I acquitting myself reasonably well, being faster than most of the others. I came in fifth out of twenty-eight students.

Managing the two weeks course, I was ok until the last test on the penultimate day when we had to jump from one base to another. It was more than I could manage. I had to admit defeat. It was the end of the course so I got permission and turned in sick at the medical centre.

This is a fairly common 'dodge' and I was viewed with some suspicion by the others. I had already been confronted and reported by a fellow student for taking painkillers every day (She accused me of taking 'uppers and downers'!!! Little did she know it was all 'upper' (paracetamol in my case) to get me through the day). However, when I reported sick and the medics took off my boot and saw the damage, they were quite impressed seeing my green and blue bruising that extended from my ankle up to the back of my knee. I was excused physical exercise for the rest of the time, really just that day.

So I 'Passed Out' as they say in military circles, and I was jolly pleased and relieved not to have to do it again.

Returning to the unit in Belfast, I was told that I was going to have a 'Baptism of Fire'—my services were needed right away. My first job was organising the visit of the Princess Royal to 40 Signals, whilst they were on their Annual two-week Camp. This was, I believe, the first time that such a visit was about to happen. Apparently, some senior Officer had decided on impulse, to write to the Princess Royal and invite her to take a visit to the Regiment, in her position as Colonel-in-Chief—and she had accepted. Marvellous news.

Now all we had to do was organise the details. As a unit in Ulster, we were planning our Annual Camp to Scarborough and we felt that we would be able to achieve better security at that location in England. The threats from the IRA insurgents were an ever-present concern for all of us.

As the Princess Royal was the Colonel-in-Chief of the Regiment, this was quite an honour for 40 Signals Regiment from Ulster—and I was a little awestruck at the prospect of planning and organising the itinerary for this very important visitor. Obviously, the Regiment was anxious that their Colonel-in-Chief received a comprehensive overview of all the training activities. Also obviously, as a new member of the Regiment, I had to be directed and guided as to which stands/activities were to be visited by Her Royal Highness. The other members of the Regiment were brilliant, advising and directing me as to which aspects of the training would best demonstrate our capability and expertise. It was my job to organise their proposed programme and ensure that they were each visited and that the Princess Royal was properly looked after. The other members of the Regiment did their stuff too.

The personal safety aspect of Her Royal Highness was also a matter of concern at that time. The insurrection campaign of the Irish Republican Army (IRA) was in full flow and security was always a high priority. Receiving support from Regiment personnel was key and they gave it wholeheartedly and because of the team effort, the job was made easy. Plans were made and a programme drawn up that was thought to be suitable for the occasion.

I was nervous, my first big job and what a job! It was definitely a 'Baptism of Fire'. On the day it all worked, the visit was a great success and the Princess Royal proved to be a much informed and entertaining guest. The Lady could discuss and debate on any subject relating to the Signal and the Regiment.

Other jobs followed. Media representation was a necessity for the part-time security services in Northern Ireland at that time. Security forces and civilians were being slaughtered at that time and despite the obdurate stubbornness of the Protestant population, there was constant fear. Innocent Catholics were also being killed; the only winners were the IRA terrorists.

It was important that a balance had to be drawn between the killing of innocent civilians on both sides of the religious divide, the killing and bombing of the security force members by the so-called 'Freedom Fighters' of the Republican movement and that of the work, wishes and desires of the average ordinary citizen, who believed in the Rule of Law.

I set to and, with the support of the TA in Ulster and the wider British Army, spent many busy evenings and weekends getting up to speed on the training exercises and events enjoyed by the many branches of the British Army, and, obviously including those members of the TA based in Ulster. These events included all their many exercises in other areas in Europe.

My training was constant. I was required to learn about all aspects of Army life, exercises and basic training of the different units. This meant a lot of weekends working with the different units in the field as well as attending specific TAPIO training, usually across the water in England but also in Scotland and Wales. It was a lot of hard work and late evenings when I had to write up stories and reports. But this was good, I was getting paid for the work and that was what I needed. It was the reason I had agreed to take on the role.

Because I was very aware of the personal security dangers to all personnel involved, including myself, I was cautious. I wrote many articles and, as I was issued with a camera, I also took photos of the activities. This was all done with due regard to the personal safety of the people involved. Specifically and particularly with regard to Ulster in my articles for publication, both locally and further afield, I stressed the normality of the activities of the part-time troops, the mundane treks over rough ground, the skills being taught on vehicle maintenance, mechanical engineering, bridge building, driving skills, map reading and generally surviving in the cold and wet whilst camping out in all weathers.

All basic life skills that could be, and were, transferred to regular living scenarios. In other words identifying the benefits of becoming a member of the TA. Many of the men and women joined the catering branch. (Obviously, there was a catering unit at each base so that each unit could be self-sufficient.) Many of the men found that they enjoyed preparing meals—some even took it up as a career. All very normal and mundane—and the bonus was that we were paid for the few hours that we were present, working within the TA.

There was also a strong medical unit with fully qualified medics of all grades who supported the TA and the regular British Army units, as and when the occasion demanded.

This TA payment system for a day's work or weekend exercise was a major persuader to many and as I pointed out, the additional earnings was an enormous help and improved the household budget—and not just for me.

Visiting the different TA units throughout Northern Ireland, whether they were on base or on exercise, practising the varying designated roles, I was struck by the comradeship among the men and women. The community spirit which brought them all together—with no regard for their individual origins or backgrounds. This communal spirit was an inspiration and boded well for the future of our communities.

Trying to put a personal work plan together so that I could identify how to handle the additional work that I wanted to do, I worked out a PR five-year plan that would demonstrate to the wider community, particularly in Northern Ireland, that the TA was very much alive and having a great time. I reckoned that this would encourage recruitment, also garner popular support (from one section of the community anyway) and, in public information terms, counter the terrorising propaganda methods of the IRA.

After the (generally) weekend visits to the units exercising their roles, I would write articles on the activities and present these articles to the respective local media within the unit base area and ask them for publicity for the unit. The media needed and asked for accompanying photos so I was given a camera and took the photographs as well. Because of the constant threat from the ever-present threat of the IRA, these photos could not identify anyone and, because of what had happened to our family, I understood and was very careful whilst taking my photographs. Once the media realised that these local guys were enjoying what they did, they were easily persuaded to join us at weekends and experience 'exercise' conditions for themselves—with the proviso that they gave us the appropriate supporting publicity. They understood and the campaign gathered momentum. The PR message became local news. TA unit activities became a constant item of the local news scene and accepted as part of our everyday non-threatening world.

As a TA Public Information Officer (PIO) I worked extensively in N Ireland but was also asked that I would expand my duties and include other units throughout the UK. As there were not many of us PIOs most of the UK units made use of my services for media work from time to time. This also meant that I had the opportunity to work with some British Army units whilst they were exercising overseas, mainly in France, Germany and Cyprus.

An integral aspect of the work was the physical training aspect where we were expected to maintain a high level of fitness. This side of the training was fairly high-octane involving actions like abseiling from over high bridges and cliffs, zip lining, crossing small ravines, shinning along ropes dangling in mid-air, scrambling over army obstacle courses involving ropes, cargo net A-frames, etc., crawling through muddy ditches and other enjoyable aspects of tough physical fitness training.

The army had its own version of 'treasure hunts' which involved map reading, compass readings and trekking miles across rough country, usually in poor weather conditions. The poor weather was a 'given'. Hill running was one of the more enjoyable pursuits, although I could have been better at it, but the activity gave me a wonderful sense of freedom and aliveness.

Weapon Training!

All this physical activity was geared towards toughening all of us up and ensuring that we were physically fit for any situation. It was also great fun.

The first Gulf War had exposed the TAPIOs, participating at that time, to the dangers of NBC (Non-Biological and Chemical) warfare, so that was added to the list of essential training. It was a scary thought that we might be exposed to this type of incident. During the training, I comforted myself that the suits were warm when we were out in cold weather—completely overlooking the fact that the NBC problem was as likely to occur in hot climates as well as cold!

All this tough training helped us all to cope with some pretty awkward moments whilst working our jobs. These 'moments' often required a cool head and quick changes of plans. This training proved itself to be very helpful many times over in the future.

An example of this was when, on one occasion, whilst working in the UN, on a job for the Special Representative Secretary General (SRSG) of Kosovo, Dr Bernard Kouchner, when I was organizing and conducting visits. During one of SRSG's visits to a remote location in the hills near Prizren. The weather closed in with dense fog enveloping the plateau we were going to use as a landing pad for SRSG's helicopter. Rather than disappoint a lot of excited residents, it was decided that the visit would go ahead. The local people were geared up to welcome the boss, and as the visit was to a fairly remote settlement, that did not have many visitors, we felt that it was important to fulfil the commitment.

We, in the escort team, were already at the location to be visited, having travelled by road. So with a very speedy revamp of the timetable and an equally speedy convoy journey down to the new landing pad within the German Camp, disaster was averted and SRSG received a hero's welcome. SRSG was adored by the bulk of Kosovars and received a great welcome wherever he went.

During my training period as a TAPIO, I was sent to the Army HQ in Lisburn at Thiepval Barracks (Northern Ireland) to learn the more administrative side of Army work. Sometimes it was as simple as writing memos to learning more about the units which made up the TA in Northern Ireland, the 36th Ulster Division. The period of training was quite intense but it had to be done, I had to learn.

One of the really good events was that in about 1990, coming up to the Anniversary of the Battle of the Somme on 1st July, the Deputy Chief of Staff for the TA in the Lisburn put together a bus load of TA soldiers from the 36th Ulster

Division to go across to the site of the battle at Thiepval Wood (France) to join in the commemorative parade to be held there.

The occasion was also to commemorate the opening and dedication of the Ulster Tower at Thiepval which was built opposite Thiepval Wood from where the 36th Ulster Division made its historic charge on the 1st of July 1916. The battle/commemoration site is in close proximity to the village of Thiepval in France. The Tower stands some 70 feet tall and is a lasting tribute to the men of Ulster who gave their lives during the First World War.

Surprise (for me) TAPIO job at the Somme Commemorations. Standing with BBC reporter Iain Munro (later head of BBC Scotland) and cameraman standing in front of the Ulster Tower at Thiepval, France

Accommodation had been arranged for us at a nearby French Army base and, thinking that I was only there to learn the ropes, on arrival, I took myself off for a walk down to the nearby village. On my return, as I strolled unconcernedly across the parade ground, I was waved over by the DCOS, who was chatting to a few others. I was then informed that, as there was no Press Officer for the forthcoming parade, I was going to do the job. I was gobsmacked. I wasn't prepared and the parade was in two days' time! That announcement took the leisure away. This was work and only my second PIO job.

With much appreciated help from a Colonel Kirkwood in the Engineers TA, who had hired a car for his personal use to go round the battlefield and many cemeteries and who kindly included me in his travels, I got to know around the area and was able to recce the main Thiepval Memorial site in France where the main parade would be held. From being on a bit of a jolly, I had to familiarise myself with two parade locations and events.

The 36th Ulster Division (Ulster TA, 107 Ulster Brigade) was having their own parade in addition to the main parade at Thiepval. This one was for the dedication of the Ulster Tower (Thiepval, France) and included quite a significant number of Ulster politicians as well as the military. Then there was the main parade at the Thiepval Memorial some distance away which included a wider range of participants involving other nations that had been involved in the original battle. These other nations also had their own media representatives to record the event.

French gendarmes were much in evidence dealing with general parade security at both locations (after all it was their home turf) and we had an interesting, discussing with them as to their tactical approach. Amicable serious confrontation would be a better term.

It was my first attendance at such an international event and it was so impressive to see how the many different national participants worked together to make the whole show a success.

There were some very important people, including Royalty, at the Thiepval Memorial, paying their respects and the whole formality of the occasion was, to me, very educational.

I had been able to bring along a couple of local Northern Ireland journalists, who had special connections to the Somme and they were well pleased to be able to attend this event. This was their first time, at this event and to these local reporters, this was a very emotional occasion. I was delighted to be able to make this happen for them, it was an honour.

The BBC were present, as was local French media and a contingent from Canada. I don't remember all of the media representatives who were present but I remember being kept busy.

The refreshments in the formal reception marquee for the guests, which was on the grass area behind the Thiepval Memorial were magnificent. The marque was really large, as one would expect, but as this was my first attendance at such an event, I was a little in awe of it all.

The French gendarmerie were very precise and particular. They seemed to be everywhere but merged into the background beautifully, quite beautifully.

A neighbour of mine was escorting her father, a veteran who had served at the Somme. I was quite delighted to see her and, at first, she didn't recognise me as I was in uniform. I didn't mind as I really didn't want to be recognised.

The parade at the Ulster Tower took place after the main parade and reception at Thiepval. We had to bus it over to the Ulster Tower and although, we were in uniform, we were stopped by the gendarmerie and I had to quickly remember some basic French in order to convince the gendarmes that we were part, a very basic and main part, of the parade to the Tower. Needless to say, my French language skills proved difficult to recall in seconds!

At the Ulster Tower, there was a large turnout of Northern Ireland dignitaries who paraded to the tower followed by the soldiers of the 36th Ulster Division easily representing both sides of the community, Protestant and Catholic alike, just as it had been at the time of the battle. During the actual Battle of the Somme, when the soldiers of the 36th Ulster Division went 'over the top' of the trenches; apparently, the Protestants donned their Orange Sashes and many carried their Bibles, as they mounted their attack. They were accompanied, side by side, by their fellow Roman Catholics soldiers who also carried their personal items. No one was bothered, each to his own. There was a job to be done and no differences were noted.

At the Ulster Tower commemoration, there had been a bit of a security flurry the morning of the parade in relation to some missing paintings. This happened well before the event took place, but that was sorted out and the parade went ahead as planned. In Ulster, we were used to these security flurries.

All in all this was quite an experience for this novice. Many more jobs followed, ranging from the mundane to the high profile.

Working as a TAPIO meant that I was kept busy. The jobs ranged from the wet weekends on exercise (often on duty through most of the night as well as during most of the day) with units practicing their role in fairly remote fields to the very high-profile Royal Artillery 41-gun salute in Hyde Park London to celebrate the Queen's Birthday. Being part of this particularly outstanding occasion in Hyde Park with all the ceremony and military precision was quite unforgettable. All these events and exercises were all part of a steep learning experience. Being pragmatic and hardworking were prime considerations for this role.

The event at the Ulster Tower and being PIO for Princess Anne's visit to 40 Signals marked the start of many such grand occasions, in which I was privileged to participate.

One of the most memorable occasions was when I was included as a member of the Public Information team that attended the 50th Anniversary of the 'D Day Landings' in Normandy France. I think that the full complement of the PIO team was present. Between the members of the team we were able to cover all the individual events planned for France. The events were very important and reflected the total effort made by the Allies to overcome the well organised German defence. Despite the importance of these events, I distinctively remember starting off the stay in France, sleeping in a sleeping bag on the bare wooden floorboards of a local school, though I hasten to add, accommodation did improve after that start.

The locations for the landings were memorable, even in their own right, as sandy beaches. Standing on one of the beaches near Arromanches it was easy to visualise the desperation of the Allied landing forces. The lovely sandy beach stretched interminably before me leading directly and bluntly to the higher ground which housed the German gun emplacements dug into the heights. As I stood on the sand with my back to the sea, I could almost feel the obvious intimidation which must have been felt by the troops as the jumped from the small army of boats, into the surf. It was such a mammoth effort made by our predecessors and one that we must acknowledge by our remembrances.

The 'D Day' commemorations took place over a number of days with parades and services taking place at key sites. I was mainly based around Merville and Caen. Princess Margaret and Prince Charles both participated in parades in my AOR. A friend of mine had the pleasure of being located near the

Bayeau Tapestry. Interested in the history of the Tapestry, he was quite delighted with this placing.

On the day itself, 6th June 1994, the events included a repeat of the Airborne Assault Landings by (originally 24,000) Canadian parachutists. I considered myself very fortunate to be included in the PINFO team that were working the landing zone/field. Interest in the events in the field was intense with many media literally dropping in from helicopters which deposited them along the edge of the field. This was much to the annoyance of those already in position at the dedicated area at some distance away towards the bottom edge of the field.

The sight of so many planes flying overhead *en masse* was something special. Being so close to the parachute landing itself was spectacular, with the parachutists baling out of their overflying aircraft, dropping down from the sky with each attached canisters hitting the ground with a dull thud. The parachutists were amazingly speedy at gathering up their gear and starting the walk down the field. The parachutists were greeted by Prince Charles and Prince Andrew who walked down the field with them, chatting away. I was tasked with accompanying Prince Andrew and found him to be a very decent fellow who was very much at home with the guys. He came across as very down to earth and ordinary.

Other TAPIOs were also in attendance at this event—as was the international media dropping down in their hired helicopters, directly onto the landing zone (DZ) even as the parachutists were doing their drop. For their own safety the media representatives had to be persuaded to get behind the line of troops guarding the perimeter of the field. A few of the media were indignant as some of them, who had dropped in on the field during the main drop, had thought themselves clever because they had stolen a march on the more managed others, in arriving by helicopter at the last minute.

After the jump, we then went on to see Pegasus Bridge (now renamed Horsa Bridge) to view the famous bridge and the surrounding area. Viewing the whole scenario made me very aware, again, of the tough conditions experienced back in 1944 by the Allied forces. It made me very grateful to those troops for the immense effort that they had made fifty years before.

The Allied Landings incorporated plans for five beach landings, Omaha, Gold, Juno and Sword. I was able to visit Omaha Beach and walk the sandy beach up to the low heights where the Germans had established their bunkers and gun emplacements. It was from this standpoint that the Germans had rained down their fire power on the advancing allies as they disembarked from their landing craft at the water's edge. It was easy to visualise the powerful scene and even, to nearly feel, the effort required by the troops as they made their way up the beach, or in some cases as they would fall wounded and dying, in the struggle to reach their objective. It was daunting just to stand and reflect on their task.

The main event as regards the attendance of the Queen and the Duke of Edinburgh, was the event at Arromanches. It was here where the Allied Forces had established a portable harbour to off load equipment following the initial landings.

When we arrived at Arromanches, after the stop at Pegasus Bridge, preparations for the Royal visitor were well under way. It was fascinating to see how the cleaned sand on the beach, was being carefully raked by individuals with garden rakes. Everything had to be pristine for Her Majesty. It was a beautiful sight to watch these careful preparations, carried out so precisely and with great care.

At the beach, I was designated to deal with the international media presence as I had had previous experience at (among other occasions) the Somme celebrations. There was an enormous crowd, especially French people, wanting to get a close view of the Queen and the Duke of Edinburgh.

The waiting crowd was not disappointed, as the Queen (despite the heavy security presence) managed to convey a sense of freedom and relaxation as she strolled through the throng of people, down to the beach, smiling as she did so. She was not in a hurry and this translated across into the crowd (of whom I was one) as her enjoying the visit and seeing all these people. It was very relaxing and wonderful. I got a real good close view of Her Majesty as she went past my position where I stood with the media crews. This visit was special to all present, including us in the military, and the Queen gained even more admirers by her relaxed smiling attitude. Having a very close view of Her Majesty, was for me, a thrilling moment of pure admiration, and I could see for myself her youthful glowing appearance.

Those of us who worked the event received a replica of the original silk map used to draw out the plan of the landings. It is special and I have had it framed as a lasting 'memento' of a very significant occasion.

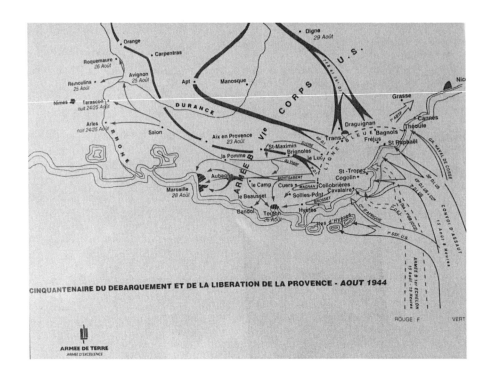

Plans of the D Day Landings in France 1944

Not all our jobs were quite so glamorous. On quite a few occasions, as a group, we slept on the floor of sheds, stables and often in hastily erected tents. Behind the scenes, it's all basic and business, the glamour is stripped right back.

To illustrate this on one occasion, the unit I was working with (5 Royal Irish) had spent two pretty tough weeks out in the ulu in Cyprus under a very strong sun. All with a view of promoting good public relations.

On this trip to Cyprus, where the soldiers were establishing a two-week camp and exercise scenario, I arrived at the same time as the troops and was therefore witness to the setting up process. As I did not normally become involved with this stage of proceedings, I was intrigued to see the soldiers rigging up a shower, using a tall standpipe and a plastic container with holes punched into it. The camp was out in the ulu and it had to be self-sufficient!

Special exercise shower

The soldiers all seemed to be thoroughly enjoyed the novelty of the outdoor showers and there was much laughter as they entered into the spirit of having to make do. The time was midsummer (June time) and it was pretty hot. We worked all day (me included) out in the open during the two-week camp.

Issued with desert type uniform, the heat was made easy. We had all the usual exercise stuff, firing weapons, manoeuvres and hunkering down in small foxholes for long periods at a stretch.

During the day, we often gathered in dusty foxholes under the beating sun and practised 'live firing' directed out to sea during which time I got some great photographs from very close range. At one point I believe a soldier was detailed to hang on to my belt as I was in danger of falling over the edge of the cliff. Mortars and Milan anti-tank missiles firing was perfected. All very exciting and dramatic. Getting the trajectory just right taking into account the distance, direction, height and precise target all had to be practised and perfected. All so very enthralling and absorbing in detail and precision.

I was able to take many photos of the soldiers at work, some quite dramatic with this wonderful backdrop of brown grass and burnt stumps of shrubs. The wonderful blue of the sea was an added bonus. Some of these pictures were later displayed within their barracks as a great reminder of an outstanding annual camp.

Even travelling in the land rovers was dusty work out here in these barren hot plains. We had had a visit from Prince Andrew in his role as Colonel in Chief, and as per usual, the visit was comprehensively covering all aspects of the training, but it was also very relaxed. Although, as you would expect, there was a few occasions when life became pretty hectic.

I was able to take loads of photographs, some spectacular views of soldiers firing their SA 80s and even catching the smoke as the projectile left the barrel of the rifle. Spectacular scenery and great photos which I passed to the unit.

The scenery around the camp site was like something out of a film set. The main operations tent was open at both ends with one open end looking towards the sea. Approaching the tent over the dry brown grass, the view was of outstandingly beautiful blue seas sparkling in the sunshine. It reminded me of scenes from the film, *Mutiny on the Bounty*!

The Duke of York meeting soldiers of 5 Royal Irish on exercise in Cyprus

Infantry business on exercise

As is customary with these exercise scenarios, there was an overnight exercise. As normal, I tagged along. The soldiers were not aware of the fact that they had a passenger. The Colonel told me to just tag along behind the last platoon. I was in uniform and no one noticed. Tabbing over the rough ground, in the silent darkness, I tried to be careful where I placed my feet. We all had to concentrate on what we were about. It's not an easy task tabbing over rough ground in the dark. The trail was rough with large rocks and I had to concentrate on the steps taken by the man in front. Sometime around the early hours of the morning, I stepped on a rock that moved and I yelped as I twisted my ankle. This was the first indication to the guy in front that he had a shadow! He was very startled and wanted me to be casevac'd off. That was not my idea at all and I asked someone to take off my boot and pack 'J' cloths around the ankle. (I had done this before during basic training and it had worked.)

After a few quick thoughts and a hurried debate, they did as I asked. It was easier than making an improvised stretcher and carrying me out. I assured them that this 'first aid' would work and I would be able to walk unaided. After the repair was made (to my instruction) and much to their evident relief, I got to my feet and did as promised.

I only had a few tough moments when the soldiers mounted the planned dawn attack and the swelling of my ankle had greatly increased. After that though, I had to go see the Doc and have a boot and leg support fitted. When the medics started taking off the boot, that was the worst part—it really hurt.

At the end of our two-week exercise, we were all looking forward to packing up and getting on the aeroplanes to go home. Assembling at the pick-up area at Camp Bloodhound, rumours started to circulate that something was happening to the Transport plane that was to take us home. Suspicions arose about leaving that day, obviously it was not going to happen that day. This was in the days before mobile phones so I couldn't let anyone at home know.

Hopefully, we would get airborne the next day—hopefully! Question was, where were we going to spend the night? The answer was simple—we would sleep on the hard standing (cemented area) that we were currently gathered on. It was hot so we just needed a roof over our heads in case a bit of a 'dew' fell overnight.

Actually, once we got over the initial shock, our 'quarters' were quickly organised. A large marque roof appeared and was quickly erected, seemingly without effort. We found ourselves organised without thought into rows of sleeping bags laid out on the concrete, parking ourselves beside whoever we had been talking to. We unrolled our sleeping bags, carrying on our conversation, totally oblivious of the unusual circumstances. Settling down for the night, lying in the sleeping bag, beside my good and protective friend, Derek, I remember looking up at the underside of the tent and just going to sleep.

There was a few hundred people who had a good night's sleep that night (we were exhausted after our two-week exercise). We were picked up the next day by Army four tonners, transported to the airfield and flown home.

Funnily enough, none of us discussed our potential travel insurance claims!

Just one of those unexpected twists that formed part of my experiences as a TAPIO. There were others, though not always in such warm climates or with such good friends.

Many weekends were spent covering events and weekend exercises. Tabs of about 25 miles in a day were common practice in Scotland. Running around the hills in Wales also seemed a favourite.

I travelled all over the UK following units as they practised their roles in different locations. I was fortunate in that I was able to write the article and also take the photographs, so it was a complete package. It was interesting work and provided valuable experience for future use.

Working with an English unit in Cyprus on one occasion, we had great support from the local British Forces (BFBS) radio station that reported on the details of the exercise and the unit involved. They guys in the unit were delighted at being noticed so far from home.

During training, I spent a lot of time in Wales with different infantry units in particular. I found that I could map read with some degree of accuracy and was able to follow patrols and had the ability to turn up at unexpected places along their route. The troops were always very pleasant to see me but I am quite sure that, there were many times, when I turned up wearing my red wellies, that they really wished me far enough away. (I had bought red wellies in a sale as the price was good and no one else wanted them, obviously not thinking of the occasions at which they would be on display!).

On one occasion, when I was covering the activities of an infantry unit, I identified a rest place and an appropriate time along their route and led a small team to the location.

The patrol was having a very well-deserved rest, hunkered down behind a wall, silently having a brew and then I leaned over the wall and greeted them. Bless their souls, I am sure they really didn't want to see me right then but they welcomed me and my companions anyway, demonstrating excellent discipline and self-restraint. I mentally saluted them all.

Military training time in 1994

This period of my life was happening during the lead up to the conflict in the Former Yugoslavia. It wasn't in my mind or plan but it worked out quite well for future needs.

When the newspaper I was working in closed down, I took a temporary job for the Ministry of Defence, HQ Land Command in Salisbury Wiltshire writing stories in support of the international peacekeeping effort to the UN Mission to the Former Yugoslavia (FRY). The region was in conflict and in the process of breaking up into separate countries. A request had gone out for anyone in the TAPIO pool willing to do a stint in support of the UN effort but focusing on the work of the British Forces deployed to the territory. There was the main focus of our attention in Central Bosnia Hercegovina where contingents of the British Forces were based at different locations throughout the central region. The supporting contingent was based in Croatia outside Split. This support sector was a little more relaxed as, although there was some emotional resentment to the presence of foreign troops by the locals, there was no physical disruption. It was safer.

My volunteer effort resulted in me going on to serve two six-month stints in Bosnia (starting in Split Croatia), both times, as part of the UN Peacekeeping Mission to the FRY. The first stint was as a Public Information Officer for the British Army and associated Coalition Forces. The second stint was that of working within the Coalition Public Information Centre based in the Holiday Inn, along Sniper Alley Sarajevo (Military Information HQ). In this CPIC all of the Nations involved in the UN Mission were represented.

Bosnia Herzegovina

The rationale behind the Bosnian War was that of a national uprising revolting against a predominant ruling nation that imposed its ideals and nationalism on a more energetic and self-identifying movement. The people in this movement had travelled, for their own reasons, to other countries and experienced the democracies of the modern western world. This movement grew and developed on its own basis into an international armed conflict that enveloped Bosnia and Herzegovina in the years between 1992 and 1995. Following a number of violent incidents in early 1992, it was commonly decided that war had started on 6 April 1992.

Recognised Dates of Conflict: 6th April 1992-14th December 1995
Ethnic Majorities
Population Structure

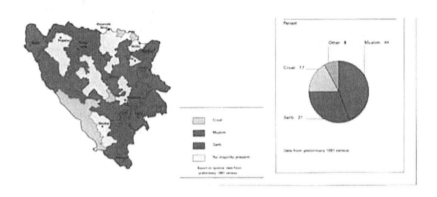

Diagram courtesy of the BiH website
Ethnic war occurred on many fronts:

1992 Croat and Muslim nationalists formed a tactical alliance and outvoted Serbs at an independence referendum. Serb nationalists were incensed as the FRY constitution stipulates that all major decisions must be reached through consensus.

As the conflict started Serbs quickly assumed control of over half the region and declared a Republic. Each faction then decided to 'cleanse' its dominant area of the minority groups. Ethnic cleansing was everywhere. The ethnic cleansing process within the newly declared Serb Republic was widespread and involved Muslim and Croat-controlled areas as well as the Serb areas.

The Bosnian Serbs, under Radovan Karadzic, lay siege to Sarajevo. The city was controlled by Muslims but they could not break out through lines set up to defend surrounding Serb villages. There was bitter fighting as well as many atrocities.

1993 Tensions increased and there was conflict between Muslims and Croats. This led to the destruction of much of Mostar, including its Old Bridge. The bridge had been built by the Ottomans in the 16th century and it was regarded as a major symbol of Bosnia's cultural diversity.

1994 The conflict was very complex and Muslims and Serbs formed an alliance against Croats in Herzegovina. Rival Muslim forces fought each other in northwest Bosnia, Croats and Serbs fought against Muslims in central Bosnia.

The declared UN safe havens for Bosnian Muslim civilians were created and included the areas of Sarajevo, Gorazde and Srebrenica.

1995 In July, the safe haven of Srebrenica was overrun by Bosnian Serb forces under the control of General Ratko Mladic. Thousands of Bosnian Muslim men and boys were separated from their families and massacred. This was done despite the presence of a contingent of much depleted Dutch UN troops. The Serbs had refused to allow Dutch troops back into the enclave when they returned from their R and R allocated breaks back home. The UN, under the terms of its peace keeping agenda were not at liberty to take any definite action to insist on the return of the Dutch soldiers.

However, when the Serbs made their moves, the UN called in NATO air strikes against the Serb positions. These air strikes helped Muslim and Croat forces to make big territorial gains throughout Bosnia. In turn, they then expelled thousands of Serb civilians from 'their now occupied' territories, taking revenge as they engaged in the deadly game of 'tit for tat'.

International negotiations and pressure resulted in the Dayton Peace Accord being signed in Paris towards the end of 1995. Dayton creates two entities of roughly equal size, one for Bosnian Muslims and Croats, the other for Serbs. An international peacekeeping force under the auspices of the UN was deployed in the Southern area of Bosnia Herzegovina.

A Civil War had erupted in Bosnia and in January 1995 I was seconded to the British Army and became a member of the UN Peacekeeping Mission. Despite, having worked, trained and travelled extensively with the British Army on various exercises and visits, this experience proved to be a bit of a revelation—awe inspiring and slightly intimidating, especially when I arrived at the departure area at RAF Brize Norton.

Immediately on arrival at Brize Norton, I couldn't help but notice that there was an awful lot of green and brown uniforms, green rucksacks and people (mainly men) who seemed to know each other very well and who looked very confident and in control. What did I expect—I don't know, but this was a new experience and after a few preliminaries, I sat and watched the ebb and flow of green on brown or brown on green as they strode around, sat, waited.

As I surveyed the other occupant in the departure lounge at RAF Brize I was again struck by the predominance of green and brown colours of the uniforms. I don't know what I expected but that is how I felt! I had travelled before with the military so should have been more used to the colours and the atmosphere, but this milling around somehow seemed more organised and defined as to purpose. I felt very much the odd person out. These men and, only a few women were used to this—going on detachment was part of the Army scene. I was part of it but detached—I was an officer (a Captain) seconded from the Territorial Army Public Information Corps, a TAPIO—a fairly new animal in the Army who was involved in the media. My job was to try and secure honest publicity for the many men and women who were going to work to try and resolve the differences between the warring factions in Bosnia Herzegovina as peacekeepers—a job that was both dangerous (when they were shot at or threatened) and compassionate, trying to get aid to the helpless individuals and communities marooned in their homes and villages, usually without electricity and/or food.

This was going to be an experience.

I think that impact of what I was heading for struck me during that flight—the seats on these transport flights was made up of webbing straps strung along both sides of the plane and directly in front of me was the cargo lashed together in an organised square that constantly reminded me of the potential deprivation that I now faced and that would go on for the next six months, with a two week break sometime in the middle for R & R (Rest and Recuperation). The comforts of tight packed seats on tourist flights did not apply. This was different, this was military and I had waited until I was nearly 49 years of age to experience this discomfort. What was I thinking of? I was slightly dazed by the noise, the unfamiliarity of it all, but the die was cast. The toilet had a curtain rigged for privacy but otherwise open to view.

I decided I had to pull myself together, settle.

The flight seemed to take a long time but eventually we arrived in Split. Airports look the same somehow, wherever you go, but stepping off a military aircraft (C 130 RAF Transport Command) at a military section of an airport, presents all things in a different light. Everything looked very Spartan and kind of makeshift—well it was to a certain extent, this was a civilian airport being used for military use.

In the arrivals hall, I was met by my new boss—a smiling gentleman with long experience in the military—who was going to direct our media-related efforts for the next six months. He knew the ropes and would guide me through the experience of signing in and preparing myself and my documents for what lay ahead. Eventually, collecting my green rucksack from the carousel (it was nearly the last one off—nothing new there) I followed my new Boss out to the land rover—a white one with UN painted on it. This was a UN Peacekeeping Mission and this was the outward sign—in Croatia.

In Bosnia, we would go around in green land rovers—former 'snatch wagons' that were much older and that had seen service in Northern Ireland and were heavily armoured. These were a little unsteady if driven at any speed—a fairly unlikely event as the roads had lots of potholes, some caused by frost and ice damage and some by shrapnel.

After a speedy, and a trifle perfunctory, induction in the former Yugoslavian/Croatian military base at Split, Divolji Barracks. I was issued with my UN allowance card and instructed on details of what was expected of me up country, I was shown to my bunk—one of many in a large room filled with bunks for those of us bunking down as we 'rotated' through, in/out of country.

I think that it was the next day that I was escorted by the boss, a former Marine, across the barracks to a helipad to board a helicopter that would take us up to Vitez which would be my base for the next six months. I knew the Colonel quite well as I had met and worked with him whilst working in my TAPIO role in media assignments in UK, Germany and France. He was a charming man who always tried to do what was right and proper. He was taking this opportunity to view the site in Vitez as he had just arrived out from UK a week or so before me and all this was new to him too. We boarded the helicopter and donned our life jackets (as the aircraft swung out over the Adriatic as part of its flight path inland).

I listened carefully to the pre-flight safety instructions. This was actually (as was explained to us) dangerous territory and we had to be aware of that fact at all times.

From Spit, the helicopter flight to Vitez was relatively short, about an hour door to door, in comparison the road trip which would have taken about six hours along very bumpy and sometimes rough makeshift roads in the land rover.

It was a good trip and soon, rounding a hill, I got my first glimpse of Vitez. It was a comparatively small town, nestled among some hills, there was a cross on top of a hill and I could see the path up to a hilltop cross, it ran from the edge of the town and was pretty distinctive with the cross sitting as it was on the crown of the hill. This cross would always remind me of Vitez a mainly Croat/Catholic town surrounded by Muslims with their equally distinctive minarets calling the faithful to prayer five times a day.

In the chopper, we approached Vitez through a gap in the hills and, as the valley spread out below us, I caught my first glimpse of the army base that was to be my main operating base for the next six months. I remember recognising that, in the main, arable farming would be the main source of income for the locals and I felt quite at home seeing the ploughed fields and meadows spread before me.

I remember that I wanted to get a better view and take a photograph as we came in to land so I leaned forward as the helicopter circled the army base for landing. I had my camera in my hand and I wanted to take a quick snap—I leaned forward thinking to myself that the seat harness will hold me back. I got quite a shock as I suddenly realised that there was no restraint holding me back. My seat buckle had not been fastened properly (by me) and I remained where I was only because of gravitational force that I was still in the aircraft! It was my first shock of the tour. The Colonel was not impressed! I knew that he was thinking of all those papers he would have had to fill in if I had left the aircraft prematurely. I had a quiet nervous laugh to myself—but it was a salutary lesson.

As we disembarked the helicopter in the field close to the camp, we were told to be as quick as possible as the farmer, who owned the field, was demanding 'landing fees'. The field seemed to be designated for grass—there could only be a small local outlet for any produce—but, in the farmer's opinion here was a sure-fire way to earn some much-needed money, I mean who knows how long this war would last and it was best to make the claim. It was the UN and they could always be made to pay up. In the farmer's eyes it was worth a try and, in the circumstances, I couldn't blame him.

Alighting from the chopper, I was met by my photographer, a girl named Wendy, who had already completed six months and who had volunteered to stay another six months to cover my stay. I was delighted to see her as I had often developed her photos on the Gretag machine back at UK Land Command and felt that I knew her really well.

Greeting each other with a hug, we got into our snatch wagon and went over to the PINFO house which was to be my base for the next six months. It was located just outside the perimeter of the camp—just across the road from the guard post. It was a typical house for the region—steps up to the front door, tiled floor, kitchen, bathroom, two rooms downstairs and a couple of bedrooms upstairs (there may have been a third but I can't remember). Downstairs one of the rooms was a 'briefing room' for journalists, complete with maps and general area information. The boiler room was in the basement—a dark and dingy place that I really did not want to identify with; I was not best impressed with the thought that I might have to take an interest in this part of the set up but it had to be done—the reality check was not welcome!

Communication with HQ Land Command in Salisbury was by a UN satellite phone in the front 'office' and a satellite box sitting on the balcony at the back of the house. There was also a desk and computer in the office. This satellite type of communication depended on the satellite passing over our area of the universe and connecting with our box on the ground. The workings of this were sometimes unreliable, but Wendy was an expert and would manage this.

Vitez, 1995

The Regiment operating in central Bosnia at the time of my arrival was Scottish and the boss was not too keen on getting publicity. This made life a trifle awkward as my role was to ensure that the wider world knew a little of the work that was being done in the region by the peacekeeping forces from the UK. Obviously, in order to do this I had to publish information about the activities of members of the unit based in the area! This reticence was understandable but a bit of a nuisance as I was keen to get out and publicise a few interesting facts—whilst not compromising or endangering the health of the soldiers.

Fortunately for me, the Devon and Dorset Regiment, under the command of a Colonel, arrived in Vitez a short time after I did, in fact I had just got myself accustomed to my new surroundings when the changeover occurred. I seized my opportunity and went to see the Colonel to ask for his support for my PINFO unit based in the house across from the camp. He was great and promised me all the support I needed—and he kept to his word for the complete duration of my tour.

The Devon and Dorset's supported us (as did the previous unit based in the camp) with food rations, we got our main meals in the mess hall, sandwiches on our frequent trips around the region, fuel for the land rover, replacement parts and tyres when we needed them. The tyres were special tyres that had to be strong enough to carry the weight of the armoured bodywork of the former 'snatch' wagons which had been a feature well known in Northern Ireland during the 'Troubles'.

Wendy resourced out trips, liaising with the OPs room to determine which unit we should visit and in what order. She was an excellent organiser and, having spent some time here already, knew the roads well. A great advantage.

The routine in Vitez for me was straight forward. I attended the morning briefing on the base, coming back to PINFO house and then briefed the journalists assembled in the briefing room with its large wall map of our AOR. Wendy and I would then take our snatch wagon to go and visit units camped from Vitez to up near Doboj.

Near to the start of my spell in Vitez, it so happened that on one occasion Wendy and I heard about a meeting that was going to take place in nearby Vitez, where the local Bosnian military leaders were convening a meeting.

Cheekily, we decided that we could call in! We did. On the morning of the meeting, we nonchalantly wandering into the centre and made our way into the conference room and took our seats at the table. No one seemed to notice until a senior rank (sporting a large pimple on the end of his nose) took a second glance at our uniforms. Dead giveaway, they weren't the same as theirs!

Needless to say, we were speedily shown the door. But it was worth a try but I don't know what we thought we were going to achieve, neither of us were fluent enough in the local language to understand what was being said. We didn't have any trouble though understanding the instruction to leave. Graphic.

The areas of importance in our region were:

Burgojno which was not too far away from Vitez. A pleasant place where there was a relatively small group of soldiers stationed. These soldiers knew the area well, patrolling the hills on foot, helping out the local people as much as possible, repairing damaged buildings and alerting others from their home base back in UK to the needs of the local people for school supplies, clothing, shoes and such like.

It was in this area that Wendy and I joined with a unit patrol of the town. The patrol was very friendly with the locals, shouting greetings using a few words of their language and lots of smiles. The locals seemed a bit bemused but friendly. Unsure what to make of these guys.

We also joined with a patrol going out of town to distribute some clothing and school related items. The unit was actively supporting a local school up in the hills by doing some necessary repair work to the damaged walls and leaking roof of the building. It was a natural progression from repairing the school to supplying some necessities and helping the locals living nearby. It gave us all great satisfaction to help the locals who very obviously needed the help.

All the men of 'fighting age' were absent from their homes so this sort of support was well received.

Gornji Vakuf was within easy reach, but was, at that time, in the hands of non-welcoming militia and therefore, not somewhere that we would be visiting on a regular basis. As members of the UN Peacekeeping force, we could travel anywhere, but local sensitivities directed mainly at keeping the peace, prevented us from being too free with our travel arrangements.

Zenica was just a few miles up the main road from Vitez. Prior to the conflict it must have been a pleasant place with trees lining each side of the wide streets and a pleasant sweeping entry/exit road branching off from the main highway. It had been a busy place with factories employing many workers and had a large sports stadium. This had been the case in most of the towns around here, prior to the conflict.

The Former Yugoslavia (FRY) had focused very much on ensuring that local people had jobs and, although the factory production did not supply outside the FRY, they did supply jobs for locals. The overall economy was not in great shape, but there was a sense of purpose locally.

On one occasion Wendy and I went to the hairdresser in Zenica to have our hair 'done'. In fact the day that life suddenly got exciting (unknown to us until after the visit to the hairdresser) as the tempo of the conflict changed, troop movement becoming more intense. At that time the world media descended on Vitez so as to be close to the action. So a very fortuitous visit to the hairdresser.

We had also visited Zenica at another time when a football match was organised between the soldiers of the UK and the New Zealanders (Kiwis). The day stands out in my memory because, as Wendy and I went up the stairs to get a seat my shoulders were squashed between two large guys who were going up the stairs at the same time. I lived in Northern Ireland and the pincer movement had happened to me once before when I had come back after a longish absence away from Northern Ireland and two 'heavies' wanted me to know that they had 'noticed' me and wanted me to be aware of the fact! The heavies in Zenica were of the same ilk and gave me the long hard stare, their eyes boring into mine and I returned the look. Maybe not the best idea in the world but I hadn't read the script and it was all I could think of doing at the time. My natural reaction to attempted intimidation.

Maglaj where the main image I have of this town was the fact that it was so obviously totally divided and silently suffering. It was much damaged by the conflict and there was a very large hole in the road right in the middle of the main bridge of the town. This made life difficult for everyone. This reminded me of

Portadown and the bridge over the River Bann and how important the bridge was to the life of the town.

At the camp, there was a small number of Engineers whose job it was to complete some vital, and emergency, repairs in the immediate area. Wendy and I were there to cover the story of a small group of engineers who had to build a non-equipment bridge over a small river in an adjacent valley. The stream would swell during the wet and would cut off the people further up the valley so a small bridge was necessary. Wendy and I set off in the 'snatch wagon', following the given directions we went up a small valley to the left (from the south side) of the town, passing the 'underground hospital' identified by a small red cross on white card, that we had been warned existed along the side of this road. The entrance was dug deep into the hill.

We identified the hospital—really just a cave-like hole in the side of the hill—at road level. Trying not to look too interested, we drove on further and came upon the six to eight engineers working at this rough bridge which forded the stream—it was a main fording place and much needed and used by the locals.

Wendy parked up and we started to talk to the soldiers who, whilst trying to be polite and answer our questions, were working furiously to get the job done and get out of there back to the safety of the camp. The attitude of the engineers was admirable—they wanted to help the people and didn't want any trouble.

Glancing up at the surrounding hills, I noticed the presence of 'OPs'— (Observation Posts)—obviously to us, manned by the Serbs from further up the valley. Currently, there was no sign of movement—maybe there was no one there?

Suddenly, around the corner of the track and from the direction of the town of Maglaj, came three or four large Mercedes, travelling at speed. The cars ground to a halt beside us, kicking up the dirt. The engineers bent their heads and worked harder.

Wendy was frantically taking photos of the engineers at work, realising that our time was going to be limited.

I was quickly surrounded by the newcomers, some dressed in parts—army uniforms part civilian dress. They had an interpreter with them and they wanted to know what I was doing there. Their shoulders were pressing against mine and I was squeezed between two of them as they formed a circle around me. They looked as if they had just got out of bed and dressed in a hurry, hair all tousled.

I expect that this is exactly what had happened and that my presence was the reason!

I quickly introduced myself to the leader of the group who barked that I had not asked permission to be there—I tried again, only to be interrupted and my shoulders were squeezed even harder. The conversation was all carried on through the interpreter—a pleasant fellow who added a few words of his own to the nature of him wanting a job with us the British military. Well, why not. An entrepreneur!

The interrogation continued and I was informed that they knew all about my photographer and myself and that we were OK. I was also told to tell my boss down in Split that he was not welcome in Maglaj; I couldn't quite grasp what he had done wrong but I was told he was not welcome. I just nodded.

The militia boss did warn me as he left our little gathering that up in the hills where we could see the OPs, that these were bad guys (Serbs) who were still in their pits but who were due to waken shortly and they would shoot at us. I thanked him for his conversation and words of warning and we said goodbye. The guys jumped in their cars and left in a flurry of dust, leaving a few traces of rubber in their wake.

I then turned my attention to the guys who were working as fast as they could to establish this non-equipment bridge. They really only had the rocks and a lot of their own physical effort. As the engineers worked, I asked questions. The guys were happy to talk as long as it didn't interfere with their work. Suddenly, I felt the wind of a bullet as it shot past the side of my head, disturbing my hair slightly and pinged off a rock in the stream. The engineer in charge never stopped shovelling stones and just remarked, 'I think someone is shooting at us, Ma'am', as he increased his rapid shovelling of stones.

It was brilliant, this nonchalant understatement of the British Army soldier. Unflappable.

Wendy and I quickly finished up our work and drove back to the camp in Maglaj, as did the soldiers. We spent a short time going round the camp talking to the other soldiers, building a picture of the conditions they were working under. In one area of the camp we were looking out of a check point area when a T54 of the (JNA) Serbian Army, rolled into view over a small rise in the field to the side of the camp. The tank stopped for a few moments, obviously watching us as we were watching it. It then moved its cannon around a bit, waggling it at us, then it retreated back behind the rise. I glanced at the soldier on duty watching from behind the hessian strip and said, it's only a matter of time, isn't it. He nodded. We left shortly afterwards and made our way back to Vitez.

Later that evening, after the soldiers' evening meal and them getting changed into casual clothes, the tank came back and fired a shell directly into the accommodation. The shell went straight through a T-shirt one of the guys was slipping on over his head, leaving a perfect circle in the material, but then tragically, it went through the calf muscle of another soldier, before going to ground.

The attack was very unexpected and alarming. The injured soldier was the one who had made the wry remark to me at the bridge. He was quickly casevac'd out to hospital in the UK.

Wendy and I learned of the shocking news the next morning in Vitez as we had left before the incident happened. We decided to go back immediately to talk to the guys at Maglaj as a show of our support in some way. There was nothing we could do, but talking often helps process the shock.

Abandoning our plans for the day, we drove up to Maglaj and spoke to some very shocked soldiers, one showing me the neat large round hole in his T-shirt. A dramatic hole in an innocent T-shirt. Thought-provoking and shocking.

Wendy and I made many journeys. During our travels around the area, we encountered many other fellow travellers, both international and local militia.

On one occasion, we came across a convoy of French troopers who had stopped for lunch. They invited us to join them. As it so happened, our lunch bag was empty as we had given the contents of sandwiches, Mars bar and apple to a group of children that we had met. The French soldiers kindly shared their provisions with us, in exchange for a brief chat, making use of their limited English and our equally limited French.

In comparison to our lunch bag, the French food was very plain but good. They had a small tin of cooked meat, some biscuits and a drink of water. It was very welcome and definitely non-fattening.

Sometimes we would see some of the local militia making their way to a guard post somewhere along the route. Wendy and I felt quite sorry for these guys as they really didn't have much. We had heard that they shared the different parts of the uniform between then, only wearing the kit (or most of it) whilst on duty.

On a particularly cold wet day, while there was still snow on the ground, we passed one such guy walking along with his AK-47 slung over his shoulder. On his feet he had a pair of white trainers that were a little too big and had seen better days. He wore a lightweight type military jacket that was quite inadequate for the conditions. He was walking fast and I daresay that his walking speed helped him keep warm. He ignored us as we drove past.

One particular encounter lives in my memory. We were returning to Vitez at the end of the day and daylight was starting to fade. We turned off the main road and rounded a corner to go under a bridge when we saw to the left of the road two men, one younger and one older, crouching around a small fire.They were guarding the route into Vitez at this point and had decided to brew some coffee. The coffee was of the thick Turkish variety that is served in small cups.

Wendy and I decided to stop as we had a couple of things left from our lunch bag. There was only a bread roll and a Mars bar but we knew that these guys were on guard for the entire night and wouldn't have much, if any provisions. Stopping the vehicle, we got out and went over to the two by the fire.

They seemed friendly and smiled as we approached and immediately offered us a coffee. We reluctantly accepted as we didn't want to offend but I was struck by their generosity as well as their obvious lack of supplies but they wanted to share.

As I sipped the thick coffee from the small cracked cup, which was white with a red design traced around the top, I felt humbled and honoured that these two guys with so little were happy to share with us, two fellow soldiers.

We didn't speak their language but the brief meeting, sharing a coffee, was a profound moment in time. We handed over our small contribution having to insist that they accepted it, and as we went on our way, the younger man eagerly tucked into the goodies. It was obvious he was hungry.

One of the things that struck me quite forcibly as we travelled around Central Bosnia, visiting and chatting to all and sundry, including the soldiers, was the generosity of the locals. We called with various local significant families, none with plenty to spare but all welcoming and eager to be hospitable. They were always keen to share, giving us coffee and slivovic (local plum brandy, a bit like poteen in Ireland). A piece of fresh bread was usually offered and the convivial atmosphere was always very welcome. The locals enjoyed the chat no matter how limited our knowledge of their language, and they practised their limited English.

I used to love watching the ladies grind the coffee beans in their hand grinders. It was a lovely ritual, pleasant and relaxing, made more enjoyable by the small glass of slivovic which we sipped as we watched the preparations for coffee.

Gorazde

Easter 1995, Wendy, my intrepid companion and photographer, and I were alerted by telephone that we were to join the military relief convoy leaving at 6.30 the next morning from Kisseljak, a relatively short distance away. The convoy was trying to gain a passage through to the enclave of Gorazde, a UN safe haven.

The idea of the convoy was to take in some relief personnel to the beleaguered garrison of Welsh Fusiliers protecting the local population. As well as the personnel, obviously they were planning on taking in some much-needed supplies of basic food stuffs plus the all-important mail for the soldiers. Personal mail is always a high priority as that is the link with home and family. Some unlucky chaps get a 'dear John' (breaking off a relationship), which is very difficult to cope with when you are working far away from family and in difficult circumstances. They usually talked to their friends and fellow soldiers. This kind of thing happens, and all too frequently.

The citizens of Gorazde were Muslim and they were surrounded by Serbian forces who were trying, and succeeding, in intimidating them out of their area. The Serbians were also trying to starve them into submission. They were often depending on handouts from the UN Peacekeepers to help them survive. The Welsh Fusiliers were also feeling the strain with restrictions of movement within the enclave and were going short on food supplies. There was no supply depot within easy reach, obviously not even a local shop!

It was also a very trying set of circumstances for the troops when they could not get soldiers back into their garrison when returning from their allocated R & R. The Serbian forces would happily agree to soldiers leave but would refuse to let anyone back in to join the others in the garrison. It was simply a process of slowly reducing numbers within the camp and eroding morale. It was a very effective method!

The route into Gorazde was circuitous, going through specific checkpoints and being checked at every turn by 'bolshi' individuals whose cruelty was legendary. Gorazde was Muslim and the blockades was mounted by Serbian militia who inspected our paperwork with a keen eye on the detail.

One of the most notorious checkpoints was at Rogatice where the local commander was reckoned to be a real piece of work, indulging in many forms of emotional stress on parties trying to travel the route. The Serbian Forces, scattered along the route between Sarajevo and Gorazde manning some highly strategic check points, had already refused some convoys passage through their territory. The Serbian Forces also checked the manifest on each convoy going through and were not averse to doing their own searches of the vehicles and personnel.

As the situation was becoming tenser, ensuring that this convoy got through to Gorazde was an important step, even considered to be vital for the good morale of the troops and even for the local citizens. It was also vital to maintain the separation of ethnic groupings in and around the enclave.

Our PINFO role was to take photographs, gather stories on the activities of the British forces in the area and generally gather as much information as we could on conditions and opposing troop movements on the ground—and to bring that information out and get it back to Headquarters Land Command in Salisbury. Wendy (the photographer) and I were telephoned, the night before the convoy move, and told to get ourselves and our vehicle (originally one of the armoured 'snatch' wagons used on the streets of Belfast during the 'troubles') down to Kisseljak. We had to meet up with the rest of the convoy vehicles and be ready for an early start the next morning. Obviously, we were expected but we had to get there on time.

The start time of the convoy was fairly critical as the information and details of the numbers of vehicles and rough idea of the contents had been passed to the Serbian Forces who had agreed that this convoy could pass through their checkpoints. We were expected at certain checks at certain times along the route and usually, unless they had held us up for reasons of their own, they would not brook any argument or discussion. The tales of their awkwardness when UN Peacekeepers failed to keep to their scheduled times, were legendary—and scary!

Based on these considerations, we decided to go to Kisseljak that evening as we couldn't depend on leaving the next morning and getting there on time. The local checkpoints did not open until about 8.00 the next morning and we couldn't afford to miss out on joining this convoy as it left Kisseljak.

Travelling down to Kisseljak that evening, we spent the night in transit accommodation specifically designated for personnel like us who were just passing through. Getting up early the next morning, we joined up with the convoy and our vehicle was positioned near the front, just behind the lead vehicle of the Convoy Commander. We departed Kisseljak at 6.30 dead on time.

Our route took us through Sarajevo and as we made our way through the ravaged streets of the capital near the airport, the effects of the conflict became very obvious. Buildings were pock marked by the shells and gunfire directed at them from the surrounding hills by the watching Serb forces.

In order to be able to move around, the locals had dug underground tunnels to connect houses across the streets which were in clear view from the hills above. Sometimes, a line of houses could be protected from the gunfire by large lumps of rusting sheets of zinc metal secured on rough frames to hold them in place. It was surreal.

The weary expressions of the people living in these difficult conditions were clear to be seen. These people were long suffering but the defiance was there too. They would not succumb to the aggressors. Seeing them watching us go past was unsettling, reminding us of their hardship and lack of basic nourishment as well as freedoms.

Just past this area was the first checkpoint. It had a difficult reputation in that they had insisted on searching a young officer on a previous convoy. The search was very intrusive and the young lady was reduced to tears. This sort of incident reflected the uselessness of the so-called authority of the UN Mission.

We approached this check with some serious trepidation but got through without incident. Continuing on our way, we navigated through the various other checkpoints without too much delay.

Passing through the countryside, the scenery was spectacular. It was wild and beautiful, with large conifers and green undulating pastures, mainly deserted, except for the odd house dotted here or there. There wasn't much sign of life.

This area had been used in competitions during the Sarajevo Winter Olympics a few years before in 1984. It was ideal for the purpose and looked absolutely wonderful in the snow. A real picture book scene.

Just as an aside, on a previous occasion, Wendy and I had been in the area closer to Kisseljak near the large Olympic Ski jump (From the 1984 Olympics) and had actually climbed the steps to the top of the run. On the way up we realised that there were occasional mines placed here close to the steps. Up or down? It was easier to continue and reached the top. The view was breath taking and the steep smooth route down was scary. The view was worth it though and we laughed out loud with the sheer exhilaration of the effort. Though we took it easy on the way down and stepped carefully.

Eventually arriving at the Rogatice checkpoint, we were met by those manning the checkpoint, all assembled at the barrier. One of the officials quickly scanned the manifest and demanded to see inside one of the large boxes that we were carrying. This particular box contained Welsh rugby shirts, a present from the guys back in Wales and definitely intended for Gorazde. The guards had probably been alerted to its presence on the manifest by a previous checkpoint, as this was usually the way it worked.

This was a strong and dreaded checkpoint, so the procedure was that they were going to demand to check inside the box and (usually) confiscate the contents, if they liked them.

But these were Welsh rugby shirts and these were Welshmen making their way to join fellow compatriots. It just wasn't going to happen.

The chap in charge of the manifest refused to let them 'interfere with the 'Queen's mail'. This guy was great, he even sat on top of the box to defy the guards. A real stand-off. The local guards were taken aback by this show of defiance. After a few tense exchanges, the guards had met their match. They gave in and waved us through. Situated near the front of the convoy we had to restrain our pleased feelings of our simple small success.

Actually, I had one really embarrassing incident occur along the route. It was about midday and I had to ask for a 'pee' stop. The convoy commander was very understanding and agreed. I could not leave the convoy and anyway, there was nowhere discreet to go 'never a tree nor bush' as in Padriac Colum's poem *'The old woman of the roads'.* The commander instructed all the guys (Wendy and I were the only females in the column) to look away. It was embarrassing but I was desperate, so I 'went', right there at the front of our wagon and behind the Command vehicle! Those guys were real gentlemen, no one said a word, at least not in my hearing. I was eternally grateful!

The road we had to take had many twists and turns as the gradient was steep. The Ghurkhas were the main drivers in the convoy and they really had large heavily laden trucks to manoeuvre round the sharp bends. It was a tough drive but they did a beautiful job, sometimes with the lorry beds overhanging the steep drops. Watching them manoeuvre was a real lesson in advanced driving techniques.

After a few delays, we arrived in Gorazde in the early evening, just before mealtime. Our anticipated arrival was such a relief to the soldiers, especially those waiting their turn to go on R & R. They all cheered when they saw us arrive at the entrance. Though I will say that, entering the enclave, I was struck by the visible apathy of the locals as we passed by. Hunger and despair were taking its toll.

Our job was to take photographs and write as many stories as possible on the activities of the soldiers working in the enclave and, to that end, the unit Adjacent, had organised a detailed programme of visits to the various OPs within their area of responsibility (AOR). This would give us a great overview of the situation, the work that the soldiers were involved in and the conditions that they were experiencing.

We were quickly informed that it was all arranged. The Adjacent was leading the patrol. The first trip was organised, we would start work the next morning early!

The plan was that the furthest OPs from the camp would be the ones we would visit first. This meant a short trip in a land rover, a speedy transfer to a Saxon armoured vehicle, which included coming under sporadic fire, and then a short fast walk to the first OP to interview the soldiers manning the site. I can still remember the ping of the bullets hitting the metal of the Saxon as we travelled along the road. This only happened to me on that trip but the soldiers had to experience that every time they made this run. Six months is a long time and includes many trips. Great guys.

The first OP (and furthest away from the camp) gave us a great view of the valley stretching out before us. It was quite a beautiful valley with the high hills rising steeply on either side. Quite spectacular. It was also easy to see the creeping line of Serbian infantry OPs coming up the valley. Intimidating and threatening as the UN was a peacekeeping force and a sitting duck.

Each OP contained a small contingent of soldiers, the number varied according to the location and strategic significance. It was at this first and distant OP that we saw an old lady from a nearby house making her daily delivery of freshly baked bread. This was a barter system; she brought bread and was given in exchange some necessary supplies that she could then use for her family. A good system.

The soldiers told us that even when there was shooting directed at them in the OP, this lady just came on, a slight figure dressed all in black making her way down the track on her morning journey. Determination was written in her every line.

During our visit and on cue, and as described to us, there was a salvo aimed in our direction and we had to make a hasty retreat into the bunker, and of course, the lady came in too. I remember being grabbed by the scruff of my neck and being hastily pushed down into the depths of safety!

Hastened by events, Wendy and I got to work. Time was precious, anything could happen.

We listened intently to the stories from the individual soldiers and Wendy took their photographs in situ.

The OP was strategically located on a piece of ground a little higher than the surrounding area with a good view looking down a valley towards a Serb occupied area. Looking down that valley we could easily see the line of Serb positions which, as we were told, were slowly advancing towards our OP. It was easy to understand the tensions and strains of the soldiers trying to maintain a UN peacekeeping presence. This was a highly sensitive and vulnerable OP.

The other OPs we visited, each strategically located were not in such an overtly sensitive locations, but each was important in their own right. Due to the lack of fuel available to the detachment, we walked to all of them.

On one occasion we passed within 100 feet of a Serb position, trying not to hear the catcalls and remarks when they realised that two of the soldiers were women.

Led and guarded by a small patrol from the camp, we climbed the hills calling in at the various OPs, talking to the troops and taking pictures.

At one point we walked along a narrow spine of a ridge between hills. I didn't mention that I had a (more than) slight fear of heights and had trouble with my balance on narrow ledges. As one who was wobbly at a few feet heights, this particular ridge impressed me as the drop on each side was very steep and I had to place my feet across the thin ridge in order to maintain my balance and progress at a decent pace. I can say without fear of contradiction, that I was not the most confident at the edge of steep drops, but I kept going, the others were doing it. I figured that I couldn't throw a female 'I'm scared' moment. It definitely wouldn't be appreciated by those daily risking a lot more and it wouldn't be fair to anyone.

Wendy and I worked hard over the four-day layover of the convoy, preparing details on nearly 100 stories and gathering other vital information relating to the prevailing conditions in the enclave. Wendy had brought extra few films to make sure we could cover all the conditions and eventualities.

Each evening, back in camp, during the period of the evening meal, the occupants came under fire. It was an intimidatingly move and the 'hesko baskian' (large pig wire and thick heavy material encasing huge amounts of all sizes of stones, grit and soil), built around the perimeter provided protection but the gunfire was annoying and threatening. It was a stark reminder of the situation we were in and I am sure that the soldiers found this bombardment nerve racking—as it was intended to do. Once again, I salute these of our soldiers for their nerve and resilience.

In Gorazde, the local people were virtually starving. They had no electricity to speak of—often relying on 'widgits'—a small very basic windmill affair bobbing about in the river and suspended on a length of electric cable. The energy generated by the flow of the water produced a small amount of electricity, usually just about enough to supply a weak surge of electricity to dimly light a small watt electric light bulb.

There was the evening run to the local garbage heap, with a load of leftover cooked food from the camp cookhouse. There wasn't much but the guys told me that even a taste of gravy in the bottom of a small foil container was eagerly pounced on by the hungry locals waiting at the dump for the truck and its evening delivery. The cooks tried to send as much as they could on the truck run, but they were on short supplies themselves, so the offerings were meagre.

After the four days of intensive work, we left with the return convoy, which got through the checkpoints without incident. Wendy and I go our photos and stories transferred back to HQ Land Command via the satellite system where I am sure, they were much viewed. From memory, I think that there were over 100 stories and many rolls of developed film.

Most times, the PINFO team travelled as a single vehicle to our various locations identified for their 'story' potential. One of our journeys sticks out very strongly in my mind. It was some time after the Gorazde trip. The situation was becoming a little bit more risky.

Wendy and I were on our way back from a 'job'—this particular job had been a rather pleasant on where we had spent a week sailing in the Adriatic, along the coast of Croatia, in a wooden boat, a Nicholson 45. The boat had been sailed out from UK with the idea of allowing troops in theatre, the luxury of a few days sailing time. The two guys crewing the boat had asked for some additional promotion in the shape of a story by the PINFO team in theatre. We were happy to oblige in return for a few days sailing!

I had done some sailing in the Far East and was delighted to get the opportunity to have a few days relaxed sailing. I always found it a very relaxing experience and we could do with the break after our intense, if, to us, our absorbing and demanding workload in Central Bosnia.

We arranged to meet the two crew down at Trogir near Split. A beautiful harbour. We introduced ourselves to the crew and went on to spend a relaxing week sailing. Travelling up north as far as Sibernik and then returning down south to the beautiful island of Hvar.

This trip occurred at the time when the warring factions were setting fire to the Knin region in Croatia. After a few days sailing along the coast, the crew decided to weigh anchor in Sibernik harbour for a bit of a rest, and, a night in harbour. We disembarked the boat in the evening to go out for our coffee but the local militiamen *masse* coming down the street to meet us was a defining message and, taking the hint, we retired to our boat for our coffee, lifting anchor and quietly departing.

Going south we were accompanied by the sounds of the war taking place inland, the boom of the heavy guns deterred us from any attempt at a sojourn on land. It was at this time we headed for the more peaceful island of Hvar. We had an overnight stop in the harbour and I stopped by the local church and joined in the service for a short time, even though I didn't understand all the words, I could relax in the tranquil atmosphere.

Returning to Split we picked up our transport and our clerical officer who had just returned from his two-week R and R back in UK. The plan was that we would all return to Vitez. It was towards the end of the year (1995) and our period on detachment. The situation was definitely tenser as it became known that international negotiations were taking place in relation to Bosnia. Local people were apprehensive as to the outcome and the forces on either side were nervously trying to get themselves in the best position possible, mainly trying to 'take' as much ground as they could and establish their 'ownership'. They figured that this jockeying for position would be helpful when dealing with whatever was heading their way.

There were many stories circulating of vehicles being stopped along the road and contents being stolen. On this particular occasion we were travelling up from Split to our base in Vitez, accompanied by our admin soldier. As we were ranked more senior than him, we both felt very responsible for his safety. Wendy, as usual, was the driver. However, we were nervous and very aware of the stories that we had heard.

We got to a point on the rough road, where we knew that some of the worst of the hijackings had taken place. Once again, we had been warned of the dangers ahead, particularly to a single vehicle. We were at the start of the reasonably recently made Route Emerald (established early on by our engineers to facilitate troop movements) and we stopped for a second and contemplated the odds of reaching our destination in safety.

Our discussion was brief. We had already travelled quite a few hours along the road from Split and the thought of going back was not very appealing, but this part was a dangerous place, fairly barren with only the odd mosque or house.

The route ahead was indeed a rough road with a very rough stone surface. There was no safe refuge between this point and the camp at Vitez. We didn't fancy going back but Wendy was concerned about the dangers ahead (as was I). We had our clerk's life to consider too. It was a big responsibility. It wasn't often that Wendy hesitated. She was a pretty pragmatic person with a no-nonsense approach. This was a heart-stopping moment for us all. We all exchanged looks, silently debating the odds.

A decision had to be made. Vitez was so close and the way was strewn with almost impossible potential obstacles. I took a deep breath and offered to take responsibility and drive this last bit. It was about an hour driving time. I think it was with some relief that Wendy agreed and we exchanged places and I took the wheel.

I was nervous but determined not to stop for anything. I told the clerk to hold on tight. He was in the back of the wagon and gripped the back of our seats with both hands and nodded. We took off at speed. It was a hair-raising ride, driving down the middle of the deserted road, bouncing over the rough surface, dodging potholes, swerving to the right and left round large stones. I held on tight to the wheel and prayed for a safe return to camp. I'm sure both passengers did the same.

Eventually, it was with some relief that we turned onto the less rough but potholed, more normal road leading to Vitez. We had made it. What a relief when we arrived at our PINFO house!

It had been an epic journey, for all of us.

Sarajevo

Shortly after I arrived in Bosnia Herzegovina in early 1995, as part of my introduction to Bosnia and the conditions the local inhabitants had had to endure for the past three years, I was introduced to the conditions within Sarajevo.

The peacekeepers were billeted mainly in the PTT (Postal and Telegraph) Building down the main drag from the Holiday Inn. Accommodation was pretty cramped with stacks of bunk beds lining every wall. But the PTT building was secure and was just beyond the main line of fire from the Serbian forces. The continual sniper fire from Serb positions up on the hills surrounding Sarajevo was a real problem throughout most of the city. But this building was outside their range and being in the PTT Building was safe, if confusing, with soldiers everywhere, working, going to eat, relaxing in small areas with friends during off duty periods or sleeping after night duty. All happening at the same time, a sea of constant activity.

The building featured strongly as a place where 'things' happened—plans were drawn up, security details were discussed and stressful political negotiations would take place, encompassing all shades of opinion, political and militaries. All sorts of important meetings took place here, including that of senior politicians involved in negotiations and senior reporters such as Martin Bell, in his iconic white suit.

Moving around Sarajevo was an experience and a careful eye had to be kept on the prevailing 'activities' from the various factions. It wasn't exactly the most dangerous thing to do, but moving from one end of Sarajevo to another in an armoured vehicle did have its exciting moments. Anyone travelling just past the Holiday Inn was in an exposed area where the Serb soldiers on the hills above had a clear view of any moving traffic or personnel along the main 'drag'. This main street down the centre of Sarajevo was known as 'shotgun or sniper alley'. It was subject to continual random shooting from the surrounding hills.

Driving down through this area, in a UN vehicle, you had to wear your flak jacket plus your helmet and you were told to hunker down in the seat thus presenting as small a target as possible. Most times you were not disappointed and you heard the distinct and unmistakeable ping of the bullets as they ricochet off the metal of your speeding vehicle. In such circumstances, it was difficult for the mind to comprehend that you are being shot at. After all you are the UN Peacekeeping Force with your blue berets/helmets in your distinctive white vehicles clearly identified as UN. At this point I was new to the concept and innocent of the reality on the ground.

During one of my jobs in Sarajevo, the boss and I went down to what was known as, the 'Residency' located between the United States Embassy and the Bosnia Hercegovina Armed Forces building. It was the UNPROFOR (official term for the UN peacekeeping mission) compound and was well guarded.

Across the road was a small kiosk selling postcards, etc., and I popped over to get a postcard. I made my choice from the small selection available. Shortly after my visit to the kiosk, I was told that a shell had been lobbed over and landed in front of the kiosk. A narrow escape for this customer. A small reminder (if one was needed) of the delicacies of the situation in Sarajevo.

I spent some time in Sarajevo, visiting different places and seeing the way the citizens had to live. Life was difficult as there was little food, scarce electrical supply and very little water. Many people had to flee their homes due to ethnic cleansing—on all sides.

During the winter, the snows came and the cold became quite intense, down in the minus 20Fs++. In order to get some heat, the beleaguered civilians just had to burn books or your once glamourous shoes. Piling on your clothes was not sufficient for warmth. Those who had to flee their homes did so within seconds, often piling their worldly possessions onto a bedsheet and making a bundle which they carried as best they could, taking turns to transport this—their meagre worldly possessions.

The young men, on the whole, had already gone, so the burden was borne by the women, the children and the elderly or incapacitated. Coupled with this severe cold and poor living conditions was the regular daily sniping from the direction of the surrounding hills from the Serbian positions. It was not unknown for a stray bullet or two to go through the window of an apartment.

Any movement out in the street was targeted from the hills. The situation for those people living in Sarajevo was indeed dire.

The main library down in the centre of town had been destroyed by fire. A few of the precious manuscripts had been saved but the impressively historic collection was effectively gone. The Sarajevo Bibliotec (library) building was destroyed.

The UN Peacekeeping Mission in Sarajevo was composed of different nations, all trying to keep the peace and quell the fighting. In all, the battle for Sarajevo lasted three years and eight months and started on the 6th April 1992.

The regular barrage of mortars and shells took over 11,541 lives and reduced life in Sarajevo to one of deprivation and danger. Civilians were dodging bullets, running from the shelter of a doorway down to the next corner, people were running out of water, with limited minutes of electricity supply and buying coffee (the main drink in this region) at rapidly escalating prices on the black market. This standard of living was just a fact of life in Sarajevo.

The main hospital in Sarajevo (which Wendy and I visited) was in a pitiful state. It was subject to constant shelling with large gaps in the walls. The doctors and nurses tried to do their job but medical supplies were always limited, medication sometimes non-existent. It was so very stressful for all.

But life and living continued for Sarajevans—somehow.

Preparations for the End Game

Prior to the fall of Srebrenica and back in Vitez, preparations were being made for the proposed assault on Mount Igman and the relief of Sarajevo. Many practice manoeuvres were being played out by the troops in the British AOR who had been pulled back and had assembling in Vitez.

Equipment was being checked and re-checked. Much attention was paid to the Warrior Personnel Carriers. A Warrior training class was set up in the grounds of the local school. Practice at driving of the warriors was in great demand as they had remained static since arriving in theatre. There was a lot of maintenance need to bring them up to acceptable operational standard for the long drive down to the fields above Tomislavgrad and Livno.

The maintenance crews were very busy at every corner of the base, checking all features of the equipment and the air bristled with anticipated action.

This international mobilisation force was name as 'Task Force Alfa'. The planning had been in place for some time but implementation was brought forward when two French peacekeepers were killed trying to recapture their Observation Posts at either end of the Vrbanja Bridge crossing the Miljacka river in Sarajevo. The Serbian forces had initiated the action and dressed as UN soldiers complete with blue helmets' and had overrun the OP.

The British Defence Secretary, Michael Portillo explained that, 'There was no shift in any sense from peacekeeping to war fighting. We merely wish to provide protection to the peacekeepers who are trying to save lives.' (BBC report)

Possibly as a result of this reorganisation of the peacekeeping role, the Muslim, Serb and Croat representatives returned to the negotiating table in December 1995 and, eventually, exhausted from the fighting, agreed to end the fighting with the signing of the Dayton peace accord in Dayton, Ohio, USA.

The subsequent Rapid Reaction Force (British and French forces mainly) which was already in existence, were now going to be deployed in Bosnia. This was the biggest Anglo-French combined operation since the Suez Crisis in 1956.

Mount Igman overlooked Sarajevo and it was where the Bosnian Serbian forces were congregated and thus holding the city hostage. Mount Igman was going to be the focus of the action and more troops would be deployed in support of those already in situ.

The basic plan was that the Devon and Dorsets' Regiment, already based in Vitez would join 500 French Foreign Legionnaires to be based on top of Mount Igman overlooking Sarajevo to the south. The 720 soldiers of the Devon and Dorsets' would secure the route around the capital using their 50 Warrior armoured personnel carriers. They would be backed up by two divisions of the Royal Artillery and a small group of the Household Cavalry, along with 180 Dutch soldiers. The dozen 105mm guns the Royal Artillery were to be positioned on the 4,500m high mountain. Air support would be provided by 664 Squadron of the Army Air Corps.

The action had been prompted by the fall of the UN agreed safe havens of Zenica and Srebrenica. It was a tough pill to swallow for the UN but they finally agreed to the American pressure to launch NATO air strikes against the Bosnian Serbs. This happened after the Serbian forces had launched a mortar attack on Sarajevo, killing 38 people queuing for their daily supplies of bread in the marketplace.

The USA had recently intimated their intention of coming in to support the UN effort and a PR team had already arrived at Split with their Starlifter Transport plane and the mighty Galaxy aircraft.

Where the planes had disgorged their payload of vehicles and forward troops, men and women, through the open lifted snout of the great jumbo plane. They were an impressive sight and the efficiency of the US PR team was also impressive, with the cameraman being first out of the plane and assiduously filming the offloading. Their PR complement were full of smiles and efficiency of purpose.

Vitez

Back in Vitez, the base was becoming very busy as troops who had manned the OPs in the surrounding areas were being brought back to camp. This was all part of the preparation for the move to join the troops of the French Foreign Legion. As the units were withdrawn from the field, they then set themselves up in their units in the camp and started to practice their roles. The 50 Warrior armoured personnel carriers were being very carefully checked. Their engines needed a full overhaul and all moving parts had to be inspected for their standard of road worthiness. All the personnel and machinery of every description needed to be good working order/road worthy condition. The entire unit, including the Warrior armoured vehicles were going to have to relocate to meet up with the French further south. It was important that all elements were roadworthy. The base was a hive of activity. The Warriors were practising their manoeuvres in a nearby yard. It was important that the tracks worked well and that the drivers felt comfortable handling these big beasts. During this training period, I even got to drive a Warrior. A very agile machine, it moves easily and it can be turned on a sixpence. Fantastic to get an opportunity to drive such an iconic machine.

On arrival down in the practice area further south, I was also given the opportunity to fire the cannon on the practice firing range. This gave me a real insight into how the troops must feel whilst carrying out their different roles. It was a fantastic opportunity as this was real anticipated live action, no pretence. It gave me a real feel for what it was like for the soldiers.

The media were everywhere, demanding information. Senior reporters calling in favours from acquaintances back in the UK. The information was freely available in Vitez but a few felt that they could add to their story line, and this additional info would boost not only their story line but their personal kudos and profile.

Back in Vitez with the troops, there really was nothing to say, other than we were preparing for whatever was to come. Preparations were obvious but one reporter actually scaled the perimeter fence to get a better view. To be fair, events do change within minutes sometimes, but wasn't this a bit OTT. Robert Burns summed it up well with this observation. *'The best laid plans of mice and men verily go astray.'*

When the order to move came, practically the entire camp emptied overnight, all in one enormous convoy. As they departed late at night, Wendy and I stood at the gate to see them on their way.

Trundling down the road, the Warriors made an impressive sight—and noise! There was a great sense of relief in the air. We were on the move, heading down South towards the fields above Tomislavgrad where they would liaise with the troops of the French Foreign Legion.

Wendy and I waited until morning and then followed. As a single vehicle, we had a little more speed than the convoy. Directions to the new site were brief, we were directed to a certain broken gate at a certain grid reference and then turn right! We found the site and reported into the OPs room.

On the new base, discussions were ongoing as to what we could do to demonstrate to the media to show them that we were ready for action. After some short debate, a night firing exercise, which was part of our readiness preparations, was proposed and I was despatched to alert the media.

I went further south, down the road and found a media crew relaxing in a hotel, on the outskirts of Split. This crew were the only ones to be found.

By this time, it had been quite a while since I had been out of a military environment and I was a little awed by the comfort and general atmosphere.

Joining the group, I passed on the details of the proposed facility and the crew agreed to pass the word along. The media guys, delighted with the news, were very welcoming and offered me some crepes and cream as a treat. I gladly accepted the proffered treat. I hadn't tasted pancakes for ages, it was not what you got in the canteen on camp. To the obvious amusement of the media crew, I obviously relished the taste of those crepes! I can still imagine them—the taste of the crepes and the cream! Outstanding.

Before I left the hotel and the media crew, we exchanged details of the forthcoming display and made arrangements on how the teams were to find the specific location for the display.

That night, the exercise, on the plains above Tomislavgrad, was a great success. The Regiment put on a spectacular display with tracer flying overhead and casualty scenario, accompanied by loud bangs. I was detailed to be part of the troops on the ground, getting the feel of the action and being an active participant. I just kept up with the troop as best as I could, running hither and thither on command. At one point, our group leader was under pressure with the casualty scenario and yelled at me to give a lift with the casualty and then realised who he was yelling at. His expression faltered for a second but then you could see him think, 'no, heck, I'm in charge'. I laughed quietly to myself. It was fine by me; he was the one in charge.

It was exciting being part of the battle scenario and considered to be part of it. The tracer flying overhead was, despite the potential serious nature, pure magic. Crazily, I wanted to reach up and catch it. A busy night and a very successful exercise.

It was a great gift to the film crew. A 'night firing' exercise, especially in the field, is a great spectacle. They media teams stationed themselves at an appropriate higher level in the field and filmed it all. The team were very impressed by the display and gave the unit full credit, also receiving much media praise themselves for their own work even being nominated (I believe) for some TV award for their programme.

Ploce Port Preparations

Ploce was located on a small strip of Bosnia wedged in the middle of the coast of Croatia, thus providing direct access to Bosnia from the sea. This was a port some distance along the coast, east from Split.

As part of the preparations for the forthcoming action, I was detailed to go to Ploce to cover details of the Engineering effort to prepare the port for the landing of supply ships that would support the military effort.

On the weekend of the job, which was scheduled for Sunday, I had been at a barbecue in Vitez on the Saturday night and hitched a ride on a helicopter which dropped me off on a deserted featureless part of the dock, with the instruction, 'they are over that way'. I went off in the general direction of what I hoped was the water and, hopefully, the docks.

The dock had been totally abandoned due to the conflict and the place looked quite desolate. The hot temperatures were made even worse by the sun's reflections on the smooth concrete. Maybe too, I was suffering a little from a late night do! No one was expecting me but I trudged on hoping for the sight of some uniformed activity.

The job of the engineers was to clear up the deserted dock through which cattle and agricultural supplies had passed. The place was messy and obviously the workers had left in a hurry.

I came upon the cattle pens and rails still stood stark, bare, useless and shiny in the bright sunshine. The place looked, what it was—deserted. As I made my way over in the direction indicated, I remember feeling that I was very much alone here!

As I walked on, I noticed a figure in the distance and made my way over in that direction. As I approached the dock, I could see where there were still stacks of torn dusty bags of lime scattered along the dockside and the railway collecting yards for the cattle still existed, rising starkly above the concrete surface. The white concrete surfaces reflected the strong sunlight and dazzled the eyes. It was difficult to see much and the sweat was starting to trickle down into my eyes.

As I progressed forwards, I came across the engineers who were working, very hard, to clear the debris of abandonment. It was hard work; all work was done by hand. The engineers concentrated on their task wanting to get it done. They only had a short timeline in which to make the port ready to accommodate the large and anticipated influx of additional troops and their equipment. The French were scheduled to be the first contingent of troops to arrive, within a few days, and they would be bringing in all their supplies through this port.

This was a dusty hot featureless place. Nobody seemed to be expecting me and hadn't noticed my arrival in the chopper. I walked over towards what appeared to be the quay area and finding a few soldiers, I enquired as to the whereabouts of the officer in charge and, finding him, I introduced myself.

The officer explained that time was so short that he couldn't stop to talk so I walked with him as he worked and as he started giving me the details for my story.

The area I had come to, was vast. A large dock area which had formerly been used for the export and importation of supplies and cattle transfer, all activity carried on in reasonably shallow craft.

However, as I was soon informed, the ship bringing in our supplies were larger and deeper and had a very small clearance on the bottom. This is known as the 'draft' and that is the vertical distance from the bottom of the ship to the floor of the dock. This clearance was a matter of concern that required careful measuring that had to take into account the weight of the load compared with the available depth of the dock. Obviously, the measurements will vary depending on the type and weight of the load, for example with a light load a ship may draw only 20' of water but fully loaded with fuel, cargo and passengers it might draw 30' of water. Usually this depth is measured at the vessels 1/2 loaded measure. This gives a general idea of how deep a vessel will sit in the water. In the case of the main vessel arriving at Ploce and carrying most of the additional resources required for the impending operation—the relief of Sarajevo—there was about 6 inches depth of water to spare on the heavily laden vessel as it eased its way into the port. A very exact calculation made by the expert engineers! This detail was fascinating to me.

When I arrived the first thing that struck me was the heat. I was full of admiration for these engineers who had to work in this heat in these conditions, with the sweat pouring off them. They were stripped down to their waist and had to do their work at clearing the docks area alongside pallets of bottled water strategically placed at intervals along the dock sides. The guys had to be constantly drinking water as they worked. They had a very short timeline in which to prepare the facility but the main overriding factors for me were the intense heat, the glare from the sun and the dust from the ripped and torn bags of lime that were lying around and blowing dust in the eyes and mouth.

I spent a couple of hours on that dock and was pleased when I saw a land rover arrive to get me back to Split. I don't think that the hard-pressed engineers saw me leave, focused as they were on the job in hand.

On arrival in Split, I was told that the Welsh Regiment in Gorazde was being flown out of the enclave and due to land in very shortly at Split airport just across the road. As I had worked with these brave men, I went out to greet them as they exited the aircraft. As they filed down the steps, you could see from their expressions how their recent difficulties had affected them. They were strained. One of the guys that I had worked closely with on various PIO jobs just hugged me with the relief at getting out safe. I understood him. He had come through a lot during those last few weeks in the enclave.

Mount Igman

Prior to the Regiment leaving Vitez, and as part of the preparations for what lay ahead, we, the PINFO team, decided that we had to make a trip to Mount Igman to do a recce of our own. Wendy was still in theatre and had got directions. This route was a little more of an adventure as we went through areas that we had never travelled before.

The trip was uneventful until we neared the Mount Igman turn off. This was my first visit and we just passed through the checkpoint and onto the way up Igman. The road up to Mount Igman covered a distance of some 11 miles but much to our surprise, the 'road' was really only a wide track. On the way up the track, we passed the odd group of Serbs soldiers in military uniform. They looked up at us as we went by and I was struck by their air of defeatism. They were tired, exhausted and they had had enough.

There wasn't much else to be seen, the odd vehicle or one or two people very desultorily wandering around. The place was not busy, pretty much empty really. Not much happening here.

Needless to say, we went further on up the track, we wanted to get to the top. As we reached higher ground, we were able to see the view overlooking Sarajevo that the Serbian snipers had enjoyed over the past few years. Sarajevo was laid out before us, buildings and streets were clearly seen, easily identified. At this height and from this angle, it was easy to see the strategic important and military superiority enjoyed by the Serbian forces over the three and half years of the conflict.

There wasn't much more to be seen, the former Igman Hotel was a ruin with green slime running down the inside walls. So, after a fairly quick trip round the area, we returned to Vitez.

As part of the preparation and planning, we, the PINFO team, made a few more visits up Mount Igman, often to confirm information on locations and prevailing conditions.

Particularly, after the French landings at Ploce, we needed to update ourselves on the situation and set off from Split in Croatia. Making our way north to the border with Bosnia and arriving at the border check, we came across a long line of the French amphibious vehicles lined up on the Croatia side trying to get through into Bosnia.

The French troops, supplies and vehicles who had landed at Ploce were now trying to provide, with a little difficulty, the appropriate paperwork to allow them access to Bosnia. As new personnel in theatre, they were being well scrutinised by the border guards.

However, as regular visitors crossing the border, with minimum baggage, we were able to pass through the check point without any bother. Though I will admit, that on one previous occasion, we had passed quite quickly on through this check point, only to have to do a fast reverse as a guard raised his rifle to his shoulder and pointed it in our direction!

On this occasion, when we arrived at the track up to Mount Igman, we found that it was blocked. There was military checkpoint (Bosnians) in place and the guys were checking everyone very carefully and refusing many. There were 27 French military vehicles lined up on the main approach road, plus other various assorted vehicles, all wanting to get through to Igman.

Exchanging a quick glance, we decided to overtake the line of vehicles and, with nerves tingling in our stomach, we arrived at the checkpoint, drawing up behind two land rovers belonging to one of the Aid Agencies that worked the region. The Aid people were talking to the guards and, as the guard walked over to lift the barrier, the Aid worker in charge swept his arm towards the second vehicle, hesitated slightly and then included us with a vague flap of his arm and we knew we were through. Bare faced cheek had won and we were through— on—on up the winding, fairly rough road that led to the top of Igman.

The Aid Agency vehicles turned off fairly soon after crossing through the barrier but we had our sights set further up the hill and we just went on. Simple really—travelling along a road that had apparently recently received fairly constant shell attacks, presumably lobbed over by the Serbs to roughen up the surface and deter visitors. The dangers of being shelled on were apparently quite high and it thus became apparent to us, that this was the reason for the barrier and the delay imposed on the French troops. A safety thing! That was a novelty to us.

Despite and because of the situation, we followed the trail right up to the top and drove around having a look to see what was in place. There was disappointedly little change.

As an aside, during one of my earlier trips from Vitez, I hadn't been able to speak to the Boss in Split and needed to let him know where I was. While I was on Igman, I stopped at a few places trying to make contact with the Boss, but without success.

During one of those stops, in a clear area near the gate, I met up with a Southern Irish lady reporter who had lived and worked in the area for a few years. Naturally, we started chatting, exchanging views. The lady and I were delighted to meet, both from Ireland and both on Mount Igman! This intrepid reporter knew her way around and we agreed that communication was a problem. There was no signal up here. The lady had been in the area for some years as she was married to a Serb and spoke the language. Reporting on the situation for RTE (Ireland TV) was how she earned her living.

The lady, viewing our land rover, explained that she had a satellite telephone but the battery on her vehicle was a bit weak and she needed a strong battery to power her phone. We agreed to do a deal. She offered me the use of her satellite phone providing she could use our land rover battery to make a call as well! No problem we attached the leads to the battery on the land rover and the calls were made—hers to home to send a report and mine to HQ Land Command in Salisbury requesting some essential supplies and to ask that they contact the Boss in Split to let him know where I was and that all was well.

The people in the Ops room in Salisbury were quite impressed as the line was very clear and the idea of me standing at the entrance to the camp on Mount Igman and casually asking them to pass on a message was very entertaining!

The Irish lady reporter and I enjoyed our brief respite and went on our way.

I was later asked by the Boss in Split what went on—I told him that I had met a fellow Irish lady and that we had helped each other out that was all, though I had the impression that something had gone on between him and HQ but I didn't ask any questions. Sometimes, it's best not to ask.

Chapter 15
Preparations on the Plains Around
TSG and Livno

Meanwhile, the combined troops of the French and British continued with their preparations and training in the plains around Livno and Tomislavgrad (TSG). The plains were ideal for the purpose, being fairly flat and not densely populated.

The French Foreign Legion was establishing their presence on a site reasonably close to the Devon and Dorset (D & D).

Before, starting any activity in the region, the Colonel of the D & D and his French counterpart had to pay their respects to the local Mayor. This protocol meeting was important to ensure peaceful cooperation and support on all sides. The mayor, as expected, gave his formal consent for the military presence, so all was well.

The D & D then had to liaise with the French Foreign Legion at their camp site, which was a former factory site beside a farm. The French General was in camp and needed a familiarisation meeting with the Colonel of the D & D regards planning etc. The Senior Officers gathered together for their chat while I and a few others went for a wander around the camp area, a former factory site.

A nearby farmer saw us strolling around and he hailed us. He could not speak either French or English but addressed us in Bosnian. As I spoke a little of the local language, I was brought out to the fore and asked to translate.

The little farmer was very worked up when he realised that we did not have an interpreter. Fortunately, I was able to get the gist of what he was saying and could explain to the soldiers that he was concerned about the men driving around the former factory yard, levelling off the surface. This action bothered him because some of the excess earth was cascading over the edge and dropping down a few feet onto his carefully tended food crops. I understood him very well as I could see the effort that he had made on this plot of ground and these crops were to feed his family over the coming winter. I was therefore able to explain to the soldiers what the problem was and they immediately understood. There was no need for any more discussion. The soldiers nodded a lot and the soothing noises did not need interpretation. We were all on the same page and the farmer was pleased—as were the soldiers. No one wanted any fuss.

Further to this meeting, the General issued an invitation to us all to join them for a further meeting when they set up camp near our site out in the training area. I was included in the invitation and the get together was to take the form of a lunch in the field above Livno, hosted by the French Foreign Legion.

When we arrived at this new location, it was obvious that the Legionnaires had only just arrived on site. They were starting to unpack and just setting up tents etc. The French soldiers worked fast and in no time, the tent, forming the meal tent, was up and the trestle tables were laid out. We were standing around and marvelling at the scene unfolding before us. Boxes were opened and the plates, silver cutlery and sparkling glasses were produced. Bottles of wine were produced and the tableau unfolded and white linen tablecloths were unpacked.

The meal itself was a real thrill. We were in the officers' meal tent which was miraculously transformed into a rather elegant dining room. The trestle tables were set with white tablecloths, silver cutlery and sparkling wine glasses with beautiful white china plates, all bearing the insignias and coat of arms of the French Foreign Legion. The transformation was remarkable. It was like a dream and I felt as if I needed to pinch myself.

The food was very basis—tinned meat and crackers was the basic fare served in true Gallic French style with a great flourish. The waiters, all French soldiers, were so very professional and everything so perfectly carried out that we could have been getting a meal in the Ritz. There was other food as well but it was the setting that enthralled me.

Wine was served that came from the vineyards belonging to and worked by the French Foreign Legion. The wine was beautiful, a very elegant full bodied red wine, expertly made and served with a great flourish. Fantastic.

It was easily the best meal I have ever enjoyed. It was truly magical and unbelievable, at a beautifully laid table, sipping wine and just a few feet from muddy tracks dug into the soft earth by heavy military vehicles.

This was one of those fairy tale moments that will always live in the memory and it was set amidst the mud and grass of a remote field in Bosnia.

"Merci beaucoup, to the French Foreign Legion."

Assault on Sarajevo

All this movement and planning was geared towards delivering Sarajevo from the clutches of the Serbian Forces that had dominated their existence for over three years.

The British and French troops made the move to Mount Igman on schedule and established themselves in their positions. I was still based in Vitez and made the journey up the trail via an overnight in Kisseljak. The camp at Kisseljak was a good halfway point. There were no checkpoints for us to get through between Kisseljak and Mount Igman which was important as the checkpoint between Kisseljak and Vitez closed each evening and we couldn't get through.

I had one experience of this one particular check point that let me know what to expect. I had armed myself with one of the local language letters allowing us Freedom of Movement through the territory. It was a copy I had picked up and photocopied. I had it carefully folded and place in the pocket of my pants, to be produced when needed. On this particular trip, we ran a little late, just a few moments.

But the check point was closed. A three-leg blue Formica-covered chair of the '60s' type had been placed in the middle of the road. We drew to a halt and the guard came out of the door of the hut. He looked us over, saying nothing. We dare not go forward. I got out and started talking, asking for permission to go through. The guy gestured towards the rickety chair balanced precariously on its three tubular metal legs. The answer was obviously 'no', we're closed. Desperately, I dug down into my trouser pocket and reached for my pass and presented it to the guard. Solemnly, he took it and started to read it—and then burst out laughing. I had gotten a note for the other partisan sector. It had no relevance here!

The only thing we could do was to go back to Kisseljak and bunk down with the rest of the transit personnel in the main bunk house. Another lesson learned.

Meanwhile, up at the camp at Mount Igman, communications were basic and very much for operational requirement, particularly in the early days of the operation.

On one occasion, I needed to talk to a senior rank and, with some support from the Brigadier (on the ground at Igman) in order to do so, I had to engage the services of a specialist comms guy. It was surreal as we had to go up on the flat roof of the former hotel while he set up the connections' lines. I sat on a brick and watched until I could speak to my contact. A marvel of military effectiveness. The line was perfectly clear.

There were many trips up and down Mount Igman. We were warned that the trail up and down came under sporadic fire and we could not get any protection while travelling the trail. Wendy and I decided, that despite the dangers, we would continue our journeys between Mount Igman and Kisseljak. It was the only way we could complete our job.

We dismissed the idea of staying on Mount Igman as the accommodation on Mount Igman was very basic and very crowded. Most of the area used for the accommodation was in the former Igman Hotel which was really very damaged by then with leaky roof and green slime on the walls.

You could nearly see the damp spores floating in the air. It definitely wasn't very healthy up here. The main reason for our constant trips was due to the fact that we needed to maintain fairly constant communication with the HQ in Salisbury. This facility was not always available on Igman.

There was one memorable occasion when we were making our way down the track, as usual. The daylight was disappearing when we set off. There had been a few reports of firing on vehicles using the trail and we were a bit apprehensive. As we went further down the trail, our headlights failed.

Wendy, who was a very good and intrepid driver, decided to pull over to try and determine what had caused the lights to go out on the vehicle. Neither of us were mechanics and not *au fait* with engines but we didn't see anything obviously wrong, so could do nothing. It was a little unsettling parked where we were, about halfway down the hill and we didn't fancy going back so we had to go forward.

Wendy was very concerned so I offered to drive. After our last adventure with me driving at speed, she agreed, just wanting to know how I was going to see where I was going but, as I said, your eyes get accustomed to the dark, as I knew from my childhood days out in the country. There was no glare in the sky from lights in Sarajevo as they didn't have much electricity. Maybe I was a little foolhardy, but I definitely didn't want to be a sitting target for any random shelling or aspiring sniper. So we set off. I could just about distinguish the edges of the track—I had to as the drop off the edge was quite steep. There was a distinct lack of safety barriers at the side of the track! The drive down was actually quite scary but we made it to Kisseljak. Another one of our nine lives gone!

The UN plan was that the 720 soldiers of the Devon and Dorsets' would secure the route around the capital using their 50 Warrior armoured personnel carriers. These would be supported by two divisions of the Royal Artillery and a small group of the Household cavalry, along with 180 Dutch soldiers. There were a dozen 105mm guns of the Royal Artillery in position on the 4,500m high Mount Igman and this fire power was the biggest used in Bosnia so far. Air support would be supplied by 664 Squadron of the Army Air Corps. According to UN spokesperson Alexander Ivanko, the task force *"would fire whenever the UN is under attack. Not just if they are fired on, not only on the Igman route but anywhere in the city".*

The day planned to mount the assault and open defensive fire on the Serbian Forces was close. This was going to be a very significant and historic moment in the course of the conflict and we wanted to be there, to finish our jobs as it were.

Wendy and I had spent the night in Kisseljak as usual, and when we arrived at the top of Igman, we found out that it was going to be that day. Tingling with nervous tension, we went to the OPs room to check. When we arrived at OPs, it was all business. The French General was the Commander and he was in direct communications with President Mitterrand. The atmosphere was charged.

During any military action, entry to the OPs room is restricted to the necessary people, but, on this occasion, I was invited to stay inside the room. The conversation between President Mitterrand and the French General in charge was on loudspeaker and we heard every word. The command to fire actually came from the President. The order was given. They fired the salvo indicating that they meant business. I was in awe. What a moment. Historic.

After the salvo of artillery fire, the General ordered everyone out of the room as he wanted a smoke. He casually mentioned that we had five minutes to spare, if the opposing forces retaliated. We stood waiting not saying another word. There was no retaliation. We relaxed. The rest would happen and it did. The siege of Sarajevo was lifted.

After this, I returned to the UK via Split. I was exhausted, mentally and physically. On my return, I was at a loose end and found it difficult to settle after all the intense activity and excitement of the campaign.

I continued to work with the Army and became involved in the training and preparation of the next contingent of troops due to depart for Bosnia on their tour of duty. It was a busy time and I spent a lot of time on Salisbury Plain and at the various bases in the area. I was very mobile, visiting units and conducting interviews, preparing the next roulement of troops for Bosnia.

Srebrenica

One other convoy of importance (whilst I was in Bosnia) was the one from Split to Srebrenica. Wendy had left theatre by this time and I was due out in the near future. I had been provided with another photographer from UK and we were down in Split at Divolji Barracks.

We got word about the fall of the Srebrenica enclave which happened on 12th July 1995 and that a hastily assembled convoy was leaving that evening. It would carry supplies of food, mattresses, blankets and other necessities to help relieve the situation. Our team had to be on that convoy.

The convoy left as planned that evening. It was made up mainly of four-tonners packed to capacity with canned food from our combined locations in Croatia as well as additional items that had already been collected and packed in anticipation of need anywhere in theatre. There were over 70 trucks in the convoy plus the usual couple of additional vehicles needed to carry support personnel. We tagged on near the front end with other support vehicles, behind the convoy commander.

The first part of the journey was uneventful, quickly passing through the Croatian Bosnian border post and we arrived on the outskirts of Gornji Vakuf in good time, just before lunchtime.

On the outskirts of the town, a local checkpoint had been established. It had not been very long since the town had been closed off to through traffic and this rather large convoy made quite an impression.

The guy in charge at the check drew himself up to his full height and made a fuss demanding documentation to show the content of the trucks and our ultimate destination. He checked our paper manifest, walking the length of the line of trucks, physically checking if the items on a particular truck complied with the details on the manifest.

I had a basic knowledge of Serbo-Croat and I was often called upon to debate with the checkers. I was asked to supply some support on this occasion as the local checkers were being a trifle awkward, demanding more info on the load. I knew some language but did not want to get into conversation. Sometimes, getting the gist of what was being said, I just nodded knowledgeably, at appropriate times, often pretending that I knew a bit more than I did. I knew enough of the language and gestures (of which they were fond) to understand what was being said and I did argue back. A dangerous game but we just wanted to get moving.

It appeared that the blue berets of the UN Peacekeeping Mission didn't count for much. The local militants, ignoring the plight of the refugees in the north, wanted to show us they were in charge.

It was a fairly hot day in July and after a couple of hours, we were all getting a bit fed up with the delay. We still had quite a way to go, with a few more checkpoints to navigate, so patience was becoming a bit stretched.

At one point I was sitting in the land rover and one of the young boys playing around at the side of the road walked past. He seemed to recognise me, maybe from a past visit I'd paid to his school with some aid, but he turned to one of the checkpoint guards and said, something like they should let us go on our way and why were we being held up. The guard looked at me and said, 'Look, she's still smiling, it's OK.' Another little pointer to me, don't smile at checkpoints!

Shortly after this incident, the convoy was released and we started on our way towards Vitez. Arriving at the outskirts of the town, just a short distance from the PINFO house, we did not anticipate any difficulty as this area was held by the Muslims. We were wrong. The guys manning the checkpoint refused to let us through.

Time was moving on and we faced the prospect of an overnight drive, but it didn't matter to these guys, they decided that we were being held there. We just had to stay put.

After some debate and negotiation we had to face the incredible fact that, in this predominately Muslim area, the blankets, food and other aid that we were taking to their brothers in arms near Tuzla, were not allowed to continue.

The guys at the checkpoint stood firm, the convoy was not moving on. There didn't appear to be any rational reason for this decision. We had no option; we were detained and would have to spend the night in our vehicles.

At this juncture, the convoy Commander sent a message down the line to me to instruct me to use my media contacts to get the word out to the rest of the world that this convoy was being held up on the outskirts of Vitez by Muslim forces, thus preventing us from proceeding to Srebrenica with our vehicles full of items that would help relieve the situation with the survivors of the Serbian expulsion from the enclave.

Without delay, and pleased to be able to do something to help, I took the land rover and went down the road to the Public Information house. The place was empty except for the BBC World Service radio team. I was delighted to see them and asked if they could publicise the fact that we (with 76 four-ton trucks packed with provisions) were being blocked from moving from outside Vitez by the Muslim command.

This situation was rich and pretty unbelievable as we were going to relieve the Muslims who had been thrown out of Srebrenica. I spoke to the journalists in the evening and at 6.00 the next morning we were rudely awakened by banging on the sides of the vehicles and told to go! God bless the BBC radio.

Without question, we started up and continued on our way. We did not meet with any more resistance. There were no check points, although I remember a low bridge where we had to let out the air in the tyres of one of the vehicles to let its load pass underneath the bridge.

Arriving at the Tuzla airfield that evening, where all the refugees were gathered, we made ourselves known to the support aid agencies on the ground and arranged to start work in the morning, distributing the food and clothing.

The provisions and clothing that we had brought actually came from our own stores, items that we had in reserve for our own use. There had been no time to have additional supplies shipped in for us to distribute.

Truth was that we were giving our own reserves of food away to these people and doing it because we wanted to help.

The refugees were already installed in tents and they had some blankets. One of the tents had been designated as a mosque so that they could pray to Allah for support. I noticed that, from time to time, a single male would appear on the perimeter of the airfield and was led to believe that they had evaded the Serbian troops. These men up here were woodsmen, used to the terrain and very capable of dodging capture. I later had the good fortune to meet up with one such guy, a young man named Mustafa, who had evaded the Serbs, ate whatever he could find whilst on the run. The UN protected enclaves in the Serbian occupied areas that Mustafa aimed for, including Zepa, had all been overrun by the time he arrived, so he had to continue running.

Eventually, after about six weeks on the run through mainly Serbian territory, he met up with his family at their other home near Visoko, Sarajevo. When I met him, he was working for the OSCE in Sarajevo and had ambitions to go to America.

The morning after we arrived at Tuzla, we joined up with the team on the airfield, we started to help give out the supplies we had brought up on the convoy,

Whilst helping distribute the items to the refugees, assembled on the airfield, I was therefore very disturbed to be told by some of those local helpers, assisting in the distribution, that the refugees were refusing the tinned food because it was out of date and complaining that we hadn't brought oil and stoves so that they could make their own bread. This was their normal routine, baking bread every day. We just didn't carry a stock of stoves on the UN bases so didn't have any to give.

I admit that I was totally taken aback. This was within two days of them being thrown out of their homes! We had made a huge effort to collect the stuff and travel up from Split in order to give them some support. Therefore, it was tough to listen to these complaints—as was the request for more blankets as they had used most of the blankets to cover the floor of the tented mosque rather than cover themselves at night to keep warm. The blankets laid out on the floor of the mosque was to make it more comfortable for the old men to kneel whilst at prayer. All the younger men had been rounded up by the Serbian forces and taken away.

We had erected tents, brought food and blankets for these people and they, in turn, demanded specific items and complained. I could hardly believe it and certainly it gave me pause for thought. Trying to be charitable, I hoped that the reaction was due to the shock and turmoil of their sudden eviction from their homes.

Shortly after this, my period of duty came to a close and I returned home. At this point, we were all aware that peace negotiations were ongoing in Dayton, so hope for peace was on the horizon.

After Dayton

After the Dayton Agreement was signed (November 1995), I returned to Bosnia for my second tour of duty, working in the Coalition Centre for Public Information (CPIC) based in the Holiday Inn in Sarajevo.

Arriving at Sarajevo Airport I saw that it hadn't changed much—but it was safer for the aircraft landings, there was no fear of shelling on incoming aircraft.

The surrounding area was much the same with the houses still bearing the imprints of the war time shelling. The major difference was that the tall defence shields in front of the houses had been removed. The defence shields had been made up of what appeared to be large sheets of heavy zinc or tin. They had proved effective in that the local residents could move around to some limited extent between houses hidden by the shields. It had not been ideal but it had provided some protection from the snipers in the surrounding hills.

I was met at the airport and taken to my first port of call which was the office. This was based in the Holiday Inn which was located just off the main drag, formerly known as Sniper Alley. The frontage of the hotel was painted yellow so it was hard to miss.

This tour of duty for me was slightly different from the first one. I was to be working in the same office with people from other nations, in a multinational coalition of Public Information Officers. The multinational aspect of the Public Information Office was going to be interesting. The mix of Americans, British, German, French, Italians and Scandinavian as well as various East Europeans (including Albanian) did indeed prove to be a fascinating mix. The different nationals focused on fulfilling their agreed roles, promoting their national troop effort. All were trying to establish and build on the negotiated peace for Bosnia, each using their particular language skills to ensure progress. It was a sincere effort.

One of the big benefits of working within this multicultural environment was the integrational aspects of working as a team. It was helpful to hear a different viewpoint on many issues. As well as this we were able to celebrate each Nation's special day, sampling their regional special foods and learn about different national customs. It was a huge bonus and very enjoyable.

I was one of three British Army Officers working in the Holiday Inn. My role was to report on the activities of the British Forces based within Bosnia. The other two Officers dealt with media reports in local newspapers and media outlets. They had their separate section within the CPIC and I hardly saw them.

I had to be constantly aware of the ongoing activities of the British Army elements based up country, set up media facilities and ensure that our troops had their fair share of general media attention. This meant that I often had to organise helicopter flights to the different areas to ferry the media around.

Sometimes we had visiting political representatives who also had to visit different bases, usually by helicopter. It was important that these politicos saw for themselves and experienced some of the conditions and drawbacks out in the field that were being experienced on a daily basis by the troops.

I was billeted with the American troops who were in a large building not far from the Holiday Inn. This building was beside a large archway that marked the route of the one taken by victorious conquering armies marching into Sarajevo. It was a pleasant spot close to the river. We had all facilities here, for eating, relaxing and exercising. The washing and toilet facilities were good, until someone would take an extra-long luxurious shower and the rest of us had cold ones! The one culprit was soon identified but she didn't care and continued, until she experienced a few cold showers herself. She wasn't happy when that happened.

For living conditions, I was sharing a corridor with six American Officers whilst quite a few others lived in the room off our corridor. I was last in and was allocated the privilege of the top bunk in the corner. This was ok with me and I unrolled my sleeping bag on the thin mattress. Beside the bed space, I also had a small wooden locker in which to store a few items. On my first evening there, I was pretty tired and the bunk was comfortable and I slept soundly. It all worked pretty well.

One of my fellow companions was an American Lieutenant Colonel from the Bronx. By virtue of being the most senior rank in the room, she was the only one with the regular single bed. She had all our respect, particularly for her bed space. A pleasant companion, she found it puzzling that I, from Northern Ireland, could work for the British Army! I tried to explain about Ulster and Unionism but she remained cynical and sceptical.

The other occupants of this corridor were all pleasant companions and I became very friendly with one on American Officer with whom I would go to the gym or run with in the early morning. She had the use of a Humvee (US Army jeep) and we often used this mode of transport around town. Though, we didn't have much spare time as I, and the rest of the girls, spent most of our time in the office or at our separate workstations, only returning to our accommodation in the evenings.

Generally, I found that the Americans were a very supportive bunch sharing their 'many care parcels' from home. I was always included in their treats and this was a great boost to morale.

I got a lift to work every day in a land rover driven by a navy guy who was more at home at sea than on dry land. A great chap and each trip was a cheerful adventure.

In the Holiday Inn, my place of work, I quickly settled into the routine of the CPIC. This was a completely different set of circumstances from the PINFO office in Split or Vitez. The scheduled press conference every day was the main focus of effort. We just had to ensure that the peace keeping effort being carried out by the different nations received adequate attention as it vied with the political decisions and tensions swirling around Bosnia.

The multinational aspect though was great and we didn't have to go out to gather the information, as we had to do in Vitez. Information came to us.

The press conference was held on the first floor of the Holiday Inn every morning except for Sundays. This first-floor large landing was a general meeting place where all sorts of information was exchanged between the multinational military personnel and journalists. The press conference was the main event and well attended.

Around the landing, there were basically three main rooms. The room for the press conference was on the right at the top of the stairs and to the side of that was another room where media reports were translated by the different national soldiers who compiled the daily report. Behind this area the male soldiers had their living area which was very convenient for work.

To the left of the rather large landing at the top of the stairs was the operations centre where the public information staff, including me, had our workstations. The head of this public information centre was an American, we had some support staff, German and American who worked extremely hard making sure that the unit was operating efficiently and effectively.

As I was the UK PIO representing UK interests, I was placed with the other two international PIOs, an American who had come over from the Pentagon (I think) and a French Major who had previously served with the UN Peacekeeping Mission based in Croatia and had a wide-ranging knowledge of the overall theatre.

Our three-person unit, with desks facing in towards each other ensured that we were always aware of events happening throughout Bosnia. A very useful setup which ensured a comprehensive knowledge and support for all units. It ensured we each had a complete picture of the other's areas and could step in at any time to give support when necessary.

The ground floor was our rather grand coffee shop where we would have the occasional coffee and relax, maybe having a meeting with someone who needed an in-depth and extended briefing. Down there, the rather nice decor felt rather grand to me, being in military uniform, and the coffee shop wasn't used all that often.

The briefing details for the press conference were fed to the separate spokespersons who conveyed the information to the journalists, together with their more detailed insight of the situation. The military spokesperson was based in the Residency, a few miles away. It was out near the hospital and beside the American Embassy and other senior military were based there. The OSCE (Organisation for Security and Cooperation in Europe), who were more involved in setting up a democratic framework on which to base the forthcoming elections, were located nearby on the other side of the river and also involved with the press conference. The OSCE contributed a large portion of the information flow on current civilian orientated events, mainly to do with the forthcoming election.

There were always a lot of multimedia journalist who would come to the press conference. The multinational military, of all ranks, sat on chairs lining the walls of the conference room. We found that it was good to listen to what was said and the questions raised by the journalists who had their particular points of view of the situation.

Each day after the press conference, we would get further updates from our national area representatives and often organise trips out into the areas. These trips were essential for our own information gathering and we also had to arrange facilities for the journalists in theatre to keep them informed on the unit activities and to get a feel for the actions and progress made by the various groups on the ground. It was very much a moveable and fluid situation outside and, even, inside Sarajevo. There had been a lot happening in Bosnia and we needed to keep informed on a daily basis and act accordingly.

Working in this international environment we were able to visit other nations' troops and get to see what was going on in their respective areas. There was much and varied work ongoing throughout the area by the forces and there was much sensitivity along the IEBL (inter-ethnic boundary lines). I felt that I, together with the others working in the CPIC, were in a very privileged position, and we all worked hard to justify our roles.

On one occasion, I was able to visit the Italian Railway Company from Bologna region in Italy. They were working on the 185 mile long (300k) damaged railway line and tunnels running north to Novi Grad in the Republika Srpska. The Italians were the railway specialists who had brought their own railway carriages and specific spare parts into theatre. They were working together with the Hungarians who were clearing the mines using their special mine clearing machines. The mines had been planted during the war and had been most effectively used to block the lines and the tunnels. There was absolutely no rail travel.

This area was sensitive, to all sides, as it had had all ethnicity living here prior to the conflict and there was much discussion about mass graves. The Serbians were still feeling a little sensitive as the accusations were still circulating and the Muslims were feeling braver and a little bit more aggressive towards their previous controllers. This particular trip was organised, taking into account all these sensitivities.

Transportation to this site was as usually via the larger Chinook helicopters for reasons of safety and time constraints. On this particular trip, we also found that, due to safety concerns within the area, we had to be ferried around by the Americans in their large Abrams tanks. This added a little excitement to the trip for everyone. The tanks deposited us beside the Italian train and we all piled aboard for our organised train ride and briefing.

The train journey covered some of the recently cleared lines and we passed an area where there were specialist teams working on exposing an area with about four or five of mass graves. I can still recall that distinct smell.

The Italian Railway Company was doing a great job and the presentation, to the assembled visitors describing the scenes that they were dealing with and it was very illuminating. The briefer, an Italian Captain dealt with the many hitherto unrealised difficulties of a country area and people in active conflict, its significant difficulties and related traumas. He opened his briefing by describing a railway tunnel containing many mines, as *potentially the best wine cellar in Bosnia*' due to its size and depth underground. A great description I thought. Good opening line!

The Italians also provided some quite delicious food and Italian wine after the briefing.

Discussing details with the briefing Captain from the Italian Railway Company in 1996

The Italian Train Company brought their own train to Republika Srpska to effect repairs to the damaged railway lines

There were quite a few other outing/facilities set up for the media. These facilities mainly using helicopter transport. In the circumstances, this form of transport was an essential element in helping keep us all informed. The advantages included the fact that there were no checkpoints to concern us. The area of Bosnia was however sensitive in many aspects and although the citizens, on the whole, were trying not to settle old scores, there were times when it had to happen and quietly.

There was one facility that I was involved with that sticks in the memory. On this occasion, the British Forces based near Banja Luka informed me that they had organised a facility and that, if I wanted, I was welcome to attend. The occasion was that there had been a huge delivery of toilet rolls to their sector and the facility was to show how these large quantities would be dealt with and distributed. A huge logistical exercise. They said that they were organising it and didn't share any details.

I was told that all I had to do was to turn up at Sarajevo airport and get the flight up country to Banja Luka base. Great. I arrived to find about 40 people milling around waiting to get onto the aircraft for transportation to the site. I looked around for the military guys organising this trip but couldn't see any. There were some very serious looking civilian type bods with briefcases, obviously very important in the group. I was then advised that there was no passenger manifest for the helicopters and that I had to get these people boarded for the helicopter trip up to Banja Luka.

At this point, all I could do was count out the passenger numbers for each aircraft and direct each group to an aircraft. The men in suits objected as I had just counted them among the other passengers. One said that 'he had never been treated like this before'. I didn't have time to explain as the authorities wanted us off the airfield ASAP. There were a lot of other things going on right there. It was an airport.

Getting everyone onto the Chinooks, we got on our way and landed in Banja Luka where we were to be transferred to another lot of helicopters in order to fly onward to the Sipovo base where the distribution of the toilet rolls was to take place.

Stepping off the Chinook in Banja Luka, I saw a chap standing on the bonnet of a land rover, loudly briefing the assemble audience as to what they were going to witness. He looked as if he was in charge as he directed the crowd towards the waiting Chinooks. I followed and as I approached the back of the last Chinook, I was grabbed by the shoulder and propelled up into the chopper into a seat and a headset was rammed on my head. I was just in time to hear the curses of the pilot as he yelled at the crewman to 'grab that girl with the clipboard as she might know where she's going' (me). This is a c****** ****.

Silently, I agreed with his description of the scene. Realising I could hear, he immediately apologised and asked for the grid reference of our destination. I explained that I didn't have one but that we were going to Sipovo base. I quickly tried to find out who was organising this trip but couldn't see anyone. The pilot assured me that he had a good idea of the grid reference and we could start.

Arriving at our destination, we could see the guys on their forklifts unloading the toilet rolls from the container. Despite enquiries, I still couldn't find the organiser of the facility.

After viewing the scene we made our way back to the landing area near the base to see about our return arrangements.

We had all assembled in the field ready for departure. I could not see any sign of anyone to organise our helicopter departure so I headed towards the FOC (Forward Operation Controller) land rover parked at the top of the field. As it so happened, we recognised each other as having previously worked together for General Jackson. He was relieved to see me as he explained that no one appeared to be organising the returning passengers, whose numbers had swollen quite dramatically. He told me that he had 28 helicopters circling overhead, all intended for different destinations—as far apart as from Sibernik, Zadar and down to Split. Quite a spread of destinations.

Passengers had to board the appropriate helicopter and there was only room for one to land on the field at any one time. He was getting a little frantic and it was obvious that we had to work together. We agreed that he called in the helicopters by destinations and I would alert the passengers as to their departing chopper. The only thing that I could think of doing, on instruction from the FOC, was to write the destination on a piece of paper and run up and down the field (like a demented holiday rep) announcing the next aircraft destination.

It was hectic but the scheme worked. The visitors got back to their appropriate destinations and all in the correct order. There was only ever one facility like that during my time, thank goodness.

There was one last flip of the coin to my time with IFOR. At the end of my six months tour, I was waiting to receive word about my date of departure but heard nothing. Absorbed as I was in the daily work of the CPIC, I just waited, secure in the knowledge that I would be told.

Listening intently to receive instruction on the headset during the epic 'Sipovo' facility

One night, back at my bunk, I was informed that a senior officer wanted to speak to me. I went to the door and discovered that a senior guy from the Residency was standing outside. Full of apologies he informed me that they had overlooked an instruction from the British sector based in the north and I was due out of theatre the next day. My first thought was the timeline and transport. I wouldn't be on time for the daily flight out of theatre! So I asked 'how' followed by, 'I'll not get there on time!'

I was quickly reassured that they had thought of that, their error and that Bill, the America Colonel in charge had to fly out the next morning and that I could have a lift in his executive jet! I was then given the time to be at Sarajevo airport to get my lift to Split to catch the flight to the UK—with the instruction to be on time.

All I had to do was pack. Well, that was easy; one large rucksack and it was done.

Attending, on time, at the airport, I got on the waiting executive jet and joined the boss. The interior of the plane was something that you see in the films, plush! We took off immediately. The boss and I were the only passengers.

A speedy flight down to Split while the boss worked on his papers. At Split, the steps were let down and I threw my bag out onto the tarmac and descended the few steps.

To be honest, it had all happened so quickly, I felt that I was in a bit of a dream. Stepping out of that jet onto the tarmac created quite a flourish to the end of a tour of duty! This was compounded by the expressions and comments I received from other Brits up in the viewing gallery at Split Airport—words like, 'It's no one important, it's just Betty stepping out of the executive jet!' Wow, thanks guys!

Receiving my service medal from the American Colonel in charge of the Coalition Centre, Sarajevo, in 1996

OSCE

As I finished my tour of duty, I was headhunted by the British Consul in Sarajevo (the Honourable Mr. Charles Crawford), and on leaving the Army, I joined the OSCE (Organisation for Security and Cooperation in Europe) January 1997, working for the Ambassador (an American) in the media office based in Sarajevo. The OSCE was in charge of the democratic election process for Bosnia Herzegovina, establishing rules and regulations as well as also monitoring the entire process.

Returning to Sarajevo, this time in a civilian capacity, I flew in via Vienna where I was due for a briefing. As I landed in Vienna, I couldn't help but compare this luxury travel with the more basic military flights that I had enjoyed previously.

Landing in Vienna amid the hustle and bustle of a busy airport, I was very aware of the fact that I was now travelling on my own and there was no 'group' guidance or just following the person in front. A strange feeling to me, but one that was rather good.

The work of the OSCE was not unfamiliar to me as, while in the CPIC, I had attended many of their press conferences, so it was just a matter of getting up to speed with their routine.

The main difference for me, with this job, was that I could go out to restaurants and enjoy the coffee shops. It made it easier to get to know the local people and their customs. This was a lot better. In civilian dress I melted in more with the local community. The military uniform set you apart a little.

My role in the OSCE in 1997 was that of Deputy Spokesperson for the elections in Bosnia Herzegovina. There were in addition, regional press offices with their own Public Information Officers who were responsible for their own areas.

During my time in Sarajevo, as well as being able to go to restaurants and enjoy the local atmosphere and food, there was one particular outstanding event. I got toothache. I was a bit wary and wondered how I was going to deal with it. In some cases of illness, different people had had to go up to Vienna for different treatments. According to previous visits to a dentist back in the UK, I had an underlying infection in my lower jaw that gave me a fairly continuous ache.

This recurrent toothache flared up during my first year in the OSCE in Sarajevo and the pain was bad. As a matter of course, and not expecting any real solutions, I asked the interpreter, Sabaheta, if she knew of a good dentist. She did and the lady had her surgery not far from our office. I was willing to give this dentist a go, so we went along.

This was just into the peace after the three years of conflict and facilities were still very much limited. I didn't care, this toothache needed attention.

On entering the dental surgery, I could see that the surgery only had a fairly ancient machine for drilling (similar to the ones used years ago back in Ulster, when I was seven). The lady dentist was most apologetic telling me she had no anaesthetic. Oh dear, this was not so good, but I needed her attention. I explained that the pain was bad and I needed her expertise. She nodded and had a look before starting to work. The lady drilled and filled and liberally swabbed my mouth with peroxide, as she explained, this was her only aid. Much to the relief of all concerned, her attention worked. It was the cure. I can confirm that I never suffered another low-grade infection of the jaw after that. It's been great.

Throughout 1997, I was pretty busy as there were many trips out of Sarajevo in order to hold press conferences and meet with the other regional information officers. The situation was in the process of change and we were the instruments required to make that change. The OSCE were there to make that change and help progress Bosnia forward into this new democracy. It seemed that most, if not all, wanted a democratic election process but wanted to make sure that their 'side' would not be at a disadvantage. My background, living and working in Northern Ireland gave me an edge on understanding their point of view.

1997 was a busy year for all in the OSCE, trying to establish the process for a democratic election. As well as progressing the election process, we had to ensure that the local people appreciated our efforts and supported us. We had to talk a lot and show our willing to work hard to achieve the objective.

There were loads of media working the area, many international media and the local national media who were working with their dedicated national contingents. The Public Information teams placed in the individual areas were a focus of attention for all, particularly explaining and promoting OSCE activities and democratic principles.

There was a big demand in Sarajevo for election related information for both international and respective national media. There were many briefing and power point presentations conducted, including to the military forces assisting in the process.

On the odd occasion, I travelled with the Head of the OSCE when he was holding media conferences or meeting with local important politicians. The

Republika Srpska, with their consent, was always included in these discussions and visits. The Ambassador was very well informed on all aspects of the situation and it was relatively easy to brief him on the latest scenarios. This was just part of the routine of the day!

When there were VIPs visiting, I was usually part of the escort, even for the visit of the Chairman-in-Office. The chief spokesperson accompanied the Ambassador most of the time, he was the right-hand man. I just filled in the gaps.

I was also chosen to represent the OSCE at a couple of international conferences, including those of local people living abroad. The diaspora was always eagerly waiting for the latest news from home. They did get copies of their local daily media, but a person who had actually been working in their home state, was a better conduit of information. In their eyes, I was actually there! To them, this info was first-hand and they could ask about this street or that street, or a particular block of flats. This was invaluable info for their hungry ears, it was a personal update

Getting through that first Democratic Election process made for a very busy year. The framework for the election was set but there were the lists of eligible voters had to be compiled, candidates had to be nominated and approved, voting rules and regulations had to be drawn up and ballots had to be printed. Local people had held elections previously, often held in secret, but they knew where to establish the voting centres and they already had a pretty comprehensive regional voters list. It was all coming together and the locals and internationals were pulling together. The election process though, only applied to the Bosnia side of the country. The Serbian side did not participate in this process.

The first Democratic Elections for Bosnia proved to be very successful and Ambassador Frowick was well pleased with the process.

After this success, there was a slight change of focus and I was appointed as Deputy Director Media Development in Bosnia, monitoring and developing media outlets with Bosnia. This meant that I became responsible for the daily monitoring of media articles, mainly newspaper report but also including radio outlets.

The media development team was separate from the main building and worked mostly in the evenings to capture media reports for that day. They prepared a daily summary for the morning report released to the international audience based in Bosnia as well as for other interested international recipients in other places.

In the monitoring outlet there was a total of 95 members of staff who read and listened to the reports and then translated them into English. The local staff employed, were augmented by a few internationals working in the evenings. This monitoring process, with translations by local interpreters, is quite precise and, based on my Northern Ireland background living in a very divided community, I was very aware of the nuances of slight word variations. It's too easy to distort the actual so careful scrutiny was needed to ensure accuracy.

The daily reports focused mainly on Bosnian media with a few reports on Croatian media outlets. The main base was in Sarajevo and it was necessary that this had to be expanded to include Croatian media, so an office had to be set up in Mostar. This was achieved.

We tried to ensure that these daily reports were a very accurate reflection of the mood and thoughts of the local media and, as such gave valuable intel to all those involved in the reconstruction of Bosnia Hercegovina.

The reports were viewed as to be of great value and were also then forwarded to Washington, Brussels and the Military chain of command.

Following on the establishment of an office in Mostar, I then had to ensure that the Serbian viewpoints were also taken into consideration. However, the area to the North, in the Republika Srpska was a little bit problematic. There was a very easily defined Inter-Entity Boundary Line (IEBL) which ran along the former military front lines as they existed at the end of the Bosnian war and defined by the Dayton Agreement of 1995.

The opinions and ideas of these people to the north of the IEBL were as important as anywhere else and they had to be taken into account, but firstly, we had to find out what these views were.

We felt, that for various reasons of sensitivity, we couldn't establish an office as easily as in Mostar, but we could have teams on the ground reporting back to the HQ in Sarajevo. The other partisan media outlets didn't have the same mistrust as the Serbs who had felt betrayed, to a certain degree, as they had formerly been the bosses in the FRY (Former Yugoslavia). Dayton had changed that but people on the ground take time to make adjustments. I had to use monitors who spoke Serbian (not too difficult as all inhabitants of the Former Yugoslavia could speak Serbia), but politics make for loyalties, so I had to tread carefully).

The first difficulty was to make sure that I could get reports from the other side of the IEBL and that the local media there would agree to the reports being made and used. Communication between the North and the rest was not always easy.

Fortunately, after some assurances of fair play and a little negotiation, they did agree to the monitoring and we made arrangements for exchanges of media reports across the IEBL. In this process I was very grateful for the help of the interpreter and former refugee, Sabaheta. I had employed this lady as an interpreter for the Sarajevo office. Formerly living in Pale with her family prior to the conflict, and subsequently becoming homeless a few times during the ensuing ethnic cleansing, she was ideal.

Sabaheta, a former journalist, could and did understand all sides. We had met a few times while she was covering stories before she was employed in the OSCE, and we had become good friends.

As I was setting up the bases for the monitoring units and personnel in Serbian territory, I felt that I had to recce the area personally. I had to make sure that the monitors were established and felt comfortable in their locations. Their personal security was a matter of importance.

I felt the weight of this responsibility heavy on my shoulders and I was very aware of the possible perceived dangers to the monitors.

The journey north was a bit of an adventure. There was snow on the ground and the road surfaces were rough at the best of times. This was not the best. But we had a good driver and found our way around in safety. It was important that the scheme would work.

During our travels, there was quite a bit of discussion with local residents and much assurances of fair play had to be given. But it worked out, the local residents, although wary were happy to have their views included in the international scheme of things.

Once established, the units worked well and we had full reports of incidents and media stories that were submitted every day in a report and, by request, forward on to the American command. Many of American units were stationed in the Republic of Serbia, and the reports were very well received by the Americans especially. The reports were regular and identified local responses to the international effort.

Establishing this media monitoring outlet, was, I felt in itself, a worthwhile achievement and I was delighted with the result, giving us a much-needed insight into the views and opinions of those in the North.

After establishing the three areas of monitoring, in November 1997, I was then sent up to Banja Luka, the capital of the Republic of Serbia (Srpska), North of Sarajevo as the Special Representative of the Head of the OSCE Mission to Sarajevo. My role as the Special Representative of Ambassador Frowick, was to ensure that the various political parties in the RS had equitable access to the media. This was the first Democratic Assembly election in the RS since the Dayton Agreement and it was important that we internationals got it right.

The instruction was clear but it didn't take into account the number of representatives already sitting in the Assembly or the fairly short time scale in which we had to achieve our aim.

In the planning of this role, I realised that one of the key elements to this project would be, for me, the interpreter. I needed really good people to keep me abreast of what was going on, I needed them to be fluent and dedicated, as I expected to have to work some long hours.

In Sarajevo, I decided to ask Sabaheta, who was already employed by the OSCE, if she would be willing to be part of the team and go up to Banja Luka with me. Sabaheta agreed to the request. We had worked together already on a few things and I had met her for the first time, when she was reporting on the situation in Banja Luka. I knew that she had interviewed Biljana Plavsic, the President of the RS at that time. She would also have decent knowledge of some of the important contacts that would need to be approached.

Accompanied by Sabaheta, we departed for Banja Luka. My main concern, which I discussed with Sabaheta, was that she might find this job to be very difficult, due to her previous experiences as a refugee, but she was able to assure me that this was a job and that she was fine with it. She also assured me that she had been on good terms with some of the major political players, and that this could therefore provide valuable assistance. She was an excellent interpreter so I decided to accept this assurance and work with it.

In Banja Luka, we found ourselves a couple of rooms and settled in. I knew that I also had to have an additional Serbian representative to interpret so that there could be no accusations of bias. After a little difficulty, I was able to find such a person. This lady also had her experiences, and, as she had also been a refugee, and been forced out of her home due to Muslim pressure, I felt that I had achieved a good balance.

The first thing we had to do was to establish a presence, so we quickly set up a few appointments with some noteworthy persons of authority. Both girls put forward their recommendations and I followed their advice.

We had the meetings with these important people in Banja Luka and made arrangements to go to the Serbian Assembly or House of Representatives to discuss with these representatives on their views and ideas regarding the forthcoming Assembly elections.

Inside the Chamber, there was a palpable air of important dissent and debate. They were very prepared for me and my two girls. They had a point of view and I was going to hear it.

That was not a problem to me, I was prepared to listen but firstly I explained who I was and what the instructions were. I understood very well that explaining who I was didn't bear any relevance. These people knew already, they do their homework when confronted by what they perceived, was an international decision. I was merely the representative of this. I explained what was going to happen during the process and they listened intently. Then the debate started.

The two girls doing the interpreting had it tough. Much was being said and they had to explain. We worked together as a team and they were brilliant. They took it in turns speaking into my ears (both sides) and they never missed a beat. I cannot remember the exact number of representatives of the people who were in that chamber but I knew that there were too many.

We needed to have a public debate on television and it couldn't last for weeks. Election Day was looming. So, I listened and we argued about everything but the bottom line was that I had to achieve this television debate with the representatives and it had to be meaningful. They knew this but they had to make their political points. They also knew I came from Ulster and there was a certain comradeship in this debate. I knew what they were talking about and, more importantly they knew that I knew and understood. It was a very important basis.

At the end of the day, I had a set of rules to establish. With the assistance of these representatives, we eventually agreed that, 27 (I think, remembering) representatives of the regions and the people were to appear on television for the debate. They represented the various area as far as I could judge and they could each make a short presentation on TV for everyone to hear. They were aghast. A short presentation was not in their 'modus operandi', the outburst was expected. Sacrilege, this was sacrilege! As with all politicians, they liked to talk. Speaking firmly, I let them know that this was the way it was going to be. They argued but after a few more points were raised, they agreed to proceed. As we prepared to depart, the Leader of the House thanked me very much for listening to their points of view and having a discussion with them. He then offered to buy me a coffee. Due to another scheduled appointment, I had to decline but appreciated the offer.

This offer of coffee was a great gesture of friendship and respect which I valued highly, particularly in these circumstances. Unfortunately I had to refuse the request due to pressure of work.

As we exited the building, both interpreters were buzzing, as was I. What an experience! There was much talk between them about where I'd learned how to debate like that. There were even some references made to Dr Ian Paisley and his speeches. Maybe I'd picked up a few tips? I felt overwhelmed but also satisfied that we had successfully established the ground rules. I felt somehow that these public representatives would make sure that they did a good job for their television audience.

On the night of the TV debate, which was held in a large auditorium, there was a buzz of anticipation in the hall as the audience filed in. The various political representatives turned up and took their place on the stage. They were sat on chairs, in a slightly curved line, at the back of the stage so that everyone could see them clearly. One or two were a little slow in turning up, and as the programme prepared to start, I was reliably informed that the politician from Pale, the home of Karadjic the former President of the Republic, had said that he would not take part in the programme. This man was an important political representative among the Serbian side, pretty hard line and his 'no show' could derail this entire effort. It was important that he, from this area of Pale, was seen to participate. All Serbian voters were watching.

The TV debate was an important part of the perceived democratic process. To my mind, this 'no-show' made a big difference and I had to think of something. After some quick thought, I asked that his name and area be printed on a large sheet of paper and placed on his vacant chair which just happened to be in the centre, a prominent place.

The programme started and after an introduction by the Chair, we settled in for the presentation and debate. The politicians made their presentations, giving their name and a summary of their policies, which were quite diverse with the underlying theme of nationalism. Taking full advantage of the presence of the TV cameras, they each made their case. It was excellent and made good viewing.

Funnily enough, in the middle of the programme, which was going out live, the missing politician from Pale appeared at the back of the platform and quietly took his seat. I admit that I was relieved.

The discussion was good and the interpreters worked hard, keeping me informed. A great effort by all. At the conclusion of the programme, their spokesperson stood up and thanked me personally for the programme they had just made and said that it had been the best presentation and discussion they had ever had, and on television too. Job done.

I was relieved and delighted, especially with the two girls who had worked so hard keeping me informed.

The election took place as scheduled and all went well for the candidates. I was relieved and could now return to Sarajevo.

On one particular occasion, when I had to make a quick dash to Banja Luka, there was one big difficulty—there wasn't a car and driver available. On being advised of this change, my contact was not happy as our scheduled meeting was important to him. Much to my surprise and delight, one of my contacts to whom I was speaking just happened to be in a position to offer me a lift but by helicopter!

There was a flight scheduled but I had to get to the helipad in a hurry as they were getting ready to depart.

I gratefully accepted the offer, promising to get to the helipad on time as it was really a relatively short distance away from where I was.

Arriving at the helipad, I could see that the chopper was preparing to take off. To my delight, the helicopter was a Bell and Howell with the glass bubble front. The crew were in the chopper and ready to depart. Quickly hopping on board, I was directed to the jump seat, joining the two crew and the chopper took off. I settled into the seat and had a first class view all the way to Banja Luka. It was a great trip.

The pilot flew the chopper reasonable low all the way up, hugging the course of the river, often flying below the sides of the cliffs on either side. A breath-taking experience. It was an absolutely superb trip and I was so grateful for that ride.

I attended my meeting and got a lift on a returning vehicle. Life was full of surprises at all times.

After my time working in Bosnia, in both capacities, military and civilian, I had quite a decent overview of what life was like for the citizens who had endured both the war and the onset of peace. Neither situation was ideal, but the Sarajevans endured and lived the best way they possibly could. A very resilient people who deserved our admiration and respect.

Working in the military in 1996 Sarajevo, we were free to take the odd trip through the town. On one occasion, I went out for a walk along one of the main streets to just to have a look at the shops as they re-opened. I was curious to see what was starting up at this early stage. At one point, I remember that I just fancied a bar of chocolate and stepped into a shop to see what was available. Basically, the entire selection was on full view. Selecting a bar (pointing to it) I proffered a couple of deutschmarks to the lady behind the counter. The lady looked embarrassed, and asked if I had the coins as she did not have any change. I did and was able to supply the necessary coins. That bar of Lindt chocolate with its blue wrapper was really tasty. It's funny the kind of detail that you vividly recall.

The reality was that this shop, in conjunction with many others, was open for business but there was very little money in the till and very little stock on the shelves. Any stock that was there was out of date.

I also noticed that the clothing in the shop were distinctly homemade, carefully smoothed/ironed, but not totally smooth and flat at the seams. I was used to making my own clothes so could notice things like this and identify reasons. Though I will say that the clothing on display was showing future promise. The ingenuous individuals were copying designs shown in magazine pictures. My personal favourite, from my own experience, was 'Burda' fashion magazine which was in great general demand at that time and circulation obviously extending to Sarajevo. I could identify the styles!

I will say that the people of Sarajevo really deserved a lot of credit for their efforts, despite their prevailing difficulties.

A great loss to Bosnia was that the once revered and magnificent central library, had been burned to the ground. Due to the desperate efforts by a few people, some of the books had been saved, but most were burnt.

Supplies of food were minimal with pizza, the main draw for those, mainly internationals, able to go out to eat. The central market had started up and the trams were running but there were no fares collected, it was free. The tram was actually a great source of comfort for a few. They could ride the tram for as long as they wanted, all day if they wanted and had nowhere else to go. It was something to do and it provided some comfort and warmth.

There was very little money out there and it came mainly from those who acted as interpreters or drivers for the international organisations. This was shared among extended families. Life had improved but poverty and poor living conditions prevailed.

This was the reality of the beginning of peace.

During my first tour of duty in Bosnia 1995, I had witnessed first-hand the results of much ethnic cleansing. This situation had not been resolved by 1998 and there were pockets of the population who were essentially homeless—and despairing. Progress toward recovery was complex and therefore slow.

I paid a few visits to one family who were living like this. They would always send out for a large bottle of coke and we would also drink coffee when I visited their house. They had lived in Pale, now they were on the outskirts of Sarajevo and eventually found a place in Hadziczi, still within the canton of Sarajevo but about an hour's drive from the centre. I visited them and tried to help a little. The war and having to leave their long-term home in Pale (members of the family had lived there for generations) was a tough pill to swallow. In the move from Pale, they hadn't had much notice and all their worldly goods had been wrapped in a sheet when they got on the bus to leave. The mother was not well, neither was the father and they had a slightly disabled daughter. Emotionally, it was too much, but like so many others, this is what happens in times of conflict and you just carried on as best as you could.

Each time, their living conditions were very poor, less than basic. But they were thankful, their other daughter earned a living as an interpreter (which is how I got to know them and was welcomed into their home). Internal refugees in Bosnia at that time usually took up residence in a house or apartment that had originally belonged to a family of the 'other ethnicity'—basically, they were squatting. It wasn't right but they really didn't have much choice

When I last met this family in Hadziczi, I was told that this was a more permanent place for them. It was more 'country' and their neighbours were nice. They were living in a small row of houses with Muslim neighbours so felt safe. Conditions inside the home were sparse but they were content, hoping for no more moves.

It was going to be my last visit and I remember talking to the father and because of my help this time, he told me that he had arranged for a supply of fuel to get them over the winter. A simple basic necessity for them. We both had tears in our eyes when we shook hands and I left.

Some ethnic groups had had to leave their homes three or four times over as the 'ethnic cleansing' process progressed. As a consequence, these families, felt totally lost, were destitute and disenfranchised. This therefore did not lend itself to a solid, safe and secure atmosphere. The Serbian people living south of the IEBL seemed to be suffering this more than the Muslims. The Serbs had had the upper hand prior to the conflict and now they were getting the payback. I felt sad for them, but couldn't make any comment as I hadn't been there previously.

Often, when out on visits to different locations, I would come across a group of families gathered in a building, huddled together for comfort and a little warmth, hoping to be left alone in their misery and hunger, but needing some basic supplies. It was terrible to witness. The aid agencies didn't seem to be able to find these people.

On one such journey, I was visiting in the Russian protected area. This was the only area that the Serb refugees felt was a reasonable safe retreat. I stopped off at a former secondary school. I was just being curious. After speaking to the soldiers, I wandered into the school and came across such a group of refugees. I was appalled at their lack of facilities. I was aware, from previous meetings and discussions, that the Russian soldiers (no disrespect to them) did not have any spare food. They had minimum rations for themselves. So I knew that there was not much to go round, and to my discomfort, I had nothing to give the refugees. There must have been about 50 people of all ages, from the elderly and infirm down to the children. They all looked gaunt. Lack of food and warmth, coupled with safety concerns, does that to you.

The conditions that those people were living in were dire beyond description. Puddles of dirty water lay on the floor. Light was that of daylight, filtering unsteadily through gaping doorways that once had doors. The smell of human waste was overpowering. There was no comfort, just a few hard plastic chairs placed in relatively sheltered areas. These chairs were for the elderly. The more able-bodied wandered around in small groups. Poorly dressed, they had to keep moving in order to keep warm.

This was the reality of a displaced people.

At the end of 1998, my contract with the OSCE came to an end and, with a sense of unfinished business, I returned to Northern Ireland.

Chapter 16
Kosovo

I left Bosnia in January 1999 and in September 1999 went to work in Pristina Kosovo for United Nations Development Programme (UNDP). UNDP is a grassroots programme under the UN banner with the role of trying to jump start an economy after a period of conflict.

In order to restart a semblance of some sort of 'normality', the UNDP organised the picking up of rubbish, cleaning of small rivers, streets and, in some cases, providing basic shelter for families returning to their homes after fleeing the conflict. The programme focuses on paying a basic wage to those members of the public and some families in return for doing this menial work in their local area.

These selected jobs include cleaning drainage channels of the accumulated debris and rubbish that had been dumped there over a time and could interfere with free drainage and which, after some time, were also starting to smell. There were other jobs that local people could do to earn a wage. There were also some approved basic community projects which would help improve general living conditions like improving the supply of drinking water. These types of programmes boosted the local economy and started the recovery process.

In some cases, where a family had lost most of the building that was their home, they would continue to occupy the damaged remains of part of the property. In as many of these cases as possible, then UNDP assistance would be given to put a roof over their heads and rebuild a wall or fix a damaged roof or floor. In many cases the floors of the temporary dwellings were just hardened earth that, in winter, became damp and muddy. This had to be remedied.

Often the family had lost a member, sometimes the father or even the grown-up sons. The decimated families were obviously feeling lost and disorientated. Bewildered by events, sad and bereft. In these circumstances, families were totally unable to see a way to help themselves or where to start. They were helpless and often felt hopeless.

In these circumstances, this support from UNDP to the families as well as to the very local economy, was much appreciated. This support often made the difference between starving and survival.

In the north of Kosovo, near Peja, close to the border with Serbia, there was much destruction of buildings and much loss of life. These people had been very resistant to the Serbian overlords and had paid the penalty, but that was true of most of the citizens throughout Kosovo. In many cases there were piles of bricks and mortar littering the streets, evidence, if needed, of the widespread destruction of homes and businesses.

Making a trip to Peja just after I arrived in Kosovo in 1999, road conditions were very bad and I had to stay overnight in Peja. I found a room in one of the houses being rented by an Aid Agency working the area. The house was well set-up with hot water and heat. It was a much higher standard than that I was experiencing in my rented room in Pristina. This house was a real oasis of comfort amidst the destruction in Peja. At the time, I didn't realise that the water supply in the area wasn't chlorinated or treated property (I would find this out months later) but I drank the coffee, which tasted good.

Peja in ruins, 1999

Mosque survived, Peja, 1999

Aftermath of Conflict

Bosnia had endured years of conflict and there was a lot of destruction but there was a rawness about Kosovo and its situation that was very distressing. Having said that, I am reminded about the refugees in Bosnia, not just Muslim, but also the Serbians. Whilst working in Sarajevo 1995, I had on a few occasions to go across the river Miljacka that flows through the centre of the town in order to visit the Serbian homes across the bridge to the far side. One of the residents acted as interpreter and we had had a chat. This girl was very good with English and made quite an impression on all our group.

Whilst in Kosovo, visiting a former large Secondary school housing refugees and protected by the Russian troops, I came across this young woman again. She had had to leave her home in Sarajevo and this was her fourth move as a refugee. The conditions she was living in were terrible. There was no heating or effective sanitation. Food was scarce. The Russian soldiers themselves had very sparse

206

rations and were continually being harassed and shot at by the surrounding Kosovar Albanians.

The girl and I met, by accident, in the Assembly Hall of the school. There must have been a couple of hundred Serbian refugees, of all ages, gathered here, ranging from children to the very old. There was no comfort. The wind and cold permeated the place. There was just a couple of the usual plastic chairs that the elderly took turns to rest on. They had to share one toilet and the smell of urine was strong. Everyone wore their outdoor clothes—it was all that they had. There were no doors left and the wind blew through without hindrance. It was very chilly and those that were fit to, wandered around aimlessly in groups. I didn't recognise her at first. She had a cloak of hopelessness wrapped tightly around her slight frame. She spoke and then the penny dropped.

Talking to her and seeing the slight hope in her eyes that I might be able to do something to help, I felt ashamed of how little I could do. These people were crushed. In order to get help and some security they (all neighbours from Sarajevo) had moved countries, but there was no respite. The Former Yugoslavia was now no more a single state but split into many smaller areas. It was hard for them to get to grips with, especially whilst enduring such conditions.

I definitely felt very bad as I couldn't help them in any way. I had only stopped and gone into the school to see what was going on and who was living there. I was being inquisitive, wanting to see conditions for myself. Ironically, I had popped into this place because I was free to do so and because I could.

The refugees had no freedom and very little food. The Russian soldiers had very little food to spare and there was no kindly aid agency delivering supplies. It was heart breaking.

I didn't stay long and as I went out to my vehicle, I shed a helpless tear for their situation.

Notwithstanding all of this, although the conflict in Kosovo had not lasted that long, the feelings of despair and loss permeated deeply. Most of the people who had left Kosovo and their homes were now back—but there were deep scars. To the Kosovo Albanians, the Serbs were occupiers whilst the Serbs regarded the Kosovars as insolent disturbers of their peace, troublemakers all.

Arriving in Kosovo in the beginning of September 1999, I was struck by their older style of life with their traditions and way of working. I was reminded very strongly of Ireland, not that there was a great similarity to Ireland as it was in 1995/6, but to the Ireland of 50-100 years before. I had been brought up, like many others, hearing stories of what life was like back then, the hardships, hunger and the need to emigrate to find work and be able to send money home. The setting here was similar to that. So, I understood their need for change and I felt quite comfortable here, in this scenario.

My role within UNDP was to establish the Public Relations Campaign and help develop the profile of the UNDP declared projects. On a wider scale, I also had to devise, organise and implement programmes for high profile visits that promoted the work of the UNDP. I also had to develop and expand media coverage, liaising and cooperating with other agencies in theatre.

There was one fairly immediate project to be dealt with. Communications, include TV signals were entirely through the satellite system, which cost a lot. There was just no terrestrial TV signal within Kosovo, so UNDP, with the technical assistance from the Japanese Government, aimed to establish a terrestrial TV transmission system to serve Kosovar needs.

First Impressions of Pristina

I had arrived in Pristina, Kosovo, after NATO forces (including General Jackson for whom I had worked for a short time back in UK) had taken over the province's peace keeping role under the auspices of NATO and the UN. To keep it in context (I was informed), Kosovo is about the same size as the County of Devon in UK with roughly the same population numbers.

The role of NATO was to maintain peace between the Kosovo Albanians and the remaining Serbs. It was not an easy task and I was witness to many disputes and had to arbitrate many times between the ethnic groups. This called into play my inherent knowledge and understanding of the arguments, and in many cases, the 'fly or crafty' moves, which I had already witnessed back in Northern Ireland during the Troubles there. I found that this situation in Kosovo had certain similarities.

Living conditions were not the best during this time (1999) and despite being careful when out and about, accidents did happen. When darkness fell, there wasn't any electric lights to light the streets and we all had the odd fall, some more serious than others. An example of such an accident/event was that on one evening as I was making my way home from work, in the dark, along the main street, I stepped off the pavement to avoid some people coming towards me. I just didn't think or look down and literally, I disappeared down into a storm drain!

During the unrest and public protests or riots (depending on your viewpoint), it had been the practice to remove the drain covers and hurl them at the opposing soldiers. The heavy metal covers were being replaced but this one had been missed and I had found it! I was wearing a long heavy coat which helped cushion me from the worst of the hard edges as I slid down, but I was a mess with mud, rainwater and dirt. My shoulder bag took in a lot of the muddy mess and my purse was ruined. The muddy mess got in everywhere. Two local guys witnessed my downfall and tried to help, apologising profusely but as I told them, it's not their fault. I was so embarrassed that I didn't feel any pain, until later, but I was lucky, no broken bones. Just a mess to sort out when I got back to my digs!

I remember very vividly my first experiences in Pristina. As usual, when I arrived, I reported to the unit office, ready to start work. They had organised accommodation for me, lodging with a lady and her daughter near my place of work. My accommodation was just off the main street, so the next day I went over to a local restaurant for a coffee.

It was the beginning of September and the weather was pleasant so the tables were placed outside, at the side of the pavement. Sitting in the sunshine, I surveyed the main drag and noticed a couple of largish balls of dry grasses, rolling along the street in the slight breeze. I was reminded of Burl Ives (an old Country and Western singer with a soft gravelly voice) singing about the *'tumbleweed drifting along'*. I felt that that song summed up the scene really well at that moment.

The dust lay heavily on the street. The buildings were covered in it and were grey. The windows were dusty. A grey street in a grey town. At that point, I had some reservations about the job in hand but I was soon jolted out of any lethargy that I felt. There was work to be done.

Chapter 17
Work and Conditions in Kosovo in 1999

Sketch Map of
KOSOVO

Apparently according to plans in place, a famous football player, Ronaldo, was paying a visit to Kosovo, courtesy of UNDP invitation. My job of organising a visit like this, in fractured conditions, was not going to be easy. Trying to talk to different areas, I sometimes had to place the telephone outside on the window ledge in order to make a connection. Organising this trip was going to be quite a task.

Communications were sketchy, roads surfaces were poor, with the need for many diversions. Ronaldo was going to visit a site in Gjakova. On the map of the area, this did not look to be far from Pristina, but the reality on the ground was very different.

Most of the road surface wasn't too bad, not too many potholes, but about halfway along the route, a bridge had been destroyed during the conflict, and this held up the flow of traffic. All traffic, cars, large freight lorries etc. laden with goods for delivery, had to carefully descend a sharp descent some 20 feet down and then slowly struggle their way up on the other side to join the road. Added to this difficulty and narrow track, traffic could only go one way at any one time. Obviously, this 'diversion' created quite a tailback of traffic, sometimes the delay stretched into an hour or more.

This was the only way in and out of Gjakova.

Such was the difficulty of travel in Kosovo after the conflict.

Organising the details of the visit meant many trips to Gjakova which were always tiring, due to the conditions and restrictions of the road trip.

The NATO troops based in Gjakova were French and they had an airfield. This made it easy for Ronaldo to make the visit, him being able to fly into the airfield. The French troops were obviously delighted to be a part of this visit and to host such a renowned footballer. Ronaldo was just passing through their base on his way into the town, but it was enough. This made liaison very easy and there was a lot of enthusiasm around these arrangements.

Travel arrangements for the visit were easy as Ronaldo was travelling by private jet. We, on the other hand, would travel by road.

All the arrangements were coming together very nicely, and then I had a call. The flight crew of the private jet were concerned about the type of fuel they could use for refuelling on landing in Kosovo. I really didn't have a clue so I said I would check details and get back to them. Time was short, so I hurtled round to the UN Air Transport section to find out about fuel! To my delight an old friend (French man) from Bosna days was manning the desk and, after greetings were exchanged, he was able to reassure me on fuel suitability.

The visit passed off smoothly, many cameras being produced from pockets as photos were taken of the star visitor, Ronaldo, on his way into the town, just about 20 minutes from the base.

Ronaldo was great. He enjoyed meeting everyone and was the perfect visitor. On the day, all of the participants seemed to have enjoyed the experience, including Ronaldo.

There were many such facilities that had to be organised. Some had to be set up with the cooperation with local military Commanders. I would go and visit them at their base, ask their permission and blessing for the event to take place and then set up the necessary visit site. The local military Commanders were quite happy to have this publicity, without them having to make any effort—who wouldn't?

Establishing the very worthwhile profile of UNDP in Kosovo was not difficult as the project manager was very active, with many varied projects on hand to support a burgeoning recovery. A former Iraqi Kurd, he spoke Arabic and understood the pressures of the Albanians and their desperate attempts to bring back a degree of normality.

The winter of 1999 in Kosovo was tough. When it snowed, it was heavy, the snow fell several feet deep, not inches. The ice was thick and we didn't have any salt to spread on the pavements or grit to spread on the roads. It would snow, then it would freeze and the pavements were lethal skating rinks for pedestrians.

Once travelling along the road to Gjakova, the car was in a traffic jam for some time and I stepped out to walk up and see what was going on. I just slid, as nice as you like, unto my back. Looking up at the grey white sky it took me a second or two to realise what had happened before I quickly got myself up, slipping a few times in the process. I gingerly slid back to the car—this time sliding on my feet. It was then that I realised that the snow chains on the vehicle wheels were the only thing that held it back from sliding all over the road.

Generally, conditions throughout Kosovo were tough. Walking with any degree of safety was a nightmare. Underfoot conditions were treacherous and there were many falls. The electricity supply was not regular and would go off abruptly at any time.

The main Obilic generating plants was elderly, some units dating from 1960s. They had not been maintained properly, if at all. The coal-powered plants produced ash from the chimneys and at one point in late '99, 20 tons of ash had to be removed from the roof of a side extension to the 'A' plant.

The Serbs had been in charge before 1999 and when they ran short on electricity, they would ask Serbia to send supplies down the transmission lines to feed the demand. The Serbs looked on Kosovo as one of their provinces and that the generators in Kosovo were regarded as being too old to be maintained properly.

Obviously, this was not the case now as the Albanians and Serbs weren't exactly on the best of terms. The international engineers of the EU who were invited over to Kosovo came with their computers and laptops to manage the generation and supply. In fact, what they really needed was a heavy hammer and a few spanners as the units were not exactly modern. The electrical generating system in Kosovo was just antiquated.

The Kosovo Albanian workers in the plants were overwhelmed, they had no knowledge of all this. Most of them had worked in a menial capacity, taking instructions, with managers mainly being Serbian.

There were just a few Kosovar managers who had been educated and trained in Belgrade. They were experts in their fields but their numbers were few. Of course, when there is minimal or no electric supply, there is no heat or light and how do you cook your food? Life, in general, was difficult, generally bereft of basics.

The solution, if you could afford it, was to purchase small generators. The noise of these generators, chuntering out their offerings of power, could be heard everywhere. It was actually reassuring.

The small generators (a little bigger than the size of a heavy lorry battery) were placed outside and on the verandas of the flats. They were powered by kerosene and the stench of fuel and (sometimes) spilt fuel, filled the frosty air. There were many tragic accidents with the generators, as flat owners sometimes tried to replenish the generators with fuel while they were still running. A dodgy thing to do. The resultant burns could be quite severe, sometimes fatal.

DFID, the foreign investment arm of the British government, realising the need, backed this striving for normality and brought in more and larger generators to be used for the business community and distributed them throughout Kosovo.

Local householders also bought small camping gas stoves, basically just small gas canisters, with which they heated soup and made coffee.

The gas camping stoves were also dangerous. They could easily tip over when in use and, in the small kitchens, a fire could start very quickly. I witnessed one such incident when the stove fell on the floor, the flames set fire to the carpet and badly burned the arms of the lady as she tried to catch the stove as it fell. The burns covered most of her arms and the medical clinic, at the bottom of the street, was closed. Medical facilities were many and well placed around Pristina but they worked social hours. In this instance, although I had witnessed this accident and stamped out the flames, I didn't have any transport and couldn't get the lady any treatment. There were no taxis.

That stoic lady had no option but to sit up all night nursing her burns, applying sliced onion to ease the pain. She went to the clinic the next morning.

It was freezing cold and dangerously slippery but she was able to get her burns dressed. I could only imagine the pain she endured whilst sitting up all night. Horrendous experience.

The depth of the frozen snow caused many people to fall and broken limbs were commonplace. The military hospitals, our main source of medical help, was kept busy. Due to the intense cold, and lack of heating, many international staff contracted pneumonia, pleurisy and other serious chest complaints.

Some had to be casevac'd out to Vienna.

I got a bad cold with a cough but remained comparatively healthy.

In an effort to keep warm, most internationals stayed at work as long as the larger generator kept the electricity running. Many of us made out our reports and articles wearing our heavy coats, woollen gloves, hats and big scarves. It was all we could do. Some lucky people, mainly Japanese who had planned ahead, had special stretch metal coils slipped over their shoes, this stopped them from slipping. The rest of us (and I was one) just slipped and slid our way home usually, in the dark.

There were very few restaurants able to open and food was scarce. Supplies had to be brought in, mainly from Turkey. Shops carried old stock and that stock was minimal. I noticed that many items sitting on the shelves needed a good dusting. The streets and fronts of buildings were also grey with the dust of neglect. Protests had occupied most of the spare time of the population. Rubbish was not being picked up but lay out in the streets, under a generous covering of snow and ice.

In the four-storey block of flats where I lived, the occupants would open a window and throw out their plastic bag of household rubbish. The bags formed quite a pile on the ground below, but it was frozen so there was no smell. After I had been there a quite a few weeks, a guy driving a tractor and trailer started to appear at reasonable intervals and lifted this rubbish. The situation was very ad hoc but it worked in its way and the rubbish disappeared.

On first arriving in Kosovo, my landlady, a lovely lady called Hilmije, organised for me to have a few lessons in Albanian. This gesture was much appreciated by me as I knew nothing about this language. The gentleman teacher was a Professor in Pristina University and he gave me a short history of Albania and its language. This introduction was very valuable to me, and although I wasn't the most assiduous pupil, this grounding was a valuable insight. I did learn some Albanian but work was pressing and I didn't do much homework.

Therefore, I was not the best of students. What I did learn was interesting and useful and I appreciate him spending the time with me.

Establishment of Terrestrial TV and Radio Link

One really important job undertaken by UNDP was the re-establishment of the terrestrial TV and radio transmission link. At that time, the link was being worked through satellite communication and was very expensive and limited. This terrestrial link was very important for the future of media development within Kosovo and our role in UNDP was to co-ordinate with the Japanese Technical team to make this happen.

The Japanese government had struck a deal with UNDP worth somewhere in the region of $14 million. A Japanese Aid Agency was already working in Kosovo and had provided basic housing for a couple of villages near Pec, which had been totally destroyed during the conflict. This technical link however was a really large investment with great future potential that would take some time to put in place. UNDP co-ordinated with the Japanese team and held meetings to develop plans. The Japanese team who flew into Kosovo were highly motivated senior technicians and, obviously, they were keen to get the job done, without delay.

At that time in Kosovo, each new journey held unseen difficulties, sometimes finding the location became a bit of a mystery tour. There were no road signs and the drivers were not totally sure of where to go in each case. It happened to me when I was escorting this team of important people to one of the proposed sites for the transmission system. The convoy turned down a road and the drivers stopped for a confab. As I thought that the direction was the wrong one, I got out and discussed with our drivers. Obviously, some drivers agreed with me and that the small convoy had taken the wrong road so we had to turn around. This manoeuvre cannot be done without fuss, when it's a convoy, however small. In this case, it was with some relief, that we did manage to get back on the right road to reach the site and that the Japanese Technical team could do their recce and formulate plans. After the inspection of the site by the team, the project went ahead and the terrestrial communications signal was established with comparative ease and in a relatively short time.

It was a great feeling to realise that I had participated, in a small way, with a very significant project which was for the benefit of Kosovo.

Chapter 18
United Nations Mission in Kosovo

After establishing the role of the UNDP and conducting an extensive PR campaign, I transferred across to the main UN Mission, UNMIK (United Nations Interim Administration to Kosovo), in February 2000. In the UN, I was engaged in general Public Affairs duties. These duties can be many and varied, but always communicating information in relation to events pertaining to the goal of the mission. In the beginning of the tour, I was tasked with writing and researching articles relating to what was happening in Kosovo. There was a lot happening in many areas, there were vineyard to be tended, local councils with rules and regulations to be confirmed and established. All very basic.

The TV and radio were wanting interviews from senior officials within the UN to give them a steer on what was envisaged for the future development of Kosovo. We, in the Public Affairs department, had to organise these interviews and escort the officials, briefing them on the latest developments. Political appointments were being made and these newly appointed politicians deserved to be interviewed so as to explain and elaborate on plans for their separate departments.

Scenes of destruction in Kosovo after the conflict in Pec/Peja Region, 1999/2000

After the destruction, life starting up again in Gjakova in 2000

Many situations and stories were being discussed, some of it pure speculation, but they all had to be checked out and verified. These stories were then written up and the articles made public on the local media outlets. It was exciting and exhilarating work. One of my important interviewees was with

Ramus Haradinaj, who later became the third Prime Minister of Kosovo, between 2004 and 2005. He was the leader of the AAK political party and a former officer and leader of the Kosovo Liberation Army (KLA), commanding the troops in Western Kosovo.

Initially, after 1999, he became a politician but quickly resigned when he became one of the KLA commanders to be charged with war crimes by the International Criminal Tribunal 'with war crimes and crimes against humanity relating to the conflict in Kosovo in 1998'. Haradinaj was tried in the court in The Hague, together with other accused associated with the conflict, was acquitted in 2008, the prosecution appealed this decision and he went through an appeal but was finally acquitted of all charges in 2012.

The man I interviewed about 2002 was pleasant, polite and had spent some time in Switzerland. He had fought for Kosovo with the KLA but had turned to politics at the onset of peace.

I also wrote an article on the Kosovar responsible for Health who had been installed under the auspices of the UN Interim Government to Kosovo UNMIK. This guy had worked in a hospital in London during the conflict and had come back to Kosovo as soon as he could. An interesting character, he seemed to know his way around.

I also knew quite well, the future Minister of Education who was the Headmaster of the Gjin Gazulli Secondary school close to where I lived in Pristina. Whilst working for the UNDP, I had visited the school to hand over some school computers donated by a school in New York, so we were old friends. I also lived in the house of Linda Mustafa, then Senior Maths teacher at the school.

The one person I would have loved to interview was Hashim Thaci, (PDK party) who was the spokesperson for the KLA (Kosovo Liberation Army) during the conflict. Thaci is from the region of Drenica which is where the KLA originated. He came to the fore during the Ramboullit negotiations when he represented Kosovo interests. After the UN arrived in Kosovo, Thaci joined the Interim Kosovo Administration. He then went on to become the first Prime Minister of Kosovo and later he also served as Foreign Minister and Deputy Prime Minister before becoming President. Although I had met him on a few occasions and had conversations with him, I never had the opportunity to sit down and interview him. Recently, Hashim Thaci was also indicted by The

Hague Tribunal for war crimes committed during the conflict but continues to defend his case.

There were many projects and interviews and many articles written and published. There was a special visit by the UN Security Council which I help organise and then had to help escort. During that visit, Sergei Lavrov, the Russian representative on the Security Council, later appointed as Minister of Foreign Affairs in the Russian Government, made a point of discussing with various Kosovars, showing his understanding of the situation of both sides of the ethnic divide in Kosovo. He held a very informed discussion with one of the Orthodox Church religious leaders who was both delighted and surprised by the visitor's interest. For me, hovering on the perimeter of the discussion, this was pleasing and illuminating. This level of knowledge and understanding was a real inspiration to all present.

Previously Lavrov had also discussed details of the difficulties experienced by the Kosovo Albanians during the conflict, once again demonstrating the same degree of understanding. Other Security Council members did have discussions with the people they met but the degree of empathy was not as strong.

During this time, I was also deputised as a Regional Administrator Spokesperson in one of the Administrative Regions based in Gjilan when the regular appointee was on extended leave. It was only for a relatively short spell but it was very enjoyable working so closely with local leaders.

Working for the UN ensured that we celebrated all National Days, of those making up the United Nations. Quite often this resulted in long weekends. On one such weekend in 2001, Linda (the lady in whose house I was staying) and I decided that we would go by bus down to Lake Ohrid in Macedonia. The lake is in Northern Macedonia, over near the border with Albania and one of the deepest lakes in Europe. The scenery is really beautiful. The bus trip took a few hours and we decided to stay overnight near the lake. The next day, when we were heading for the bus to get back to Kosovo, we learned that the area along our route and around Skopje airport had been occupied by some militants who were stopping free movement in Northern Macedonia. Apparently, there was an armed conflict between groups of ethnic Albanians living in Macedonia known as the Albanian National Army (NLA), who had attacked the Republic of Macedonia Security Forces. As we had to pass the airport, it just meant that we would not be able to get back to Pristina.

Linda and I decided to go our different routes, as she had some family living in Macedonia and declared that it was best that she stayed with them for a few days, but I had to get back to work, so made my way to Skopje. In Skopje, I was quite surprised to find that quite a few of my colleagues from Pristina were also there. Gathered together, there was about a couple of hundred of us and we assembled at the OSCE building to try and determine a collective course of action.

As it happened, we just milled around for a few days, trying to determine details of what was going on around the airport. After a few days, we got some transport organised and received the political clearance necessary for us all to be allowed to get back, via road, to Pristina.

Some of the groups were lucky enough to get back via a hastily arranged helicopter ride but I missed out on that. Instead, I was able to get a seat on the first bus out.

It was an uneasy wait for the bus. When it arrived and we took our seats (I was in the front row), I glanced around at the other passengers and realised that we were all very nervous (naturally enough). My fellow passengers were a mixture of internationals and Kosovars who were working for various international organisations. To my mind, the mix of different nationalities just emphasised the fact that we were all in this together. None of us knew what to expect on the road from Skopje to the border. As we started our journey, rumours were flying around. There was talk of groups fighting in different locations and unknown gangs stopping traffic on different routes. The tension on the bus was palpable, we were all nervous, especially as we approached the border.

There were a few tense moments along the way. There were some checkpoints but they allowed us through without incident. The combined feelings of relief came out in one collective sigh as we crossed the border and reached the territory of Kosovo.

When I eventually arrived home, I discovered that Linda was there already. Linda had travelled home by another route, this one via Tehran. An easy route, apparently, and one we hadn't thought about.

We were really so delighted and relieved to see each other and even more relieved that we were both safe. After all the excitement, I somehow didn't manage to get down to Lake Ohrid again.

Once back in Pristina, we learned that the militant troublemakers had been granted safe passage out of the area and peace was restored! On learning in what manner this was achieved and implemented, I was unimpressed. To my mind, a few troublemakers, when their little rebellion had failed, had apparently been bussed out of the area under international protection. Meanwhile, the personal safety concerns of some Macedonian citizens had been discounted and therefore nothing had been resolved and the same thing could happen again, anytime. The temporary sticking plaster, of a safe passage to militants, just covered a running sore, leaving it messy and unresolved.

However, for the rest of us, safely back in Kosovo, work resumed and was, as usual, varied and very enjoyable. We did what we had to do to get the job done.

Political Reporting of KTC

As a member of the Public Affairs team, one of my main roles was to write articles for publication. It was as part of that role I was asked to attend the main meeting of the appointed executives trying to establish an interim governing body. This meeting was chaired by SRSG (Special Representative of the Secretary General of the UN). Dr Kouchner who later became the French Foreign Minister in the French Sarkozy Government.

I was sent to sit in on the regular (weekly?) KTC meeting with the aim of writing a report for release to the local media. The experience provided a fascinating insight into the political practices of an emerging State. I found that reporting on the discussions taking place in the Kosovo Transitional Council (KTC) was extremely revealing and I knew that the local population would be equally enthralled by all the goings on. I sat at the side of the room making notes, fascinated by the discussions, trying to ensure that I got it right for the outer audience. It was also quite an experience.

President Rugova was president of the partially recognised Republic of Kosovo 1992-2000 and President of Kosovo from 2002 until his death in 2006. A prominent Kosovo Albanian political leader (LDK party - Democratic League of Kosovo), scholar and writer, much revered. He oversaw the popular struggle for independence, advocating a peaceful resistance to Yugoslavian rule and lobbied USA and EU during the War in Kosovo

SRSG Kouchner on the left and President Ibrahim Rugova on the right with his back to the camera but with his distinctive scarf clearly visible.

President Rugova, as a 'man of the people' never shied away from discussion and debate on the subject of Kosovo.

SRSG had insisted on making sure that the political representatives on the KTC really did represent each section of the community within Kosovo. Some were a little hesitant at first, but then, seeing the benefits of being part of such a Council, agreed to take part.

Chairing the discussion, SRSG was very even handed, and everyone had a chance to make their political point and discuss the requirements of their specific interests.

The KTC met regularly (weekly) and the reports, which promptly appeared in the local paper, detailing the political progress, were well received by the Kosovars. After each meeting, I returned to my office and would write up the report of the discussions. The report was then translated and published in the local paper, Koha Ditore.

As anticipated, this report on Council business was eagerly received by the readers, both in the local community and in the diaspora spread around the world. Everyone was keen to hear how the situation was developing, especially after the significant struggles of the past few years, and they were also eager to see what the future would hold for them and their country.

Working on the various articles, researching and interviewing the contributors, I got to know Kosovo and its people really well, from their villages to their towns. This information gathering involved much enjoyable travel throughout the area and it was good to see the new Kosovo evolving from the ruins.

The Kosovars are a fascinating mix of modernity and tradition, moulding in together to form their unique populace. There was much to admire and respect in their traditions and culture. I visited their homes, shared meals with them and took part in their customs, including attending a few funerals.

One of the most difficult funerals that I attended, in Kosovo, was that of Xhemail Mustafa who was a cousin of my friend Linda with who I stayed. He was gunned down in the entrance to his apartment on 23rd November 2000. Xhemail was also a political adviser to President Rugova and his senior media adviser. A member of the LDK, at the time of his death, he had written an article condemning the criminal violence that had taken place in Kosovo post 1999. This death hit home hard for me.

I did attend other funerals of prominent Kosovars, including that of the Chairman of KEK, with whom I had many good discussions on the subject of electricity provision and maintenance within Kosovo. All of the deaths were difficult.

In the case of all the funerals, I knew the individuals pretty well including their extended families and I wanted to express my support as well as my sincere condolences for their loss. I also found that I could easily relate to the people and understand their genuine strivings for a better future.

As part of a very acceptable routine, my friend Linda and I would often, with a few of her other friends (one friend Besire Domaniku and her husband were owners of a shop in Pristina), would get an overnight bus to Istanbul or Sarajevo. The bus was not that modern and it rattled a bit as it went but it was quite comfortable and took us there overnight in safety. We would get the same bus and crew on their return to Pristina a few days later, laden with their load of parcels and packages from the shops in Istanbul to shops in Pristina.

The border customs guys were used to this traffic and were pretty thorough with their checks, but didn't hold us back for long.

These trips were always enjoyable and I felt quite at home with the company. I became a familiar face among the other passengers and got quite used to the idiosyncrasies of the routine of trade and bus travel between Turkey and Kosovo.

Chapter 19
Outreach Campaign

Working at my desk on one occasion, I answered the telephone and received an unusual call. The voice on the other end introduced itself as that of Prince Hicham El Alaoui and informed me that he was organising a programme of visits all around Kosovo on behalf of SRSG Kouchner.

Hicham went on to explain that this 'Outreach Campaign' was going to require a small team to travel around Kosovo, identifying places and towns that SRSG could visit and hold 'town hall' meetings with the citizens. The team would have to develop a programme, suitable and appropriate, for each location. By mounting this 'Outreach Campaign' it was estimated that these visits would play a very significant and important role in the future development of relationships of all citizens within Kosovo.

SRSG Kouchner was already a much-respected figurehead within Kosovo, based both on his then current role as SRSG, his determination to get all parties involved in the government of Kosovo and on his previous position as leading figure in *Medicin Sans Frontier* which had been very active and relevant within Kosovo, prior to the conflict. He was also on great terms with President Rugova.

The visionary for this 'Outreach Campaign' was that of Prince Hicham who envisaged that SRSG would speak directly to an assembly of the people in their own town halls, discussing with them, their past experiences as well as their future hopes and plans.

At the time of the call, I was not fully aware of all this, other than that there was some scheme being planned to promote the Mission and its objectives.

The caller introduced himself (the name sounded different but not significant) and asked me if I would be part of this team, planning and organising these visits. He explained that a meeting was planned for 12.00 the next day, so would I please go along. The proposition sounded very attractive but a little of a fairy tale, so I said 'yes, I'd love to do that' and sat the phone down, thinking, someone is pulling my leg.

I went back to work and forgot about the call.

The next day, I was at my desk, when I heard footsteps coming down the corridor and looked up to see a gentleman standing in the doorway. He said, 'You didn't come to the meeting today'. I was totally taken aback and embarrassed. I could see at a glance that this guy was serious! I stumbled a bit and told him that I had thought the call was a leg pull at my expense. Fortunately for me, he kindly accepted my explanation and apology, but I did feel an idiot. He then asked me if I wanted to do this task and I quickly accepted. Only an idiot would turn down such a PR jobs and I wasn't that stupid!

As he spoke about the project and his concept, I realised it was a great plan and would give UNMIK a great boost. It had great potential as a morale booster for the people trying to surface from the conflict and distress of the recent past. I felt honoured to be asked to be one of the team to plan and organise this project. I must admit that I studied this guy for a moment or two, as I had never seen him before, and then I realised there were two other sturdy souls standing in the doorway and the penny dropped, this guy was really important and they would be his close protection team!!!

Prince Hicham explained that he worked in the Cabinet of SRSG and this was a pure Public Relations exercise which would boost the profile of the UN Mission to Kosovo. It did sound good and I was looking forward to working on it but I must admit that I was extremely embarrassed as he explained the rational and I realised how I had snubbed a very serious proposal from a very Senior Official!

Prince Hicham El Alaoui was/is a Moroccan prince and closely related to the King of Saudi Arabia and a real gentleman. He was also a great modernising influence back in his own country as well as being a great believer in democracy. In the interests of total disclosure, Hicham explained that he worked for UNMIK for $1 a year and supplied all his own security, accommodation and food, because he believed in what he was doing. Quite remarkable in its own way, and a remarkable individual.

Prince Hicham had decided on his team which consisted of me plus two guys, a French man (Francois) who had served with the military in Kosovo prior to the entry of NATO troops and an American (David) who had arrived with the ceasefire.

The experience of Francois was a great asset as he had travelled extensively around the region, monitoring the ceasefire during his former military associated role.

Almost immediately, our team were given an office and allocated telephone connections. After a brief meeting to draw up some plans for what we had to do to organise this campaign, we were ready to start. The temporary/permanent use of a vehicle was authorised and it was solely for our use. Quite a remarkable fact within a mission where vehicles were a shared asset. Having agreed a rough agenda for our survey trips to towns, we set off on our visits. It was imperative we get started.

Over the preparation and planning period, we often referred to Hicham to ensure that he was *au fait* with what we were doing or maybe had some suggestions for us to follow. It worked out to be a good team effort and during the planning stage, we visited every main town and area within Kosovo.

Our visits followed a rough pattern, first we would telephone the officials at the location and arrange to meet. When we would arrive at our pre-appointed location, we would introduce ourselves and our Mission to the local officials in the towns and discuss with them, our plans for a visit by SRSG Kouchner.

The team worked hard and the local officials were very helpful, regarding the visits as a stamp of authority on their town and their management of it.

These Town Hall meetings were very important to SRSG personally as he wanted to explain and emphasise that the UN were here solely to guide and assist in the transition to a full local government to be manned solely by Kosovars. SRSG felt a huge degree of responsibility to the people of Kosovo and he felt that he understood them and they him, so the dialogue was always two way. An important concept.

These planning meetings were met with much enthusiasm, as SRSG Kouchner, whilst working for '*Medicins Sans Frontieres*' prior to 1999, had been a recognised and appreciated personage by the Kosovo Albanians. He had officially recognised some of their difficult episodes including a particularly unpleasant gas attack by the ruling authorities.

Proposed programmes for the visits were quickly drawn up, taking into account specific local requests. Venues were agreed and inspected for viability of purpose. SRSG insisted on the presence of a wide range of locals in his audience, emphasising that he didn't want to see just local officials, but ordinary citizens. As he said, he wanted to speak to all the people.

Initially, Hicham was consulted after each programme was set up to ensure that they were fully compliant with his overall vision before we proceeded. After a few such checks, he was reassured that we knew what he wanted and that we did not need the detailed thorough checks.

The team also worked on the logistics of the project. This meant that we liaised with all the other international agencies based in the different towns and areas as well as with the local officials and local military. We became adept at organising car convoys or arranging helicopter transport for the Cabinet and Advisers of SRSG who accompanied him on these visits.

There were many times that the visit programme had to be re-arranged due to some last-minute hitch, but for me, this just added to the challenge. We were a busy team. The idea was that all towns within Kosovo were going to be visited by SRSG.

After the first couple of visits, the 'Outreach Campaign' was declared a great success. Much of this success was due to SRSG himself and the rapport and reputation he had built up in Kosovo even before the conflict. As he had envisaged, SRSG was able to discuss with the people directly in the meetings. The whole of Kosovo had suffered and was sensitive, but SRSG connected with them. It even got to the point where he could even touch on the very sensitive subject of 'the disappeared'. The 'disappeared' were those men of all ages, who had been involved in the struggle against the Serbian domination and who had literally disappeared. Probably deceased, but their women folk found this idea difficult to accept.

SRSG dealt with this subject with great understanding and sensitivity, addressing the assembled audience in such a way as to make them feel that he was speaking directly to each individual. Gjakova, in particular, had been an area of much conflict and destruction and there was much distress relating to the many missing. At that Town Hall meeting, when SRSG addressed the audience on the topic of the missing, the silence was deafening. Many of the audience were women who had lost their husbands and sons and held out for the hope that they would return one day. As SRSG spoke on the subject closest to their hearts, many cried quietly and with great dignity. The audience listened and absorbed his words. They knew he was doing this for their sake, helping them come to terms with the reality of their situation.

The address was historic, moving and absolutely what was needed. SRSG Kouchner, in my opinion, was the only person who could have tackled this subject and have his words be received with such respect.

SRSG was making one of his scheduled 'Outreach' visits to Ferizai when we learned that, Javier Solana, Secretary-General of the Council of European Union also known as High Representative for Foreign and Security Policies (CFSP) within the EU, was also joining us for the event. This made the event very high profile. The meeting was well attended. The stadium was packed with assembled Kosovars and there was a great air of anticipation. There was the usual display of local talent, breakdancing, traditional dancing, etc. to honour SRSG and his guest.

The town was historically important, dating back to the days of the Ottoman Empire and the people were determined to put on a good show. SRSG as usual, was well received and Javier Solana was included in the welcome. Solana had flown in especially for the event, co-ordinating his arrival with that of SRSG and landing just outside the stadium. The Turkish forces were the ones working in this area and a Turkish Colonel was on hand to welcome this important guest.

The local participants were very enthusiastic and the timetable over ran somewhat, much to the disappointment of the local Kosovo Army soldiers who had decided to make a presentation to SRSG but were unable to do so as, due to time constraints, their guests had to leave. This over run of the schedule was part and parcel of the welcome and enthusiasm generated for SRSG. However, the local KLA officials were disappointed.

Over the span of the campaign, nearly all towns in Kosovo were visited by SRSG and wherever he went, he received an enthusiastic welcome.

There was one occasion when we organised an Outreach visit to Dragash, near Prizren. The area to be visited was on a plateau high above Prizren and the road up to it had many twists and turns so we decided, due to many considerations and time constraints, SRSG had to be brought in by helicopter. That was easy to organise but on the day of the visit, the cloud base came down and the mist hung over the plateau. There was no way that we could use the helicopter.

Our team had already travelled up to Dragash, with the vehicles. We were ready to ferry the Boss around. When we saw the low cloud base and heard the official weather verdict, the first thought was that the visit would have to be abandoned.

I thought of the preparations that the people of Dragash had made and I could see the awful disappointment on their faces if the visit did not happen. I couldn't let this happen. Plan B—which didn't exist—had to make an appearance.

Fortunately, we had seven or eight vehicles at our disposal on the site, so we called down to Prizren to talk to the German base command near the town and ask for a weather check. This was quickly followed by a request for their help. We were assured that there was no mist or fog down at their LZ and they agreed to assist us and allow the helicopter carrying SRSG to land on their base. Now all we had to do was organise a helicopter. This was done and the programme for the visit was quickly reorganised to allow for the delay. We just had to transport the Boss from the LZ on the base up to the plateau and Dragash.

The only way to get SRSG and his entourage up the hill was to take our vehicles down the hill to meet the helicopter. Shades of the 'Grand Old Duke of York' came to mind.

It was quite a drive down the hill for the convoy of cars. The road was not ideal for fast moving cars. There were too many twists and turns, with steep sided drops on the steep slopes.

But we (the drivers were excellent) made it, arriving at the helipad just minutes before the helicopter carrying SRSG.

I can say, from the relieved smile on his face, that SRSG was pleased and relieved to see us waiting for him. Nadia Youness, our Public Relations chief accompanying SRSG was also much relieved, going by her smiling expression. The security detail from Pristina arrived by road, just as the helicopter landed. Phew!

We picked up SRSG and, with the rest of his entourage, in convoy, we started the drive back up the hill to Dragash.

It was a Saturday and market day in Prizren and, passing the market stalls along the side of the road, progress was slow due to the people milling around the stall. The usual market scene. Then one of the traders recognised SRSG Kouchner and the whole market was alerted. They cheered and clapped, chanting 'Kouchneri, Kouchneri'. It was a very emotional drive.

SRSG was amazed and delighted at his reception as he smiled and waved.

He hadn't realised that he was such a celebrity, but deservedly so in the people's opinions. Kosovars genuinely loved him.

The visit to Dragash was also important as these people sometimes felt a bit isolated and apart from the rest of Kosovo and it was very important that they felt included in SRSG's plans. In any event, the visit was a great success, working out pretty much as planned. The important thing was that everyone had a good day and difficulties making it happen were forgotten.

We often witnessed demonstrations of the regard Kosovars had for SRSG. On occasion, when he went out for dinner in the evening, especially after a tough day, the whole of his Cabinet was invited along, much to the delight of the restaurant owner chosen on that day.

SRSG and his staff (including me from time to time) walked down the street to whatever restaurant was selected for that night. If SRSG had to cross the street (followed by his staff), without hesitation, the traffic would come to a stop blasting their horns. Mr. Kouchner would cross the street waving to the cars and they hollered back. The adulation and affection were so very evident but then SRSG did respect the Kosovars and their struggles over the past. It was a two-way street.

I feel that I was privileged to have worked in the Cabinet of SRSG Kouchner during this period and to be part of his entourage. Working for Prince Hicham El Alaoui, a Muslim prince from Morocco who sincerely believed in freedom, charity and democracy was another privilege. Hicham worked for the UN Democracy programme paying all his own expenses. His bodyguards were his own hirings and he evidently commanded their respect. A favoured past time for Hicham was playing football with his bodyguards. It was fun for all. On one occasion, Hicham organised a visit by his uncle the Sheik, who had come to view some of the educational facilities that he had funded. The Outreach team were included among those honoured guests welcomed into the Sheik's tent. We were not fully aware of whys and wherefores of these things and Hicham had to explain that it really was a great honour to be invited into the tent and included with the other important guests (local dignitaries) who were being welcomes by the Sheik.

During the reception, as was customary, a large traditional open fronted Bedouin type tent was erected for the Sheik and his party in which they entertained all the important people.

Our Outreach team had assisted, in a small way, in the organisation of the event and Hicham made a point of coming over to us and inviting us, on behalf of the Shah, to join the dignitaries in this very traditional way.

It was a magnificent tent and its occupants were all dressed in their traditional regalia. They all looked magnificent, especially from such close quarters, especially here in Kosovo. This scene made me think of the desert and expanses of sand.

The tent was furnished with very luxurious rugs strewn around and the display of food on the low tables was quite splendid. The bowls and dishes holding the food gleamed richly in their opulence. The rich display of the food appeared to be vying with the richly ornate outfits and tent dressings.

When we entered the tent, the grandeur, the atmosphere and the delicious aromas of the food enclosed us with their ambiance and splendour. I felt so honoured to be perceived as important enough to be considered as a guest.

That was the measure of this guy, Hicham was always considerate. In Pristina where he lived, he was also known for his fondness for football too and would often play with the kids in the street outside his house. The game could happen anytime anywhere, whenever he had a few minutes to spare, and the kids had a football. If he saw kids playing football in the street anywhere and he had a few minutes to spare, he just couldn't resist joining them.

A sincere and dedicated democrat, well-educated having studied in the Sorbonne in Paris and graduated from Princetown. He was a very genuine individual. I admired his ideas and achieved great satisfaction working for him. It was a thoroughly great experience on all counts.

On a daily basis, the complete Public Information team, made up of film crews, radio presenters and officials working on PR related projects, met in the office of the Head of Public Affairs, Nadia Youness. Prior to coming to Kosovo, Nadia had worked in the Cabinet of the Secretary General of the UN in New York. She was a great boss. She was later blown up in her office whilst working for the UN in Iraq, near the beginning of that mission. We all felt her loss very keenly and held our own Memorial Service in Pristina.

Chapter 20
European Union

As the winter of 2000 approached, I made plans to return home. I knew what a winter in Kosovo was like and I didn't fancy spending another one in those conditions.

Just as I was making my plans to depart, an acquaintance of mine in the Public Affairs department asked me to assist him when he was attending a radio interview with his boss. He explained that he was leaving the mission soon and his associate was a lady named Joan who was the Chief of the EU Public Utilities Sector, who was nervous as this was her first radio interview in Kosovo and, he felt, that she might appreciate the presence of another female. Both of our experiences of radio interviews were limited but he felt that, based on the additional experience that I had gained during the 'Outreach Campaign', I would be able to guide them through any awkward moments as the programme was going out live.

It was a Saturday morning job and everything went well during the interview, the programme went out live and afterward, we went our separate ways.

This incident was apparently the catalyst for what came next. A few days later, I was literally walking down the back stairs of Government Building (UN headquarters in Pristina) when I met Joan, the lady interviewed on the radio. We greeted each other and she asked if I was going to join her team in the Public Utilities Sector. As I was not aware of any such approach, I said that I wasn't and went on my way.

Shortly after this, the approach was made and after some negotiation, I agreed to work as Spokesperson for the Public Utilities Sector dealing with Electricity, Water and Waste issues.

In the interests of clarity, UNMIK had been divided into four Pillars or sectors. They were:

- Pillar I: Police and Justice (United Nations-led)
- Pillar II: Civil Administration (United Nations-led)
- Pillar III: Democratisation and Institutional Building (led by the Organisation for Security and Cooperation in Europe)
- Pillar IV: Reconstruction and Economy (EU-led)

So, effectively, I was moving to Pillar IV but remaining within the UN Administrative Mission to Kosovo. Spokesperson for the Public Utilities, I also later became Deputy Spokesperson for the EU mission.

Working in the PUD (Public Utilities) was much the same as in the UN, but with smaller numbers of people. Everyone was very welcoming and I soon settled in. The first job I had was to write the weekly report and, as I knew little about the department, the report required me to do a lot of research on departmental activities. This meant quickly talking to a wide range of people to get the facts. They were happy to help, though I did get a few bum steers.

The big item on the agenda was the difficulties experienced with the electricity supply. The Kosovo Electrical Corporation (Korporata Energjetike e Kosoves) had been in operation since the 1960s. There were two plants, Plant A was commissioned in 1962 and Plant B in 1983. Prior to the conflict, units A and B supplied the needs of Kosovo but with a lot of support from the Serbian Electrical supply (EPS). The perceived predominance that the Serbian authorities had over Kosovo affairs and operations was evident in this set up, with dependence on Serbia. This explained why there was sparse attention paid to maintaining the energy setup within Kosovo. Everything was reliant on Serbian input and engineering superiority. However, despite this approach, in the past, many Albanian senior engineers had been educated and trained in Belgrade.

The, then (2000) current, situation, within Kosovo, with electricity provision was very precarious. There were many outages of power and citizens had to resort to using small generators for their homes in order to have electricity for essentials like cooking and minimal heating. In areas where people lived, when the electricity failed, there immediately arose the heavy drone of generators with a hint of a smell of kerosene.

Sometimes, the outages ran for extended periods, often days, and the general population, including the internationals, were fed up and demanding a better service, especially now that the international organisations with their deep pockets, were here.

One big problem existed though, most of the people in Kosovo weren't able to pay for their electricity and the jobs were few. Some diligent souls did pay but they were very much in the minority. Most families within Kosovo had close relatives (usually sons or brothers) working overseas and they would send monies back home to support the family 'back home'.

Electricity was to be one of the main issues during my time in the EU.

There were many important people who wanted to visit the two generating plants (A and B) at Obilic. Some visitors were energy experts, others visiting were politicians. All visitors wanted to see for themselves the existing conditions at the plants and if there was any progress in getting the plants up and running efficiently or even constantly. There was a large degree of scepticism among most people in Kosovo, at that time that the generators could not be in 'that' bad of a condition'

All visitors were welcome. The generation of electricity was a huge issue and presented many great difficulties. It wasn't easy to understand the problems until you saw the age of the generators, their condition and the fact that the generators were usually in the midst of a repair to some part or other. It was sixties technology, huge heavy boilers and bulky parts, poorly maintained over the years, that had just run out of their expected lifespan. It was simple really, to all intents and purposes, they were done.

After familiarising myself with the issues relating to generating electricity and the necessary running repairs needed, I started to help escort some of the many visitors around the generator plants, Plants 'A' and Plant 'B'. I gave many briefings on the history of the plants and their daily generating output.

Many other visits were also conducted by plant engineers who could get into deep engineering detail. The aim of the chiefs was to garner support of some kind, any kind, for their objective of trying to supply Kosovo with regular and continuous electricity. In such situations, political wherewithal and tacit support, can rescue many a failing enterprise.

Visiting the plants for the first time though, I was struck by the enormity of the generators and the fact that their inner working was, obviously carefully, laid out on the floor. The insides of the machines gaped blankly out at me.

On enquiring, I was usually told that the necessary parts were on order from the supplier and we had to wait until the parts arrived. This seemed to be an ongoing state of affairs as the working parts were very much worn and constantly needed to be replaced. I was also told that, that as the generators in the 'A' plant had been commissioned at the beginning of the 60s, that these parts were difficult to resource and deliveries would therefore take longer. The 'B' plant, under the supervision of German engineers, seemed to be little more efficient, but it too had difficulties. Nothing was working well.

The picture for future electricity generating efficiency wasn't great. But it was what it was. Meanwhile, the customers and users were refusing to pay for the energy they consumed. Sometimes the users didn't have the means to pay for their electric consumption, and you can't get blood out of a stone, as we say in Ulster. It was not a good situation and I was the newly appointed spokesperson for the PUB.

It was at about this point that the local Kosovar spokesperson for Kosovo Electric (KEK) called me and asked for some support when dealing with a group of individual energy users who happened to be Serbian and living in a small area within Pristina. Fadil was a Kosovo Albanian and felt that he needed an international mediator to allow him to ask them for payment for their electricity usage and/or hopefully negotiate terms of payment. He knew the situation, having been here throughout, but firmly believed that the point had to be made, despite not holding out any hope for money.

I agreed to act as mediator as he obviously needed support in this new Kosovo and I went along to the meeting he had arranged. Fadil briefed me thoroughly on the circumstances surrounding the meeting and I could understand his point of view but I also felt that he was on a mission to nothing as these ethnic Serbians didn't have any source of income and I told him so. These people had to keep a low profile from the surrounding Kosovars and there weren't any jobs for them. Where then would they get any money to pay for electric, but he had to make a point. I went along to the meeting and Fadil introduced me and stated his case.

There was a good attendance and we were met with polite attention but no answers. These people couldn't pay. They had no money or any way of making money. The finances weren't available. The difficulties of the situation were now underlined.

It was a difficult situation and you could see the sense of defeat and despair in the eyes of everyone present. The non-response was what Fadil expected but he had hoped for more positive.

However, the role of the EU in Kosovo was that of reconstruction and economic development and we had to think of something; we had to make this situation work.

There were many other areas that required EU involvement such as in general administration. The EU had established their Regional Administrators in each region or sector as agreed under the UN reorganisation agenda. These regions had many different issues, some common to other areas, others specific to their area, all requiring some inspired solutions. In order to get some coherence between regions, meetings were held at regular intervals, usually weekly, and the representatives updated each other on the progress in their areas.

Over all of this was the issue of needing a regular and constant supply of electricity. This was the main stumbling block to reconstruction and economic revival. In an effort to support this aim DFID, the financial arm of the UK Foreign Affairs department, had brought in approximately 40 large generators to be distributed throughout Kosovo. It was the best they could do at this time. A few years later, with improved supplies of energy, these large distinctive yellow generators were being sold off by certain individuals who no longer needed them. But the original purchase made by DFID had been essential in that an effort had to be made to support areas of the economy which was trying to regenerate itself.

Chapter 21
Waste Company Strike in Pristina

While in the PUD, I also turned my attention to include the issues in the waste sector. This sector had improved drastically from its difficult beginnings in 1999 when individuals with tractor and trailer had travelled the streets picking up the plastic bags of rubbish lying in piles near homes. Prior to the conflict and the Serbian withdrawal, there had been the usual garbage disposal trucks working throughout Kosovo. When the Serbian population had to leave in a hurry in 1999, they used any mode of transport that was available to them to transport their belongings, including the garbage trucks.

When Milosevic had surrendered control to the international community, the situation was clear for the Serbs. As far as I could find out, any previous collection truck, or indeed, pretty much anything that had an engine, had been commandeered by the departing people as they made their way out of Kosovo and into Serbia. The fleeing Serbs made a sorry sight as they made their shambolic, and sad, departure. They had to take as much of their belongings as possible as they knew that they would not get back to live in Kosovo.

It was because of this lack of appropriate vehicles that the men used tractors and trailers to collect rubbish in the early days of 1999. For me, the penny had eventually dropped!

In order to establish a reliable and effective waste sector, the EU brought in experts in planning and waste management plus essential supplies of equipment, including modern garbage collection trucks and machinery for use on the actual depository/garbage collection depots.

The EU recruited range of experts in the Waste Sector were busy organising the depots in the various towns, planning collection routes and ensuring that they had adequate machinery and collection trucks. This equipment brought the sector up to a good standard and a collection routine was quickly established under the guidance of these experts.

Pristina, the capital, seemed to be the exception. Prior to my employment in the EU, I had been aware that there were difficulties in Pristina with the waste company frequently going on strike. There didn't appear to be any resolution to the difficulties and the international experts seemed to be at a loss as to how to achieve a regular, uninterrupted service.

In mid-2001, another strike had been called in Pristina. I became aware of the strike when a marquee was erected in the central square, outside the (Korporata Energjet e Kosoves) KEK electricity company building HQ. The strikers were sheltering from the increasing heat, reclining underneath the large canopy. The atmosphere was relaxed and passing citizens were handing over contributions of food etc. It seemed to me that due to their past recent history, the public had a lot of sympathy for the strikers, believing that they were hard done by, same as the perception held whilst under Serb rule. Many of the people making the contributions to the strikers were related to them in some in some way. There were many extended families in Kosovo, and in any smallish country, they all knew each other.

On one occasion, as I was passing the square, I noticed that they had the services of a barber and I was informed that this man was volunteering his service for free. None of the authorities were paying much attention to the strikers. The protest was a peaceful one, but a very visible one, and it went on for a few days before the protest changed course, aiming for a more effective delivery, and it was at this juncture that the canopy and strikers disappeared from the square.

The strikers had retired to the main landfill depot on the outskirts of town. I found this out when the Local Waste Manager, a Kosovar Albania, came into my office and asked for help with the public perception of the strike. The strike was continuing, but not in such public view as before but with much more militancy out at their depot. Meeting were being held with all parties but listening to all points of view was not resolving anything. Negotiations were getting nowhere and the strike just continued and the refuse in Pristina was just piled up in the streets.

Workers were not being paid but extended families went out of their way to help, mainly with gifts of food as well as small financial support. The strikers reported each day to the depot and held meetings. There was one or two drivers who tried to work on but the strikers were belligerent and refused to let them break the strike line and one strike breaker was even arrested by the local police. On hearing this news, and understanding the close nature of local families, I immediately understood the delicacy of the situation. I alerted another international, working with the police. He was equally alarmed by the developments and used his relevant position to gain the speedy release of the imprisoned strike breaker, who had been roughed up a bit, but not seriously.

The general situation within the Pristina Waste Sector was not good. The vehicles that the EU had contributed to the Waste Company were held by the strikers in their compound behind a high wire fence. As a security measure, the strikers were manning the site 24x7, taking it in turns to guard the entrance. It was an efficient and effective strategy.

Many high-level discussions were held between the strikers and senior politicians within the EU plus other associated agencies. Despite all the talks, there didn't appear to be any solution, the strikers were determined to continue with their action. It was not totally clear where the problem lay or what they wanted, but the strike continued. I attended a few discussions and the strikers were very strong in their resolve to continue the strike.

It was at this point that the EU decided to act and take some counter measures. Approaches were made to different sectors to try and work out a solution, but no real way out could be found. No one wanted to confront the strikers, the situation was a delicate one, fraught with difficulties but not solutions. The whole situation was balanced on the knife edge of democratic principles and freedom of expression. In the emergent democratic state of Kosovo, this situation, the actions and reactions, were establishing precedents for the future.

Trying to find a way through the difficulties and potential solutions was not easy. I was facing the reluctance of any agency to support any positive action by the PUD or to get involved in any meaningful way that would disrupt the strike. The freedom to strike was sacrosanct. This strike action by the Waste Company though had developed into a regular habit, with many different reasons being named by the strikers. As far as I could tell, the only ones to suffer were the general population of Pristina.

The political advisers were very much involved and many views were put forward. The Ambassador responsible for this area of the economy decided to pay a visit to the site and discuss directly with the strikers. I was a member of that party.

On the day, the word had leaked out as both sides of the road to the dump site were lined with people. Walking down that road was a bit intimidating as we were met with much abuse and, strikingly to me, even one international security policeman, was shouting at us 'to observe the strikers human rights'. I don't know what he knew about the background to this scenario but it was inappropriate. Obviously never being concerned with the fact that the population of the capital Pristina was being held to ransom as was the EU and the UN! Incredible thought process.

We, the EU, were trying to assist in the rebuilding of Kosovo and trying to uphold the rule of law. Rubbish was starting to pile up in the streets of the capital and the environmentally designed disposal schemes, introduced by international experts and, at this stage, half constructed, were lying abandoned. This was not the time or place for international hecklers. I must admit I stepped over to this guy and we had a few words. He didn't expect that and looked surprised but stopped his heckling. I turned away and joined the others from the EU.

The group of politicians and their advisers continued on to the barrier at the depot.

During the meeting, now confrontation, thanks to the crowd lining the route, the Ambassador tried his best to discuss with the strikers but, as he wasn't giving them pots of cash, there was no agreement. The strikers, although very polite, were adamant that they were staying where they were, occupying the site and refusing to work.

We had to think of something. The feeling was that the situation had to be resolved in some way.

Speaking to some people in the transport sector, I discovered that the only neutral agency was the UN transport contingent based a little way outside town. Possibly they could help. The latest contingent of the UN Transport Company was just arriving in Kosovo.

The replacement Transport Troop were from Ireland and they were just settling into their new abode, preparing to carry out their role to look after the heavy vehicles deployed in Kosovo. As UN they were totally neutral and would act only in accordance with the rule of law and with military approval and discipline.

Our hopes for support got a little boost. Subsequent tentative enquiries were not totally demolished altogether. There might be some way to resolve this issue.

Discussions were held with the Commandant who, after questioning me in great detail on the feasibility of the plan, appeared to be satisfied that all avenues had been covered. The request for support was justified as we only wanted to retrieve EU supplied heavy plant equipment that was intended to support an economic recovery. After considering our plans and reviewing the situation, the Commandant then requested permission from the NATO appointed General to use these UN forces in this rescue mission. These EU supplied garbage trucks were an essential for the waste collection programme. After some discussion within the NATO and the UN, permission was granted and the action could go ahead, depending on a final decision by the EU.

As no agreement or way forward had been achieved during the meeting at the dump site, the EU reluctantly made the decision to go ahead with the plan formulated to retrieve the dump trucks languishing on the site.

The Irish Army Transport Troop were alerted as well as was a company of the international riot police force based in Mitrovice. Permission was again sought and granted by the General in charge of the UN International forces and within hours the operation was made ready. I was part of the team that were going in and we congregated at a UN base outside Pristina. We were nervous.

The convoy of low loaders, drivers and various tow vehicles set off in the early hours of the morning. It was all a little surreal in the grey light as we trundled along the road in convoy. I was dressed up in camouflage gear and supplied with a video recorder to record all details of the operation.

Assembling at a point some short way from the dump site, we were joined by the Indian Army riot troops from Mitrovice. The troops formed up and started the slow walk forward. There wasn't that many of them but they were impressive. Quiet, except for their boots hitting the road in unison, they went forward steadily.

No one was expecting us at this time, there was no guard or shouting citizen.

As a group we arrived at the locked barrier and requested admittance. The strikers were all asleep and after a few moments of bleary-eyed shock, we were allowed forward to collect the EU trucks parked behind the wire fence.

The Indian police squad stepped back, seeing that their services were not required.

On request, bunches of keys were reluctantly handed over and, needless to say, they didn't fit the vehicles. No worries; we had expected that development. We didn't have replica keys but we had our ways of starting the vehicles and

242

moving them onto the low loaders where necessary or filling up with fuel in order to get them moving. Yes, we had even thought of the fact that the vehicles might be low on fuel.

The Irish Army drivers were magnificent, quietly moving around the vehicles checking for what was needed and getting it organised. Great guys. Experts at working with vehicles and reluctant engines, in no time at all, the EU vehicles were heading out of the gates, under the control of the Irish Army Transport Troop.

The action was over in a short time and we left, leaving behind a few, by now, wide awake strikers standing at the gates. The entire action was filmed by myself and the operation was completed using only Internationals, thus protecting local staff. Interpretation was not required.

Next morning, when I arrived at my office, the media crews were waiting for me. They were lined up in the corridor outside my office, armed with accusations of abuse by the Internationals and wanting comments. I explained that I had the tape and that all was done in accordance with the Rule of Law. The reporters melted away.

During the retrieval process, a high fence around the compound had been demolished but seeing as the EU had supplied it, they would replace it. The important thing was that the trucks had been recovered and collection of waste would resume.

By morning, a local waste management team were already on the dump site going over the office records. This management team actually discovered a couple of nefarious moves that had been hidden by the previous site team and when that was brought into the open, the debate died a death.

The workers decided that it was best to have a job and they all went back to work. Strike over.

After the Strike

In the aftermath of this turmoil, I was invited to have a meal with the family of the local manager of the Pristina Waste Company (Abid) who had tried so hard to negotiate a settlement with the strikers. I considered this to be a great honour and was delighted to accept. My friend, Linda, advised me of the protocol and she came along to act as interpreter.

The family were very welcoming and indicated that I should sit in a place of honour in their home. The food was lovely, traditional Albanian food that I enjoyed, and the evening passed off very pleasantly. A lovely social occasion.

As I was leaving their home and driving out of the compound, I noticed that one of the workers that I recognised from the waste company was patrolling along the top of the walls of the compound with an AK-47 slung over his shoulder. On asking, I was told that they had to do this as a security precaution during my visit as there had been threats and troubles made previously to Abid. It might have been solely for my benefit or it might have been standard procedure but, in that moment, I felt humbled at the thought of how they might have had to do battle, maybe to protect me, or maybe on their own account. Things were not always as they seemed.

Shortly after the waste strike was settled, Abid, the local manager, asked me if I could help him do something about the amount of white plastic bags that were littering the landscape. Every purchase made in the shops was placed in a white plastic bag. They were plentiful and easily escaped. In order to deal with the issue, he needed to request additional funding and therefore needed something on paper to substantiate his case. The white plastic bags were an eyesore, they were everywhere. These bags were made of very thin plastic and not strong, but when discarded, and placed in the rubbish bins they had a tendency to blow away and ended up flapping in all sorts of unusual places.

Often in fields by the side of the road, there would be 10-20 waving in the breeze. So action to stop this happening was most welcome. I was only too pleased to help and wrote up a proposal. He supplied the brief outline of his plan to deal with the bags and he went out and took the photographs. Between us, we compiled a good argument for the extra funding.

As part of the role during my time with PUD, I also got to know the Water Management Company of Battlava and its manager, Causch Berisha. A very experienced and efficient manager, Causch ensured that the water supply in Pristina and elsewhere was fit for consumption. Supplies for chlorination were always difficult to maintain for Kosovo for some reason but Causch knew the ropes and made sure that supplies for Kosovo, especially for Pristina, the capital were maintained at correct levels.

During my time in the PUD, I was also aware that from time to time, there was some concerns over the water levels of the reservoir, Battlava Lake, the reservoir for Pristina region. However that was not something within our control being dependant on prevailing weather conditions. Simply if there hadn't been enough snow or rain, then the water levels dropped but the public demand for water remained the same. I could only assist when water became scarce and the public had to be alerted to conserve usage. Everything else seemed to run smoothly under this manager, who was also a lovely gentleman.

Battlava Lake was quite a tourist spot with a restaurant and coffee bar. Particularly on a Sunday afternoon, Linda and I would often take the bus out to the lake and spend a couple of hours sitting out there, drinking coffee and chatting. On one particular occasion, sometime in the summer of 2000, when we were trying to get back home, we hopped on the bus. It looked a bit battered but that was normal and we didn't think anything of it. However, along the road, the bus stopped and the driver and his helper got out and got the petrol can out. Apparently, there was a hole in the petrol tank and so they had to refill it. They were definitely demonstrating the 'make the best of it' approach. More power to them.

A hole in the petrol tank so we needed a refuelling stop on the way home

Prior to 1999, the monetary policy in Kosovo was linked to the Serbian dinar and inflation was rampant. After the UN and the EU arrived in Kosovo, the decision was made to transfer to using the deutschmark. Therefore in 2002, it was a natural process to transfer to the new currency of the EURO. It replaced the deutschmark and was in a ratio of 2:1, deutschmark to euro. I was appointed manager of the large PR campaign which was established. In the event, the introduction of the Euro passed off smoothly but with one big difference. The cost of living doubled virtually overnight. It was quite a dramatic increase and not one that had been taken into consideration by all accounts, especially by the Kosovars. Their personal budgets were tight enough as it was, but they swallowed hard and got on with living. This was all part of the path to Kosovo becoming part of Europe.

As the EU continued their reconstruction plan and integration of the population, they improved the physical connection via a train service, available between the Serb enclaves and Serbia to the north. It wasn't that easy and again, railway experts were brought in to ensure that this happened.

There were many meetings and much deliberation over this event as neither Serbia nor the enclaves in Kosovo were part of the euro zone. This meant that the Serbian people couldn't purchase products brought into Kosovo as they only had the dinars.

All these seemingly endless issues had to be considered, but the people living in the enclaves needed to have some freedom to get out and about. It just wasn't always safe for them to do so within the wider Kosovo. Those in the enclaves were also keen to visit their friends and relatives in Serbia, some had not been able to meet up for some time. So, it was very important that these difficulties had to be resolved. On their side, the Serbs in Kosovo were keen to avail themselves of this protected train service and it meant that travellers from Serbia could come south to see their relatives and friends. Thus it was that this EU sponsored service was much appreciated.

Because of the work I had done with the Irish Transport soldiers, during the Waste Company strike in Pristina, when their President came over for a visit, I was invited along for the display and I was presented to President Mary Robinson a dedicated advocate for Human Rights who later became the United Nations High Commissioner for Human Rights. I was also introduced to her successor, President Mary McAleese (who actually came from the Belfast in Northern Ireland), when she made her visit to the troops. Again, I count both occasions as a privilege and an honour.

KEK

In July 1999, when NATO troops viewed the situation at the Power Plants in Obilic they felt a total sense of despair—the place was a mess! Many of the units had been cannibalised, the acrid taste of ash dust filled the throat, making it difficult to swallow. There was so much dust in the generating hall of the A Plant that it was impossible to see the full length of the hall. There were more broken windows than whole ones and the engineers of NATO forces shook their heads— this plant would never work—it was impossible. Other sources had to be found to provide electricity for Kosovo.

However, the returning Kosovars did not agree—'this will work'; 'we will make it work'—they said.

Well, with the help of some specialist engineers from among the NATO troops, they eventually got it started—one painful start after another. Thousands of litres of diesel were used with little effect—a contractor was brought in—large quantities of diesel and mazut was brought through the border points. Only with the help of KFOR troops was this achieved—and still the units did not remain in generation. What was the problem—the units were old; they had been sadly neglected and they needed to be stripped down and thoroughly overhauled—but there was no time—winter was fast approaching and Kosovo needed electricity—and so was the Kosovo power situation created.

A hopeless task built on a memory of the past that like all memories is always better when viewed from the present.

Since then, over 400 million euro has been spent on much needed repairs to the generating plants and the mines. Included in this amount, 20 million euro had to be spent on the transmission system, damaged during the conflict but the rest has been spent replacing parts, cleaning and overhauling the units trying to make them serviceable. This may seem a lot of money to be invested in a system but it is calculated that a unit of this size and type requires 50 million euros to be spent on it in maintenance every year in order to keep the unit in good operating condition and if you consider that there has been no maintenance carried out on these units for about 15 years—the total maintenance bill runs in around 750 million euro. Working on this calculation, at this point, we have only reached slightly over half of what should have been spent on the units in order to keep them operating at a reasonable standard.

There was much work needed on the transmission system—Kosovo was not a standalone unit but part of the larger Yugoslav system and the connections to that system had suffered as a result of NATO bombing. These—connections had to be repaired before any of the much-needed electricity could be imported from outside of Kosovo. Also we have to take into consideration that the cables were 20 years old and had deteriorated quite considerably and therefore could not carry the load (even when the links had been reconnected). Much of the cabling had to be replaced.

The units are powered by lignite, extracted from the mines and when work was restarted in 1999 it was discovered that two of the huge excavators had not worked for some time and were actually covered by the overburden (topsoil) which then had to be removed—a painfully slow process. Some of the other excavators were still working but the parts that had been repaired and replaced had been done so by poor quality workmanship/spare parts and broke down very quickly once the machinery was started up again. It is amazing how expensive these nuts and bolts are and how long they take to be delivered—meanwhile the unit is inoperable.

The story repeated itself time and again, throughout the mines and the generating plants. Ash had to be removed from around the generators and broken windows replaced in the generating hall.

Deterioration of the working parts of the generators had taken place plus the walls of the boilers were paper thin. The generators could be started but could not be brought up to high pressure as the boilers leaked and threatened to explode—new ones take about one year to be ordered and brought into Kosovo—meanwhile, the unit cannot run without a boiler.

After the lightning strike and fire in July 2001, the rehabilitation programme suffered a serious setback and alternative, more immediate, programmes had to be embarked on in order to provide some electricity for the winter of 2002/3. This extra work was supplemented by additional 20 million euro of funds to be used solely for imports over the winter. Only one of the units in the **B** plant was repaired with the remaining unit to be repaired during the summer of 2003. However due to time constraints during the summer, not all the work had been completed on the first of the **B** units and it would have to be taken out of service in July in order to complete the repairs required.

Working in conjunction with this effort on the **B** plant, additional works were carried out on the **A** units to strengthen them and make them more sustainable. They were in a delicate state of reliability and could not be relied upon to work for long periods of time without breaking down. The fact that the units were old—the **A** units are over 30 years old and the **B** units over 20 years—that they have been seriously neglected with poor maintenance—all contributes to the fact that the supply of electricity in Kosovo still needed a substantial amount of funding for the essential repairs and until that basic work was completed, sometime in the future, (dates and time lines had been established before and none had been fulfilled so none could be given) Simple fact was that Kosovo would not be able to maintain a reliable supply of domestically generated power supplies.

The only hope of maintaining a reliable and sustainable supply of electricity was to supplement the domestic supply with a supply of imports. Imports have to be paid for and the only way that KEK could pay for those is if the consumers pay KEK for the electricity that they use so that the company, can in turn, pay for the imports that are needed. The contracts already in place would improve the standard of the units and by restructuring the company, focusing on the main role of providing power and thus reducing overall expenditure, it was anticipated that the situation would gradually improve but no estimates could be made for a guaranteed supply until a new power plant was established. However it was guaranteed that a sustainable and reliable power supply would require a lot of money and would take years to be constructed—once that money was made available.

However, the main focus of my effort was on KEK and the supply of electricity. I had to keep track of the daily generation of energy and of any repairs that were being worked on. It was on these issues that most questions were raised by the media at the daily press conferences.

A continuous supply of electricity was difficult to achieve given the current state of repair and operation of the generating units. The International experts were in agreement that, in order to try and achieve a continuous energy supply, the only way would be to enlist support from the Serbian Electric Company in Belgrade.

Obviously, the political turmoil and separation had stopped all of this cooperation but the specialist engineers were still in place, in their now separate entities, but surely the former relationships could well be re-established. All that was required was an approach by the current authorities in Kosovo and with a negotiated payment, this partnership could be re-established.

The Serbian units were running well and had the capacity to support the demands of Kosovo, after all, this had been the plan prior to the breakup of

Kosovo. The EU agreed with this new planned cooperation and also agreed to fund a negotiated settlement.

Under EU oversight, negotiations were established between KEK and their opposite numbers in Belgrade and a deal was quickly struck.

Prior to the conflict, any additional supplies had been automatically forwarded from the electrical company in Serbia. The overall plan was that the aging Kosovo generating plant would be run down and replaced by their more modern systems. At that time, Kosovo was regarded as an integral part of Serbia and the additional energy did not require payment. Neither were they charged for transmitting the electricity over the distribution network. It was an accepted fact that Kosovo was part of Serbia. This had obviously changed since the end of the conflict.

As the generators in Kosovo were in pretty poor condition with many parts needing replaced and this need for additional energy being a fairly constant one, this would work out to be pretty expensive. However, the need was there so the energy had to be paid for.

As part of my repertoire of knowledge, I had to keep myself informed of all of this and, as luck in the shape of my friend Linda would have it, a great acquaintance of hers, Ramiz, was one of the engineers specialising in the electrical consumer demands required to keep Kosovo operating with a decent energy supply. Ramiz, due to the position I held and my need for relevant information, was happy to brief me on the methodology, needs and requirements for the transfer of the power. In the main control room, I was able to see the large banks of knobs and controls that monitored the demand and supply of the energy, as it happened.

These complete and complex briefings proved to be an invaluable source of information to me. I was also able to go and see him at work in KEK and thus get to understand in better detail all the exchanges, friendships and experiences of this engineering brotherhood. Serbian or Albanian, they had been trained together, all been colleagues in the past and there was mutual respect, one engineer to another. This inside view and insight into such a complex and specialised engineering capability was invaluable and I really appreciate their support and understanding of the need for this international to be aware of the details and needs required. It was heartening for the future prospects of the new Kosovo.

KEK, as an organisation, was large. There were approximately 10,000 people working within the entire organisation. The operation ranged from the mining of the coal in the open cast (ground level) coalmine to the final product of energy being delivered to the citizens. It was an enormous undertaking and completed within Kosovo. I had never walked a coalfield before and never been anywhere near such large operating machinery. I was fairly familiar looking down at a car engine, I had been close to aeroplane engines and was impressed with the huge blades of rotors on helicopters but these giants were huge. Out in the coalmine, the huge revolving excavator wheels were as high as houses. I was dwarfed by it all, a small particle in this vast dirty, earthy and gritty coal mine.

I had many conducted visits to the coalfield, getting to know and appreciate what I was representing and speaking about. It was quite an education. This farmer's granddaughter from Ulster had stepped into this unknown world and had a lot to learn. My grandfather had always said that God had given us all our seven (later thinking determines about nine) senses plus a brain and all we had to do was to use them, otherwise we could lose them. We just had to give of our best every day and we could then rest content at night. It is true.

The local Kosovars working in the mine were nonchalant and completed their roles with a kind of pride, they were working for their state of Kosovo, no longer subservient to the all-encompassing arms of a Serbia having shaken off the shackles. The EU and the International community were here and there was no looking back.

The enormous machinery towered above us as we made our rounds of the open cast mine (1999)

My escorts, including the boss, Fadil Ismaili (leading, me third from left) with senior managers, during an inspection of the work (1999).

General view of the coalfield and the machinery below

One small section of a cog wheel dwarfing a workman. He was nonchalant; I was impressed.

Workers were very much dwarfed by the machinery they worked on in the coalmine. The misty conditions were normal as the seams of coal combust (smoulder and burn) constantly

Being a large Corporation, KEK had its own spokesperson, Human Resources branch and ran its own internal newspaper. The KEK newspaper was published locally and contained updates on all the many branches within its control.

The articles were accompanied by photographs of managers sitting at meeting and, although, it was a trifle old-fashioned in its way, it was a great update for all workers. Fadil, the KEK spokesperson, asked me if I had any ideas that might improve the publication seeing as I had been in newspapers myself.

I definitely did and between us, we decided to increase interest in the photographs by picturing more workers, rather than just managers doing their jobs. Guys on the generation floor or miners working on the raw coal, with dirt marks on their faces and spanners in their hands, close to the machinery they were repairing or working on. The workers were photographed and named, sometimes with a comment. All matters of interest to the many workers.

The dull photos of the managers at meetings, sitting solemn faced staring at the camera became a thing of the past. The idea was generally well received and along with additional new ideas and articles, the publication improved, the profile of KEK took on new vision and circulation increased.

It struck me many times, in my various discussions and dealings, that prior to 1999, Kosovo had been multicultural, Albanians, Serbians, Roma and Askali had been educated, or not, worked and socialised in close proximity to each other. Many remained friends, but there was bitterness and disparity and it would take time to resolve these deeply ingrained issues. I could understand this as 'sides' had been taken in the past and not so recent past. Having to decide which faction is going to rise to the top is not always easy to judge when you're down at ground level. However, I found them all to be basically good people and I could work with each and every one of them.

Fairly soon after I started work in PUD, as part of my familiarisation of the area and its needs, I visited the Serbian enclave of Gracanica. I had often passed through this area in the past as the main road between Gjilan and Pristina, just passed through the village which was close to the old bauxite mine tailings. Kosovo has many mineral deposits to be mined, including those in Trepce near Mitrovice.

In Gracanica, there was a quite a large electrical substation, serving the surrounding area and this then became of some importance to me in my dealings with KEK. On my way through the village on one occasion, I had called in at the substation, to have a look and a possible chat. I had checked with the production manager in Pristina that this substation was being maintained. The three men manning the station told me that they were only there to look after it, they weren't getting paid but they wanted to keep it safe and working for the local population.

These guys had worked for KEK before the conflict and knew the value of the station to their area and were hoping that some resolution would be made. They had no idea what that could be, but they hoped for something. Their quiet acceptance of the current situation and their hope for a better future was heartening. In the meantime, whilst guarding the station, they worked the small plot of ground at the back and side of the station. They were growing essential foodstuffs for their families. They were concerned that I, as an EU representative might object to their growing of the much-needed crops but I assured them that I had no objection. Though I did notice that on my subsequent visits, the growing of crops had stopped. I said nothing.

Gracanica village is centred on a Serbian monastery and the nuns and priests still lived there behind the walls. As in all monasteries, they were totally self-sufficient and I found them very welcoming. As well as their basic food stuffs, they produce the most delicious full-bodied red wine. I purchased a few bottles. Very enjoyable.

After my first visit to Gracanica, I approached a senior KEK manager, Nazmi Gashi with whom I had been working on various matters, and mooted the idea of employing Serb engineers living in Gracanica. After some discussion with Nazmi who obviously had to discuss with Vizar Kelmendi the KEK Company Accountant, among others the benefits of getting local employment back into that area, and therefore possible payment for electricity, it was agreed that we would liaise with local community officials and set up interviews. Nazmi, as a fluent Serbian and Albanian speaker would do the interviews. Nazmi had employed workers from here before the conflict and had no problem dealing with them or them with him. In fact they all knew each other well.

The process of advertising and interviewing staff began. There was a definite flurry of anticipation on all sides. Nazmi quietly organised the process. On the day of the interviews it was such a treat to see the renewed hope and friendliness that existed between them all. It was a golden moment for all. A real boost for the whole community.

This policy of cross community working and integration continued, with varying degrees of success, extending as far as up to Mitrovice and the north where, as far as I could tell, they actually received their electricity supply from Serbia. Simply because I was a neutral international, I was very much involved and met many Serbian officials for discussions and general liaison. This was done always with the support of KEK managers. This was great progress and as we continued the process, the atmosphere became more relaxed and more emphasis was placed on the different factions working together for the benefit of all. Beautiful.

On one particularly memorable occasion, I was asked to meet up with some Serbian citizens who were really in revolt, I think it was a town called Strepce. This town was an important Serbian town, the people were suffering severe isolation, poor finances and vague fractured supplies of electricity. This was the case until they took matters into their own hands and through support with spares from Serbia, managed to improve their supply. Though there were difficulties obtaining these spares, mainly financial similar to the generating problems re spares, but on a smaller scale. Needless to say, the people of Strepce weren't paying for their electrical usage but, due to energy experts within, they were able to maintain periodic connections and even repair distribution lines.

Out of need, these citizens had developed a good enterprise. There were great difficulties and this situation couldn't last but it was what they had for now, it had to do. This level of maintenance though was coming to an end, spare parts were more difficult to obtain through Serbia and the situation was worsening.

My brief was to let the people know that KEK workers had to gain access in order to maintain the supply and that KEK had to be paid for that supply. Apparently on a previous recent occasion, a senior energy expert from the international sector, had been sent down to discuss with these citizens about supply and payment. After his apparent abrupt departure from the meeting (I was told he had to leave in a hurry), the locals erupted in a fury and burnt the bridge at the entrance to the town, thus restricting free passage! I only found this out on my way to the meeting which was to be held at the local school/community centre. Arriving at the meeting site, I found that quite a large crowd had congregated outside the school. The American military were also present which was very reassuring, except for the fact that they were carrying their carbines in the ready position and it was obvious that the troops were alert and ready for action.

The soldiers approached me and warned me of the dangers, intimating that I should think twice about staying. It was evening time and I had my interpreter and a driver so felt that I should, even for the sake of those gathered there, try and hold the meeting as planned. Working on the knowledge that nothing annoys more that cancelling a meeting at the last minute, I felt that we had to go ahead. The soldiers also advised me that the crowd had been on the slivovic (local plum brandy and as potent as poteen) since midday so the talk would be very forthright and would be difficult.

Light was fading and I wasn't about to go into any meeting room. There was no electrical supply to the area at that time, so I asked the soldiers if they had lights and a megaphone. They didn't have a megaphone but they could supply lights, two strong lights on top of each of the two patrol vehicles. I addressed the crowd, introducing myself and our discussion started, (erupted would be a better word) loud and aggressive, everyone wanting to get their point heard. The soldiers, bless their souls, were concerned for my safety and crossed the barrels of their weapons across my chest as a means of separation and protection, successfully distancing me from the crowd. The soldiers were on high alert.

The men (there were no women present) in the crowd were loud shouting in a mixture of English and Serbian. I understood their desire to make someone listen and hopefully to understand. I could do that. I listened and I answered back (shouting really), the shouts quietened and the discussion, although not resolving anything, became a debate. I answered their points about supply as best as I could and stressed that the big problem was payment.

After a good solid discussion, I left. My meeting buddies must have felt that I had heard them and the parting was civil. My friends back in Pristina were quite relieved when I reappeared. I didn't feel endangered, these were citizens, customers needing a service and deserved a hearing. I just gave them that honour and had it returned.

Back in Gracanica, once Nazmi had successfully employed the necessary Serbian workers for Gracanica substation and they were at work and receiving a wage, the atmosphere did ease. These people had regained some self-respect and held their heads high. There was now hope for the future.

Nazmi was well known to these workers and respected for his expertise, fair minded approach and pleasant steady way of working. A gentleman with a level-headed approach to the situation. There were other managers like him in KEK and they all supported his actions. The Company accountant Vizar Kelmendi was a great example. This was a big landmark for KEK.

There were many meetings with different agencies where I was present but I remember one in particularly. It was between some financial experts from the IMF and the KEK Board. The financial experts were examining details of expenditure and the members of the KEK Board were under pressure. One of the visitors was a young Serbian lady and, it was obvious to me, that she was antagonistic toward the KEK Board and wanted to find fault. That was fine, many mistakes had been made in the past but I found myself having to defend some unfounded accusations as the Kosovars were at a loss as to how to deal with this, without appearing rude. Understanding the undercurrents and sensitivities I was able to intervene in a level manner and appeal for reason. The debate settled down. Once again, an example of how delicately balanced was this new entity of Kosovo.

The next step in the forward progress of Kosovo towards its new identity, was that we had to explore better cooperation between Mitrovice and the Northern areas with the rest of Kosovo. This was the core of the problem and produced much resistance from all sides. This resistance was hard core and vocal. There were a few who realised that resolution of this was the way forward but many were holding back. Forward steps of this nature will not be achieved easily or quickly. The idea had been planted and the fruit would take time.

Approximately 30MW of electricity were produced by a hydroelectric scheme near Radavci and this was in better working order than KEK as it produced a constant supply. The EU specialist for water, Richard, checked it out and made a few minor adjustments, but it worked well and consistently and all it needed was to be maintained.

As part of my job, I was required to negotiate many times and I will say that I always received respect from all sides and I was able to respond in the same manner. They respected the fact that I was doing a job to the best of my ability and gave me the credit for trying. On my part I understood their differing viewpoints and respected their views.

At one point, I was asked to go down to the monastery in Gracanica to ask for the support of the Orthodox clergy to support cooperation between the communities. In the event, some highly respected and prominent Orthodox clergy were listened politely and intently but they really didn't have any room to manoeuvre and I could read it in their eyes. They didn't have any space to move, their backs were against the wall and they were willing to defend their faith. I was impressed. It was defending their faith that held them, politics were not their motivation.

On this occasion, this discussion didn't result in any success but, at least, there was a discussion.

On one occasion, something that I found to be quite ludicrous, KEK had difficulty being paid for electricity usage by a section of the International Organisation, the UN in Kosovo. KEK had been refused payment on many occasions in the past, usually from citizens in Kosovo who had various reasons for non-payment, usually personal finances.

As an organisation, KEK did not have the best of reputations for supply of electricity to various regions and that was due, on the whole, to old, poorly maintained generators prior to 1999. Sometimes, the supply was interrupted for other reasons of general maintenance but the accounts section had organised themselves very efficiently and were accurate in their record keeping. Electricity supply was now being tracked and monitored quite efficiently.

So when the accounts sector approached me, in visible distress, claiming that these international sectors had not paid, I was bothered. The sector who did not pay their bills was that of the Human Rights Sector of the UN. It was embarrassing all around but the Human Rights sector refused to accept that a mistake had been made at their end and accused KEK of misrepresentation.

Because of who it was, there was a lot of fuss and double checks and triple checks were made of accounts. One UN lady, in particular, was very vocal in her defence of the Human Rights sector. KEK people were embarrassed but adamant. The bill had not been paid and they could prove it. After some political discussion at a very high level (SRSG), it was agreed that this sector had to suffer the same fate as any other Kosovar organisation—they had to be cut off. With many issued warnings, this was done. KEK workers had to be escorted by some internationals (I was one and the political adviser to the Head of the EU Mission was another) to ensure that all protocol was followed.

Needless to say, this process created quite a furore and the internationals involved in the UN sector affected were extremely indignant. However, sauce for the goose, etc. Very reluctantly, the UN sector paid up but with extremely bad grace. I believe that they even complained about me back to London and the vocal lady from the UN was really very vocal on many subsequent meetings with other internationals. I remember thinking that the UN Human Rights sector in this instance seemed to be very selective in their methodology, whenever confronted or crossed.

On my part, I really felt embarrassed by their approach as they wouldn't accept the proof of non-payment and they refused to listen to reason, continuing to badmouth KEK.

Kosovars generally had a reason as to why they didn't pay the bill as they had no money, but an international organisation that was well funded! It raised many questions for locals.

I did work hard in both Bosnia and Kosovo but I was also able to visit adjoining countries when I had time off. In the case of Bosnia, as a civilian, it was easy to get a bus down to Croatia and spend the weekend there, enjoying the food and relaxed atmosphere. In Kosovo, we had a little further to travel, but again an overnight bus ride from Pristina, took us over the mountains to Turkey, to Istanbul.

Istanbul is a fantastic place with its secular outlook (2000) and historic location on the Bosporus. It is beautiful and the food is great. I was also able to spend some very pleasant weekends visiting Greece.

Security in Kosovo became a problem after the year 2000. There were many break-ins of houses occupied by internationals and we had to add security grills to the doors and windows. These were installed courtesy of the UN. These heavy metal grills were to prove to be a deterrent. Unfortunately, at my first attempt to have grills fitted, after a break-in to the house, I hadn't made sure that the appropriate cementing of the grills into the brickwork had been completed. I came back a few days later and the house had been broken into again. The burglars even left my very distinctive purple torch, stolen during the first break-in and used in the second break-in, lying discarded inside the wardrobe. I just had to laugh, what else could I do. The thieves had taken some money but had not bothered with anything heavier. An opportunist burglary.

It was about this time that the Public Affairs chief wanted me to move from the Public Affairs office and be a political adviser to the Kosovo Prime Minister at that time. I wasn't totally comfortable with this move as there had been an international already installed in this role and he was ousted by the Kosovars. I saw the writing on the wall, so asked for time to think.

Just about this time, KEK public affairs team were also asking for my support. They were in the process of making big changes and needed to be able to contact me frequently to discuss things. These guys wanted to get everything right, and I supported their efforts as much as I could. In view of the situation, it was requested that I move into a spare office in the KEK HQ building, not too far from Government Building. This meant that the KEK guys had unfettered access to me, which they valued. The chief PIO, Monique, agreed but was not happy.

In late 2001, the work in KEK was progressing well. The majority of the staff had welcomed the new concepts of 'inclusiveness', although, naturally, there were some who were hesitant, even resistant.

The latter were watching the situation and reserving judgement. But KEK, as a whole was moving forward, and the Serbian authorities in the north were hesitant but wanting to join the movement.

Within KEK, I noticed that some of the workers were wanting better wages and conditions. The agitation was slightly subdued but the feeling was there.

On one area of the coalfield, there was a small collection of houses and, due to subsidence of the coal seams, these householders had to be rehoused in a more secure area, but close by to where they now were. The EU provided them with new homes and added a few more to accommodate the usual extended households. This having happened with homes, the generating plant workers reasoned that this was their time to raise a few issues on pay and conditions. I was not involved in this at all, but, as usual, I seemed somehow to get drawn.

The occasion was when I was escorting a German media crew (ZDF) around the plants at Obilic. I was showing them the huge generating floor and the surroundings, when an innocuous looking group of workers appeared and started addressing me and the camera crew. The interpreter quickly updated me on what was being said and there was no escape. The men had seized their opportunity and wanted publicity for their cause. The camera crew were all on for this item of news and all I could do was defend. I had been ambushed by professionals.

A very detailed debate ensued, sometimes in English, sometimes Albanian. I was fortunate that I could remember details that I had heard during many different meetings of senior KEK management. I was therefore able to answer most of their points in a reasonable manner. The debate must have lasted about 30 minutes and fortunately, I was just about able to hold my own.

Eventually, when all points had been thoroughly discussed, the men drifted away. I was left with a film crew who had been filming events. Congratulating me on my debating ability, they left, happy with their scoop, and I went back to the office and reported the incident. The CEO, Ali, was not happy but, as I pointed out, it would have looked even worse if I had not engaged.

At the end of 2002, beginning of 2003, I retired, going back to live in Northern Ireland.